American Furniture

AMERICAN FURNITURE 2015

Edited by Luke Beckerdite

Published by the CHIPSTONE FOUNDATION

Distributed by University Press of New England

Hanover and London

CHIPSTONE FOUNDATION BOARD OF DIRECTORS
Edward S. Cooke Jr.
Kaywin Feldman
Michael W. Hatch
Charles Hummel
Ted Kellner
Peter M. Kenny
W. David Knox II   *Chairman and* CEO
John S. McGregor
Jonathan Prown   *Executive Director*
Alison Stone
Stanley Stone III
Gustavus F. Taylor

EDITOR
Luke Beckerdite

BOOK AND EXHIBITION REVIEW EDITOR
Gerald W. R. Ward

EDITORIAL ADVISORY BOARD
Glenn Adamson, *Nanette L. Laitman Director, Museum of Arts and Design*
Eleanore P. Gadsden, *Carolyn and Peter Lynch Curator of Decorative Arts and Sculpture, Art of the Americas, Museum of Fine Arts Boston*
Leroy Graves, *Upholstery Conservator, Colonial Williamsburg Foundation*
Erik Gronning, *Senior Specialist in American Furniture, Sotheby's*
Robert Hunter, *Editor, Ceramics in America*
Alan Miller, *Conservator and Independent Furniture Consultant, Quakertown, Pennsylvania*
Lisa Minardi, *Assistant Curator, Winterthur Museum*
Sumpter Priddy III, *Decorative Arts Scholar and Dealer, Alexandria, Virginia*
Jonathan Prown, *Executive Director, Chipstone Foudation*
Robert F. Trent, *Independent Furniture Consultant, Wilmington, Delaware*
Gerald W. R. Ward, *Katharine Lane Weems Senior Curator of Decorative Arts and Sculpture Emeritus, Art of the Americas, Museum of Fine Arts, Boston*
Philip Zea, *Executive Director, Historic Deerfield*

Published by the Chipstone Foundation
Distributed by University Press of New England
1 Court Street
Lebanon, New Hampshire 03766
upne.com

© 2015 by the Chipstone Foundation
All rights reserved
Printed in the United States of America   5 4 3 2 1
ISSN 1069-4188
ISBN 978-0-9827722-7-0

Cover: Detail, chest, probably made for Eva Koppenhefer, Lebanon County, Pennsylvania, 1785. Walnut and sulfur inlay with white pine and tulip poplar; iron, brass. H. 28½", W. 54⅞", D. 24⅜". (Courtesy, Philip H. Bradley Co.; photo, Gavin Ashworth.

Back cover: Detail, chest, made for Veronica Miller, southeastern Pennsylvania, 1785. Walnut and sulfur inlay with tulip poplar; iron, brass. H. 20", W. 52", D. 23¾". (Courtesy, Clarke Hess; photo, Gavin Ashworth.)

Design: Wynne Patterson, Pittsfield, VT
Copyediting: Ironia Simpson, Bennington, VT
Printing: Meridian Printing, East Greenwich, RI

Contents

Editorial Statement *Luke Beckerdite*	VII
Barnard Eaglesfield: A Prominent Philadelphia Cabinetmaker Revealed *Jay Robert Stiefel*	1
The Notebook of Philadelphia Joiner John Widdifield	16
Sulfur-Inlaid Furniture: New Insights on Materials and Techniques *Mark Anderson, Brenda Hornsby Heindl, and Jennifer Mass*	68
Sulfur Inlay in Pennsylvania German Furniture: New Discoveries *Lisa Minardi*	86
Book Reviews	200

Kem Weber: Designer and Architect, Christopher Long; review by Nonie Gadsden

In Plain Sight: Discovering the Furniture of Nathaniel Gould, Kemble Widmer and Joyce King, with essays by Glenn Adamson, Daniel Finamore, Dean Thomas Lahikainen, and Elisabeth Garrett Widmer; review by Joshua Lane

Made in the Americas: The New World Discovers Asia, Dennis Carr, with contributions by Gauvin Alexander Bailey, Timothy Brook, Mitchell Codding, Karina H. Corrigan, and Donna Pierce; review by William Sargent

Early Seating Upholstery: Reading the Evidence, Leroy Graves; review by Jonathan Prown

Recent Writing on American Furniture: A Bibliography *Gerald W. R. Ward*	222
Index	232

Editorial Statement

American Furniture is an interdisciplinary journal dedicated to advancing knowledge of furniture made or used in the Americas from the seventeenth century to the present. Authors are encouraged to submit articles on any aspect of furniture history, essays on conservation and historic technology, reproductions or transcripts of documents, annotated photographs of new furniture discoveries, and book and exhibition reviews. References for compiling an annual bibliography also are welcome.

Manuscripts must be double-spaced, illustrated with black-and-white prints, transparencies, or high resolution digital images, and prepared in accordance with the Chipstone style guide. The Foundation will offer significant honoraria for manuscripts accepted for publication and reimburse authors for all photography approved in writing by the editor.

Luke Beckerdite

American Furniture

Jay Robert Stiefel

Barnard Eaglesfield:
A Prominent
Philadelphia
Cabinetmaker
Revealed

▼ SIGNIFICANT NEW information on early Philadelphia furniture makers and their work has been published since the Philadelphia Museum of Art opened its seminal exhibition *Worldly Goods: The Arts of Early Pennsylvania, 1680–1758* in 1999. We now know of additional pieces signed by or attributable to members of the Claypoole dynasty—Joseph (1677–1744), James (1720–1796), George (1706–1793), and Josiah (1717–1757)—and that joiner John Head (1688–1754; from 1717 in Philadelphia) was one of the city's most prolific and innovative craftsmen. Insights into Head's work originated with the author's discovery of that cabinetmaker's account book, which resulted in several publications and attributions of more than forty pieces of case furniture to Head's shop. The author's present discovery of unpublished manuscripts pertaining to Philadelphia joiner Barnard Eaglesfield (d. 1732) reveals that his stature and influence as a furniture maker may have been comparable to that of Head and the Claypooles.[1]

Previously, scant attention had been paid to Eaglesfield because no one had attributed objects to him or cited primary sources that document him as a furniture maker. A nineteenth-century genealogist cited a 1726 charge from a "Barnard Eaglesfield" to the estate of Philadelphia merchant Hugh Lowden for a coffin; however, coffins were produced by a variety of woodworkers including house joiners, carpenters, and cabinetmakers, so furniture production cannot be inferred from this reference. Similarly, William McPherson Hornor Jr.'s *Blue Book Philadelphia Furniture* (1935) identified Eaglesfield as a woodworker but failed to demonstrate that he was a furniture maker: "Bernard Eaglesfield, joiner, worked for Hugh Loudon, 1722–23; died 1732." Because Hornor did not cite his sources, this and much other information on Eaglesfield in the *Blue Book* could not be verified. Moreover, not every joiner made furniture. Hornor's reference to a "Buffett" (corner cupboard) purportedly made by Eaglesfield in 1735 was problematical since Eaglesfield died in 1732. Quoting from an unidentified "list," Hornor stated that Eaglesfield had "13 Setts bedstead stuff," "73 yds Calico in remnants," and a "stock" of lumber. The last was especially tantalizing as it included walnut, mahogany, and cedar—all woods then common for making furniture in Philadelphia and readily available from lumber merchants. But without a reference to tools with which to fashion it, this was no confirmation that Eaglesfield was a maker rather than a merchant. In contrast, Joseph Claypoole's advertisements and John Head's account book, which also refer to quantities of materials, clearly relate that each is making furniture.[2]

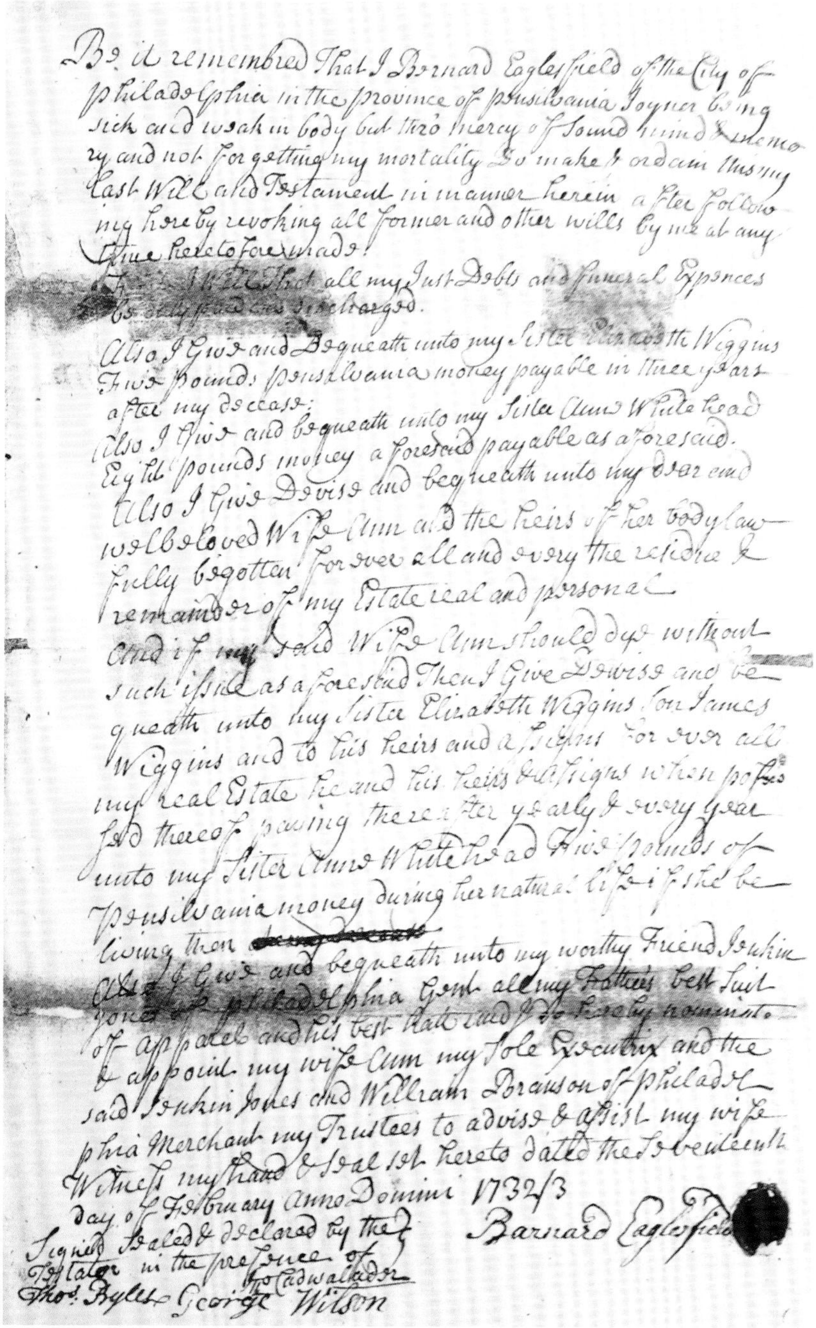

Figure 1 Will of Barnard Eaglesfield, Philadelphia, Pennsylvania, dated February 17, 1732/1733 and probated April 13, 1733. (Courtesy, Philadelphia Register of Wills.)

Eaglesfield's name came to this author's attention when researching John Head's account book. On June 13, 1724, Head charged "Barni Eagelsfield" for twenty brass knobs. The following day, Head credited him for 9½ feet of "mohoganey plank" and made separate payments to Eaglesfield and his wife for the difference in cost, but there was no indication that Eaglesfield was using the hardware or wood to make furniture. "Barnard Eaglesfield" also appears in a ledger maintained by Philadelphia merchant James Logan (1674–1751). A 1725 credit entry recorded Eaglesfield's payment of £180 in "cash," and a debit was entered the following year for his purchase of two dozen looking glasses—a commodity Logan imported in large quantities.

In an era when many transactions were conducted by barter, as ready money was being siphoned abroad to pay for finished goods, £180 was a significant cash sum. Although informative, the transactions in the Head account book and Logan ledger still were insufficient to show that Eaglesfield was a furniture maker. Indeed, his sale of mahogany to Head and his purchase of looking glasses from Logan lent greater weight to his being a merchant rather than a working craftsman.[3]

The manuscripts that are the subject of this essay reveal that Eaglesfield was a prominent and prosperous furniture maker who occupied premises on the busiest street in Philadelphia's commercial center and had commissions for large and complex forms at premium prices; ties to more than one hundred members of Philadelphia's commercial, political, and religious elite; and patrons as far away as the West Indies. Eaglesfield's probate records are also the most extensive, detailed, and comprehensive found to date for any Philadelphia furniture maker. At his death, Eaglesfield owned at least seventy-two pieces of furniture—some of which were clearly stock-in-trade or unfinished commissioned work—and large quantities of materials, hardware, and tools. Previous researchers may have overlooked Eaglesfield because his prominence was not suspected and his probate records are not listed in the standard index used to locate such records in the City of Philadelphia archives.[4]

At first glance, Eaglesfield's simple, one-page will appears to provide little information other than documenting his signature and describing him as a "Joyner" (figs. 1, 2). He left his estate to his wife, Ann, with the provision that, if she died without lawful issue, the estate would pass to his sister, her son, and his heirs. As no children are named, Barnard and Ann may have had none. When Eaglefield's will is considered in a broader historical

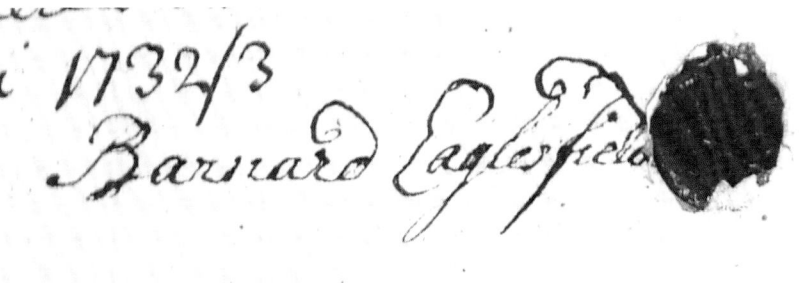

Figure 2 Signature of Barnard Eaglesfield on his will, Philadelphia, Pennsylvania, dated February 17, 1732/1733 and probated April 13, 1733. (Courtesy, Philadelphia Register of Wills.)

context, it sheds light on his business and personal relations, particularly with those of the Baptist faith. Barnard left "all my Father's best Suit of Apparel, & his best hatt" to his trustee, "Jenkin Jones [1696–1760] of Philad: Gent[leman]." In 1726 Jones became a minister at the Baptist church in Philadelphia, succeeding George Eaglesfield (d. 1730). Logan's ledger, in an account for "George Eglesfield," records cash payments partly coming "from his Son," between 1720 and 1724, and, in Barnard's account, £10 in cash paid for "balancing his father's Acco[unt]" in 1724. No other Eaglesfield or variant of that name appears in the ledger. Given that Jones and George Eaglesfield served the same congregation and that Barnard's estate listed "6 folio Book[s] belonging to ye Baptist meeting," the elder Eaglesfield appears to have been the cabinetmaker's father.[5]

The other trustee of Barnard's estate was also a Baptist, "William Branson [1684–1760] of Philad: Merch[an]t." A convert from Quakerism, Branson transitioned from joiner to shopkeeper to one of America's first iron industrialists. Branson may have supplied Eaglesfield with furniture hardware as he later did John Head. Barnard witnessed the will of another Philadelphia Baptist, James Tuthill, a gentleman. A provision in that document manumitted a "Negro Man Sharper," who would later be paid for helping to bury

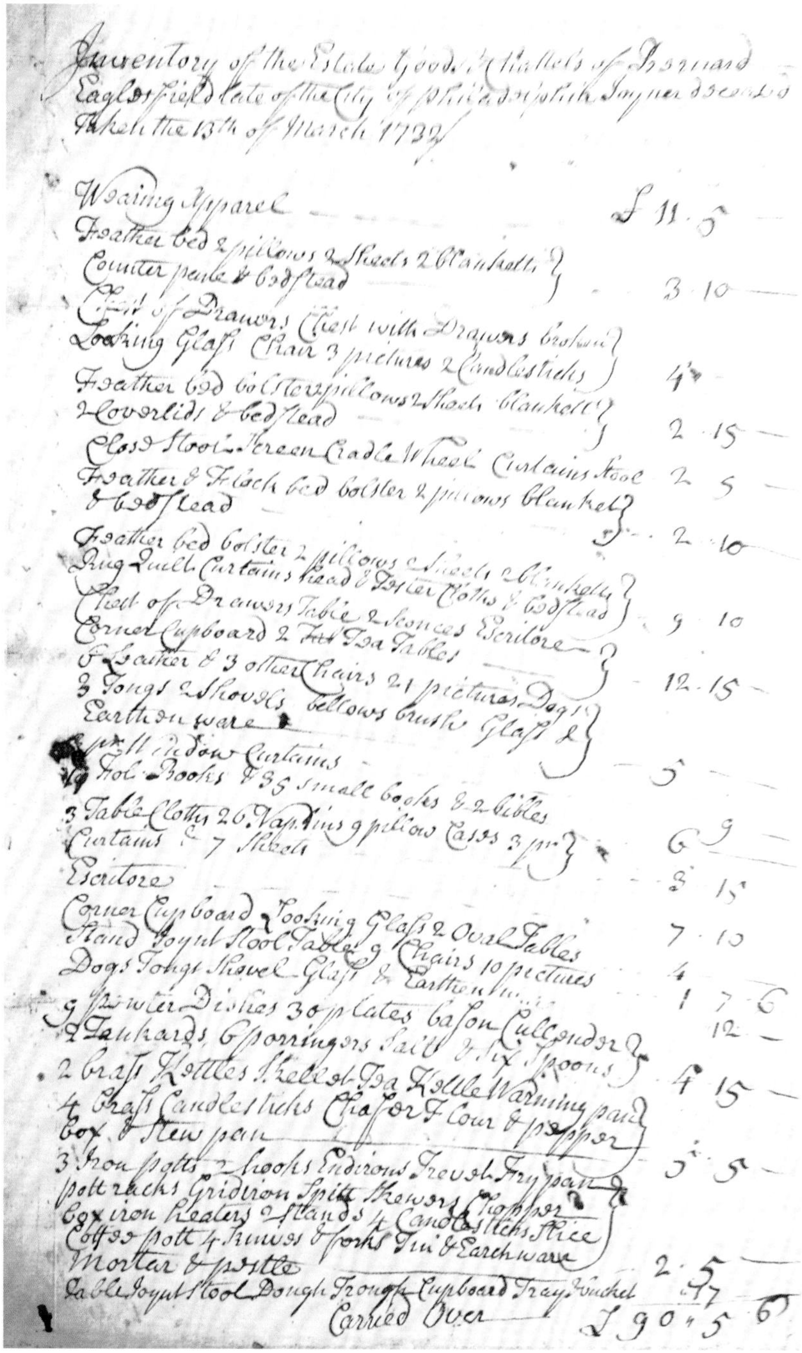

Figure 3 First page of the probate inventory of Barnard Eaglesfield, dated March 13, 1732[/1733]. (Courtesy, Philadelphia Register of Wills.)

Barnard. Barnard himself was probably a Baptist as, in 1724, Ann Eaglesfield was disowned by the local Quaker meeting for marrying outside the faith.[6]

In addition to his will, Eaglesfield's probate records include a one-page affirmation by witnesses Thomas Biles, George Wilson, and John Cadwalader, dated March 12, 1732[/1733]; a five-page inventory of "Goods & Chattels" in his house and shop (including furniture, materials, hardware, and tools totaling £355.4.4) appraised by Cadwalader and Edward Roberts, and dated May 15, 1733; and an eight-page accounting listing more than a hundred creditors and debtors (totaling £681.18.11½) signed by Thomas Hine and dated July 18, 1735. A decade later, Wilson made furniture for Philadelphia merchant Nathaniel Allen. The fact that Wilson was a joiner and witness to Eaglesfield's will suggests that the two may have done business and possibly worked together.[7]

The first page of Eaglesfield's inventory appears to list household objects, as it starts with a valuation of his "Wearing Apparel" and ends with smaller domestic wares (fig. 3). In between are entries for at least forty-eight pieces of furniture (of which thirty-eight are case pieces), evidence of his prosperity but also illustrative of the range of his output, as many of those objects were probably made in his shop:

> Feather bed & pillows 2 Sheets 2 blanketts Counter pane & bedstead £3.10
> Chest of Drawers Chest with Drawers broken Looking Glass Chair 3 pictures 2 Candlesticks £4
> Feather bed bolster 2 pillows 2 sheets blanket 2 Coverlids & bedstead £2.15
> Close Stool Screen Cradle Wheel Curtains Stool £2.5
> Feather & Flock bed bolster 2 pillows blanket & bedstead £2.10
> Feather bed bolster 2 pillows 2 Sheets 2 blanketts Rug Quilt Curtains head & Tester Cloths & bedstead £9.10
> Chest of Drawers Table 2 Sconces Escritore Corner cupboard 2 Tea Tables £12.15
> 6 Leather & 3 other Chairs 24 Pictures Dogs 3 Tongs 2 Shovels bellows brush Glass & Earthenware £5
> Escritore £7.10
> Corner Cupboard Looking Glass 2 Oval Tables £4.10
> Stand Joynt Stool Table 9 Chairs 10 pictures £1.7.6
> Table Joynt Stool Dough Trough Cupboard Tray & bucket 17s

Remarkably, Eaglesfield owned two "escritores," a double-case form with a fall front also referred to contemporaneously as "scrutoire," "scrutore," "scrudore," "screetore," and "scriptor." With its two sections, fall front, and varied drawer sizes, the scrutoire was one of the most elaborate and costly furniture pieces produced in colonial America and required an accomplished craftsman to make it. As no furniture by Eaglesfield has yet been identified, one or both escritores may have looked like an example bearing the mark of Philadelphia joiner Edward Evans (1679–1754) and the date 1707 (fig. 4), which has a lockable fall front and no exterior doors; or possibly resembled a scrutoire that once had a fall-front writing surface originally concealed behind two lockable doors (fig. 5).[8]

The second through fourth pages of the inventory list items in quantities and types so extensive that they appear to have been for resale. Some of the "9 small Looking Glasses" recorded on the third page may have been simi-

Figure 4 Edward Evans, scrutoire, Philadelphia, Pennsylvania, 1707. Walnut with Atlantic white cedar and white pine. H. 66½", W. 44½", D. 19⅞". (Courtesy, Colonial Williamsburg Foundation.) The scrutoire is stamped "Edward Evans 1707" on the inside bottom drawer centered above the open well in the upper section. It is the earliest dated piece of Philadelphia furniture marked with a maker's name.

lar to those Eaglesfield bought from Logan and thus not necessarily made in the joiner's shop. There are also more hardware and tools than Eaglesfield would have likely have required for his own work:

> 9 Compass & 1 handsaw. . . , 6 Sett Coffin handles. . . , 2½ Doz: ditto handles & Squares. . . , 19 Drawer & 10 Chest Locks. . . , 11 Nippers Dantzick Lock & 7 pr. Spurrs & 3 smaller Locks. . . , 10½ Inch and 10¾ & 13 Inch Augers. . . , 12 m of 2d nails. . . , 4 m of 3d ditto. . . , 12 m Tin Lackerd & other small nails. . . , 13 box irons. . . , 4 doz & 8 pr butts [i.e., butt hinges]. . . , 15 Socket Chisels & 8 Caulking Irons & 29 Chisels. . . , 2 Lotts Desk Locks & 1 box ditto. . . , 2 Drawer Locks & parcel [of] Screws. . . , 8 rass Locks & pins. . . , 6 Doz: handles & Scutcheons. . . , 16 pr. Hinges. . . , 8 Doz Scutcheons. . . , 2 Doz Knobs & 18 Drops. . . , 8 Doz & 10 Drops & Latche. . . , 3 Doz plane Irons & 16 padlocks & Spri[n]gs. . . , 3 Doz Small knives & 10 pr bright hinges. . . , 7 Doz: Dove Tails. . . , 2 Doz H hinges. . . , 22 files & 24 Scissors. . . , 15 Rules. . . , 4 Addices & 24 Hatchets. . . , 18 broad & 1 narrow Axe. . . , 20 Doz: Gimlets & 6 Chest Locks.

The third and fourth pages of the inventory also list substantial quantities of fabric, tape, ribbon, clothing, spices, spectacles, knives, and other items. These goods are evidence that Eaglesfield, like John Head, expanded his business to encompass distribution and lines of merchandise beyond furniture making, which was essential in a barter economy.[9]

The fifth page of the inventory appears to relate exclusively to Eaglesfield's shop (fig. 6), which, judging from the quantities and types of wood, appears to have been active at the time of his demise: "285 Walnut

Boards at 2127 foot, 133 Ditto plank at 861 foot, 39 Cedar boards at 195 foot and 5 ps Mahogany plank & boards at 144 foot." The "3 Work benches" are an indication that others, perhaps including George Wilson, worked in the shop. The range of tools indicates that Eaglesfield could produce both joinery and turning, and their quantity is small enough to suggest that they were not items for sale: "53 moulding planes. . . , 2 Joynters, Strike block. . . , Skew planes Long & 2 fored. . . , 2 Holdfasts hatchets & Six Saws. . . , 4 Mortizing Chisels & formers 2 rasps & 7 files. . . , Morris Saw bow Saw 4 hamers pinchers & Shears. . . , 3 Augers Ladle & Glew pott. . . , 7 Turning Tools Fraw [froe] Compass Sens & Screw Key." The last two listings—compass centers and a screw key—were parts of a lathe.[10]

Figure 5 Scrutoire, Philadelphia, Pennsylvania, 1715–1730. Walnut with Atlantic white cedar and hard pine. H. 64", W. 32", D. 20". (Courtesy, Dietrich American Foundation.) This scrutoire is illustrated open with the fall missing in William McPherson Hornor Jr., *Blue Book Philadelphia Furniture* (Philadelphia: privately printed, 1935), p. 15, pl. 1.

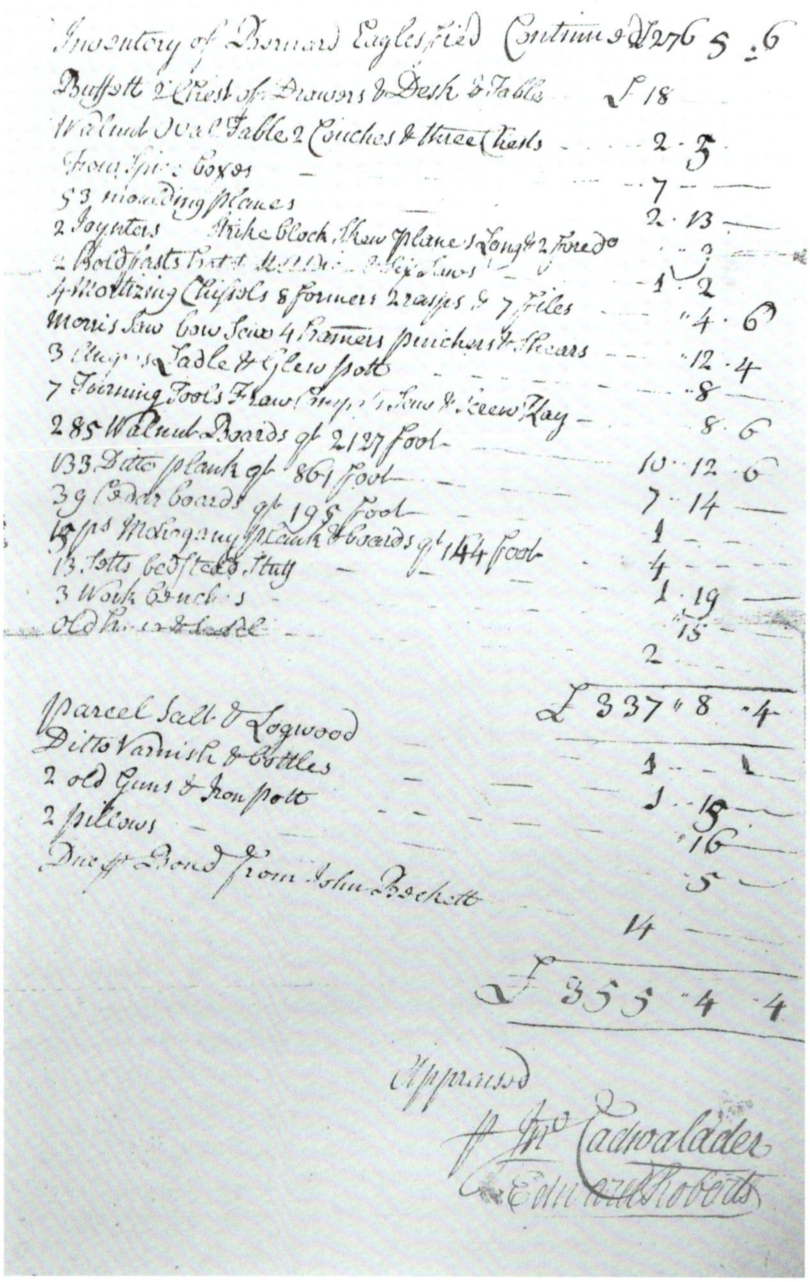

Figure 6 Last page of the probate inventory of Barnard Eaglesfield, dated March 13, 1732[/1733], listing 15 pieces of furniture; tools; varnish; planks and boards of mahogany, walnut, and cedar; and three work benches. (Courtesy, Philadelphia Register of Wills.)

The furniture in the shop consisted of a "Buffett 2 Chest of Drawers & Desk & Table" valued at £18, a "Walnut Oval Table 2 Couches & three Chests" valued at £2.5, and "Four Spice boxes" valued at 7s. Given their low valuations, the oval table, couches, chests, and spice boxes may have been incomplete at the time of the appraisal. If so, then several of the pieces of furniture listed on the first page of the inventory may also have been for sale, particularly one of the "escritores." That form usually does not appear in duplicate in household inventories.[11]

Eaglesfield's probate records indicate that he was financially successful, transacting business with prosperous mercantile firms and numerous members of Philadelphia's elite, including Samuel Powel Sr. and Jr., Jonathan Fisher, Israel Pemberton, Lawrence Growden, William Chancellor, Anthony

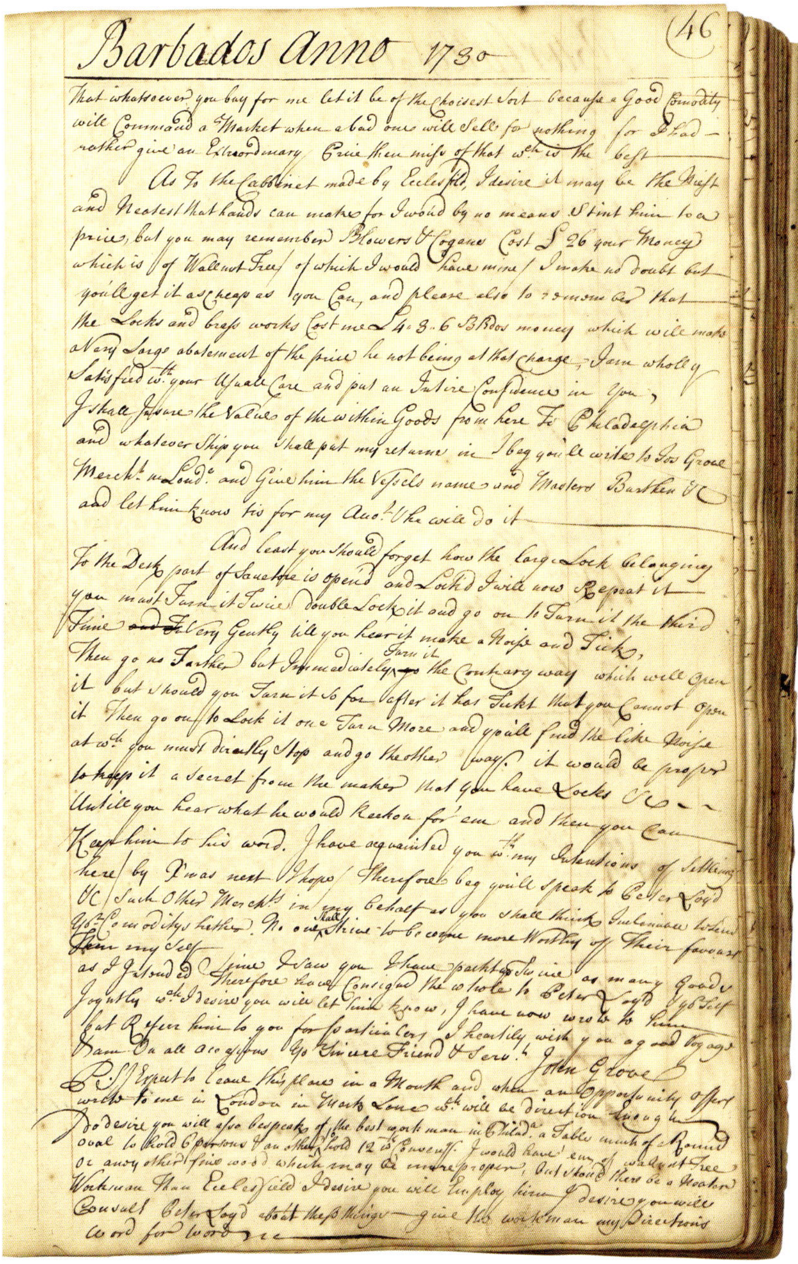

Figure 7 *Opposite* and *Right*, Transcription of a 1730 letter of instructions from John Grove to Thomas Chalkley in the Thomas Chalkley Account and Letter Book, 1729–1732, p. 46. (Courtesy, Historical Society of Pennsylvania.)

Morris, Logan & Shippen, and Willing & Shippen. Befitting his status, he may even have had his likeness painted by Philadelphia's leading portrait artist, Gustavus Hesselius (1682–1755), as suggested by the latter's March 3, 1734 charge of £1.13.3. Eaglesfield's funeral costs were also substantial, totaling £14.17.4, of which £3 was Sharper's charge "for work & Horse & at Burial." A further indication of the cabinetmaker's prominence is a November 6, 1730, indenture recording his acquisition of premises on a 24- by 102-foot lot on the north side of High Street. This property was in the commercial heart of Philadelphia, on the city's widest thoroughfare, at the location of its market, and close to the businesses of others with whom Eaglesfield dealt, such as Head and Logan.[12]

Figure 8 Henry Popple, *A Map of the British Empire in America with the French and Spanish settlements adjacent thereto*, [1733] ca. 1735. Engraving on paper. H. 15", W. 20½". (Courtesy, Colonial Williamsburg Foundation.)

Presumably, most furniture commissions in Philadelphia were conveyed orally from a patron (or a patron's agent) to a shop master like Eaglesfield. As a consequence, only sparse documentation has survived to show how patrons contributed to the design and production of objects or to illuminate the negotiation process. A notable exception is a previously unpublished letter wherein John Grove, a wealthy Barbadian merchant, instructed ship captain Thomas Chalkley (1675–1741) to procure furniture from Eaglesfield (fig. 7). Grove's letter is transcribed on two pages of an account and letter book kept by Chalkley. Being in a remote location, and wanting the finest furniture with no expense spared, Grove put his "Directions" in writing and insisted that they be transmitted "word for word" to "the best work man in Philada."[13]

On the second voyage of the *New Bristol Hope* from Barbados to Philadelphia (fig. 8), April 28–May 30, 1730, Chalkley took on board a trunk and "Bale of Merchandise" with a combined value of "£225.2.5 Barbados Money." Grove consigned the merchandise to fellow Quaker Chalkley and Philadelphia merchant Peter Lloyd (d. 1744/1745). To prevent the hardware for Grove's furniture order from being mixed up with the consigned goods and inadvertently sold, Chalkley added the notation, "There is in The Trunk the brasses Locks etc for the scrutore."[14]

Grove authorized Chalkley to spend the proceeds of the consignment but specified that "whatsoever you buy for me let it be of the choisest Sort because a Good Commodity will Command a Market when a bad one will sell for nothing for I had rather give an Extraordinary Price then miss of that wch is the best." Given the fact that the Grove family had amassed considerable wealth in the triangular trade and that one of their kin acted as their agent in London, it is significant that John chose to patronize a Philadelphia joiner rather than an English one, particularly since cost did not seem to be an issue. "As to the Cabbinet [scrutoire] made by Ecclesfild," Grove wrote:

> I desire it may be the Ni[c]est and Neatest that hands can make for I would by no means Stint him to a price, but you may remember Blowers & Cogans Cost £26 your Money which is of Wallnut Tree / of which I would want have mine / I make no doubt but you'll get it as cheap as you Can, and please also to remember that the Locks and brass works Cost me £4-3-6 BBdos money which will make a Very Large abatement of the price he not being at that charge.

He also assured Chalkley, "I am wholly Satisfied wth your Usuall Care and put an Intire Confidence in you."[15]

Grove's letter did not specify features for his scrutoire, probably because Eaglesfield had likely made, or was at least intimately familiar with, the one purchased by Grove's competitor in Barbados, Blower & Cogan. By ordering a similar piece from the same source Grove would have known essentially what he was getting. Grove did, however, provide instructions as to the operation of the locks he furnished:

> And least you should forget how the larg Lock belonging To the Desk part of Scrutore is open'd and Lock'd I will now Repeat it—you must Turn it Twice & double Lock it and go on to Turn it the third Time Very Gently till you hear it make a Noise and Tick, Then go no Further but Instead immediately Turn it the Contrary way which will open it but should you Turn it so far after it has Tickt that you Cannot open it Then go on to Lock it one Turn More and you'll find the like Noise at wch. you must directly Stop and go the other way.

As a negotiating tactic, he also advised Chalkley to get a price for the locks and brasses before disclosing that he already had them in hand: "It would be proper to keep a secret from the maker that you have the Locks etc. ~ Untill you hear what he would Reckon for 'em and then you can Keep him to his word." Grove may have gotten the hardware in London and thus was confident that he had them at prices cheaper than those at which Eaglesfield could buy them in Philadelphia.[16]

Although scrutoires were among the most expensive case forms available during the first three decades of the eighteenth century, £26 would have been an extraordinary price for a standard example. Of the two scrutoires listed in Eaglesfield's probate inventory, one was valued at £7.10 and the other was included in a group of eight pieces valued at £12.15. By further comparison, Chalkley debited Samuel Collynns £7.10 for "a black Wallnut Scutroir" in 1730.[17]

Grove's reference to Blower & Cogan's walnut "scrutore" costing £26 raises questions about the appearance of that object as well as of the piece Grove wanted Eaglesfield to make for him. During the first quarter of the eighteenth century, the term "scrutoire" generally referred to a double-case piece with a fall front similar to the Evans example (fig. 4). Any such piece costing in the vicinity of £26, especially if primarily in walnut (a wood plentiful in Philadelphia), must have had additional features. Possible options include an elaborate interior or pediment, veneers of exotic woods, or mirrors. Given the 1730 date of Grove's order, it is also possible that his use of the term "scrutore" referred to a desk-and-bookcase (fig. 9). In 1736 John Head charged James Steel £15 for "a scrudore and Bookcas apon a Chest of drawers," one of the most complex and costly pieces recorded in Head's account book, and perhaps the same "Desk and Book Case wth Glass Doors," valued at like amount in Steel's probate inventory.[18]

In a postscript, Grove expanded his order to include two tables:

> I do desire you will also bespeak of the best work man in Philada. a Table much of a Round oval to hold 6 persons & an other to hold 12 is to Convenss. I should have 'em of wallnut Tree or any other fine wood which may be more proper, but should there be a neater Workman Than Ecclesfield I desire you will Employ him & desire you will Consult Peter Loyd about these things ~ give the workman my Directions word for word.

Gate-leg tables seating six were the norm; those seating twice that number were uncommon and expensive (fig. 10). Grove's caveat regarding "a neater Workman" implies that while he knew of no one better than Eaglesfield, he may have been uncertain about the cabinetmaker's ability to do turning for the bases; however, the tools and lathe components in the latter's inventory indicate that such concern was unnecessary.[19]

In England, the importation of walnut was still popular in the 1730s, despite the greater availability of mahogany. Grove requested that his tables

Figure 9 Desk-and-bookcase, probably Philadelphia, Pennsylvania, 1715–1730. Walnut with tulip poplar and walnut. H. 90", W. 40", D. 22¾". (Courtesy, Philadelphia Museum of Art; gift of Mrs. John Wintersteen.)

Figure 10 Oval table, Philadelphia, Pennsylvania, 1715–1730. Black walnut with Atlantic white cedar. H. 28¾", D. (top) 59¾", W. (open) 73". (Courtesy, Dietrich American Foundation.)

be made of walnut or "any other fine wood which may be more proper." This calls into question why a Barbadian would order walnut when mahogany was plentiful in the West Indies and could readily be shipped to Philadelphia. Indeed, we know that Eaglesfield had it in his inventory. Grove may have deemed walnut a desired novelty, especially if imported from Pennsylvania, which some Barbadians held in high esteem. A year before, the governor of the island had told Chalkley, "Whoever lived to see it, Pennsylvania would be the metropolis of America, in some hundreds of years."[20]

Now that Eaglesfield has been documented as a prominent early cabinetmaker, scholarship can focus on finding his furniture. Objects made by him may have descended in the families of fellow Baptists or the many individuals listed in his estate accounting. It is even possible that the scrutoire and tables mentioned in Grove's letter have survived. Since Eaglesfield did not die until 1732 and Chalkley made many more voyages to Barbados, there would have been time for the fulfillment of Grove's order. Should any marked objects be discovered, the script can be compared with Eaglesfield's signature on the original will. Similarly, additional documents pertaining to his life and career may survive in archival collections in Philadelphia and Barbados, as well as in other areas where Eaglesfield had patrons. It is hoped that the manuscripts discussed in this essay will prompt further revelations about Eaglesfield and his work, just as the discovery of John Head's account book did for his production.

ACKNOWLEDGMENTS For assistance with this article, the author thanks Adam Bowett, Wendy A. Cooper, Beatrice B. Garvan, Laura C. Keim, Deborah Rebuck, Christopher R. Storb, Philip D. Zimmerman, and the staffs of the Dietrich American Foundation, Historical Society of Pennsylvania, and Library Company of Philadelphia.

1. Jack Lindsey, *Worldly Goods: The Arts of Early Pennsylvania, 1680–1758* (Philadelphia: Philadelphia Museum of Art, 1999). Jay Robert Stiefel, "Philadelphia Cabinetmaking and Commerce: The Account Book of John Head, Joiner, 1718–1753" and "The Head Account Book as Artifact: A Supplementary Essay," *Library Bulletin* (American Philosophical Society), n. s., 1, no. 1 (Winter 2001), http://www.amphilsoc.org/bulletin/20011/stiefpdf.pdf. Jay Robert Stiefel, Alan Andersen, and Christopher Storb, "The John Head Project, Part 1: Documenting His Work," *Antiques & Fine Art* 9, no. 1 (autumn/winter 2008): 190–93. Andrew Brunk, "The Claypoole Family Joiners of Philadelphia: Their Legacy and the Context of Their Work," in *American Furniture*, edited by Luke Beckerdite (Hanover, N.H.: University Press of New England for the Chipstone Foundation, 2002), pp. 147–73. Alan Miller, "Flux in Design and Method in Early Eighteenth-Century Philadelphia Furniture," in *American Furniture*, edited by Luke Beckerdite (Hanover, N.H.: University Press of New England for the Chipstone Foundation, 2014), pp. 30-86.

2. Mrs. Thomas Potts James, Memorial of Thomas Potts, Junior, etc. (Cambridge, Mass.: privately printed, 1874), p. 381, citing ledgers given to the Philadelphia Library by Robert Grace. "Lowden" is the spelling also found in his will. Will of Hugh Lowden, Philadelphia Wills 1726, Will Book D, 355, no. 276, Philadelphia Register of Wills. William McPherson Hornor Jr., *Blue Book Philadelphia Furniture* (Philadelphia: privately printed, 1935), pp. 2, 3, 26–27, 39, 66.

3. Stiefel, "Philadelphia Cabinetmaking and Commerce," sec. X. C. 4, p. 45; John Head Account Book, p. 60, Vaux Papers, 1738–1985, American Philosophical Society, Philadelphia, Miscellaneous Manuscript Collection 73. James Logan Ledger 1720–1727, p. 180, collection no. 0379, vol. 3, Historical Society of Philadelphia, Pennsylvania (hereafter HSP).

4. Will of Barnard Eaglesfield, February 17, 1732/1733, probated April 13, 1733, Will Book E, 231, no. 310, Philadelphia Register of Wills. Probate administration documents filed with the will include a one-page affirmation by the witnesses dated March 12, 1732[/1733]; a five-page inventory of his house and shop dated May 15, 1733; and an eight-page list of creditors and debtors dated July 18, 1735. (All of these will documents will hereafter be cited as Will of Barnard Eaglesfield.) None of the foregoing is listed in Richard T. Williams and Mildred C. Williams, *Index of Wills & Administration Records, Philadelphia, Pennsylvania, 1682–1782* (Danboro, Pa.: Richard T. Williams and Mildred C. Williams, 1971–1972), Index KFP 144.8.P5 W54 1972, HSP. The probate inventory of Philadelphia joiner Charles Plumley (d. 1708) lists many tools, materials, chairs, and unfinished furniture, but only a few case pieces (Benno M. Forman, *American Seating Furniture, 1630–1730* [New York: W. W. Norton, 1988], app. 1).

5. Will of Barnard Eaglesfield. Early Baptist records are notoriously sparse, particularly as to congregants. No records were located for the birth, baptism, or marriage of Barnard. There are references, however, to the ministry of George Eaglesfield (*Minutes of the Philadelphia Baptist Association from A.D. 1707 to A.D. 1807*, edited by A. D. Gillette [Philadelphia: American Baptist Publication Society, 1851], pp. 12, 16; David Spencer, *Early Baptists of Philadelphia* [Philadelphia: W. Syckel Moore, 1877], chap. 5, pp. 58–59, 78). The only other Eaglesfield connected with Baptists in Philadelphia in the generation of George Eaglesfield is a "John Eaglesfield." His name appears in the Will of William Elton (shipwright), June 22, 1702, proved December 15, 1702, Philadelphia Wills, Book B, no. 258. In 1698 Elton and his wife were baptized and became part of the first Baptist congregation to convene in Philadelphia (William Williams Keen, *The Bi-centennial Celebration of the Founding of the First Baptist Church of Philadelphia* [Philadelphia: American Baptist Publication Society, 1898], p. 468). George Eaglesfield's purchases from Logan were all in 1720 and included nothing related to furniture. Logan Ledger, p. 28. Two other sons of George Eaglesfield are noted as non-Quakers buried in Philadelphia: William, on August 19, 1701, and Benjamin, April 9, 1703 (William W. Hinshaw, *Encyclopedia of American Quaker Geneaology*, 7 vols. [Ann Arbor, Mich.: Geneaological Publishing Co., 1938], 2: 443).

6. Will of Barnard Eaglesfield. Branson sold Head 7½ dozen escutcheons and drops in 1721, and butt hinges in 1737 (Stiefel, "Philadelphia Cabinetmaking and Commerce," nn. 310–14). Branson had sold James Logan a bedstead and sacking bottoms and "Cornishes for the Bed and 3 Windows" in 1712. Laura C. Keim, *Stenton Room Furnishings Study* (Philadelphia: National Society of the Colonial Dames of America in the Commonwealth of Pennsylvania, 2011), p. 46. Will of James Tutthill [Tuthill], February 9, 1727/1728, proved February 9, 1727, Philadelphia Wills, Book E, no. 71. Keen, *Founding of the First Baptist Church*, pp. 457–58. Ann Eaglesfield, formerly Bellows, was disowned by the Philadelphia Monthly Meeting for marrying "out of unity" on 1 mo. 27, 1724 (March 27, 1724) (Hinshaw, *Encyclopedia of American Quaker Geneaology*, 2: 510).

7. Will of Barnard Eaglesfield. Stiefel, "Philadelphia Cabinetmaking and Commerce," n. 44.

8. Will of Barnard Eaglesfield. For more on scrutoires, see Peter Kenny, "Ark of the Covenant: The Remarkable Inlaid Cedar Scrutoir from the Brinckerhoff Family of Newtown, Long Island," in *American Furniture*, edited by Luke Beckerdite (Hanover, N.H.: University Press of New England for the Chipstone Foundation, 2014), pp. 2–29; and Sumpter Priddy III, "Musings on a Scottish-Irish Desk Form in Colonial Virginia: The Scrutoire," *Journal of Early Southern Decorative Arts* 33 (2012), http://www.mesdajournal.org/2012/musings-sottish-irish-desk-form-colonial-virginia-scrutoire/.

9. Will of Barnard Eaglesfield. See "The Limitations of a Barter Economy," in Stiefel, "The Head Account Book as Artifact," sec. 1.A., pp. 82–85.

10. Will of Barnard Eaglesfield.

11. Ibid.

12. Will of Barnard Eaglesfield. Indenture from Joseph and Elizabeth Richardson to Bernard Eaglesfield, November 6, 1730 (collection of the author). This was the merchant Joseph Richardson, not the silversmith Joseph Richardson Sr., whose wives were Hannah and Mary, respectively. Jay Robert Stiefel, "All in the Family: Joseph Richardson's Earliest Silver," *Catalogue of Antiques & Fine Art* 5, no. 1 (Spring 2004): 145–49.

13. Thomas Chalkley, Account and Letter Book, 1729–1732, p. 46, collection no. 3215, location: 3V, 118F, HSP (hereafter Chalkley Account Book, 1729–1732).

14. Ibid. For other furniture entries in Chalkley's accounts, see Stiefel, "Philadelphia Cabinetmaking," nn. 494, 654.

15. Chalkley Account Book, 1729–1732, p. 46. John Grove appears to have been the son of another John Grove, "one of Barbados' largest slave importers" (S. D. Smith, *Slavery, Family, and Gentry Capitalism in the British Atlantic: The World of the Lascelles, 1648-1834* [Cambridge, Eng.: Cambridge University Press, 2006], p. 29). The elder Grove's will mentions his widow "Rebeckah" and a minor son John (Will of John Grove, St. Georges Parish, Barbados, May 31, 1717, proved June 18, 1717, RB6/4, 151, compiled and edited in Joanne McRee Sanders, *Barbados Records Wills and Administrations*, vol. 3, *1701–1725* [Houston, Tex.: Sanders Historical Publications, 1981], p. 147). Rebecca Grove also appears in Chalkley's accounts. In 1718 he transported sugar for her from Barbados and sold it in London, and clothing and goods in silver, brass, and pewter from London were consigned to her by Chalkley for his own account. John's mother had ordered a tankard, salvers, and other silver. Thomas Chalkley, Account Book, 1718–1727, pp. 2, 7, collection no. LCP in 132, location: limbo 3C, HSP. The "Jos Grove Mercht. in Londn," mentioned in John's letter appears to have been the son of his uncle Joseph Grove (d. 1713), a merchant in Bermondsey, Surrey. Sanders, ed., *Barbados Records Wills and Administrations*, pp. 147–48. Chalkley may have been transcribing Grove's spellings when he referred to Eaglesfield as "Ecclesfild" and "Ecclesfield". In Chalkley's earlier accounts, Barnard's father appears in transactions in 1720 and 1722 as "George Eaglesfield" (Chalkley Account Book, 1718–1727, pp. 7, 30.) No persons named Eccelesfild or Eccelsfield could be found in contemporaneous records pertaining to Philadelphia or in a READEX search of local newspapers of that era.

16. Blower & Cogan imported slaves into Barbados (Eli Faber, *Jews, Slaves and the Slave Trade / Setting the Record Straight* [New York: NYU Press, 2000], p. 96). Chalkley Account and Letter Book, 1729–1732, p. 46.

17. Will of Barnard Eaglesfield. Chalkley Account Book, 1729–1732, p. 55.

18. Stiefel, "Philadelphia Cabinetmaking and Commerce," sec. X. E. 12, p. 15, and n. 681. Will of James Steel, Philadelphia Wills, 1741 Will Book F, 261, no. 289.

19. Chalkley Account Book, 1729–1732, p. 46. Lindsey, *Worldy Goods*, p. 144, nos. 50–52.

20. Chalkley Account Book, 1729–1732, p. 46. Adam Bowett, "After the Naval Stores Act: Some Implications for English Walnut Furniture," *Furniture History* 31 (1995): 116. Thomas Chalkley, *The Journal of Thomas Chalkley: A Minister of the Gospel in the Society of Friends* (1870), p. 295. Will of Barnard Eaglesfield.

Figure 1 John Widdifield notebook, northern England and Philadelphia, ca. 1704–1720 with later inscriptions. Leather, paper, and ink. 6½" x 4⅛". (Private collection; photo, Gavin Ashworth.)

The Notebook of Philadelphia Joiner John Widdifield

▼ ON SEPTEMBER 17, 2015 Swann Galleries of New York sold a rare manuscript notebook kept by John Widdifield, an English furniture maker who immigrated to Philadelphia by 1705. The collector who acquired the book has generously allowed the Chipstone Foundation to publish it in this volume of *American Furniture* and make it, along with a keyword searchable transcription, available on the foundation's website, www.chipstone.org, and that of the University of Wisconsin-Madison. Widdifield's notebook will also be designated as an ongoing research project on Chipstone's website, thus allowing scholars, students, and others to publish work related to that manuscript. This introduction to the book is intended to begin that dialogue.

John Widdifield was born on September 13, 1673, or "ye 13 ^{dy} of ye 7 mo," as recorded in the Julian calendar in his notebook. The notebook also states that his father was Peter, which, with the aforementioned inscription, contradicts several online sources giving his father's name as John and the joiner's birth date as 1676. The joiner's father may have been Peter Widdifield of Bishop Auckland, a market town in County Durham in northeastern England. Bishop Auckland is about thirty miles south of Newcastle upon Tyne, where John lived at some point before immigrating to Philadelphia (fig. 2). His will indicates that he kept his "messauge" (dwelling house with outbuildings) in Newcastle upon Tyne, and that it was located "between Pilgrim Street and Upper Draw Bridge." John's mother may have been Elizabeth Marlys of Sadberge, a town about fifteen miles southeast of Bishop Auckland. She and Peter married on May 12, 1663.[1]

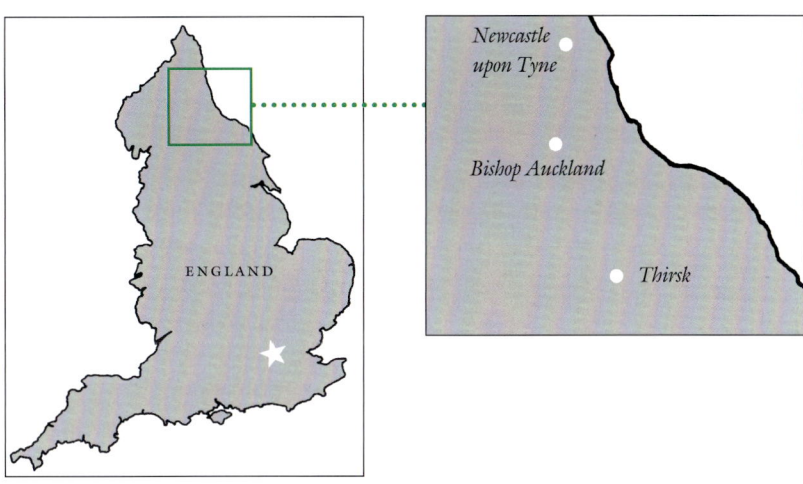

Figure 2 Map of England showing towns associated with Widdifield.

John Widdifield may have moved to Newcastle upon Tyne by early adulthood. His residence appears to have been on the western side of present-day Pilgrim Street near its intersection with Highbridge Street. According to R. J. Charleton's *A History of Newcastle-on-Tyne* (1887), that location was near the meetinghouse of the Society of Friends, which was built in 1698. Earlier meetings were held at Gateshead, just outside the city limits. Assuming that Widdifield began his apprenticeship at the customary age of fourteen he would have completed his training about four years before the meetinghouse was erected.[2]

Throughout the seventeenth century, Newcastle upon Tyne had a guild for joiners (as well as separate guilds for several other woodworking trades), but a 1656 order denied membership to Quakers, Scots, Dutch, and Catholics: "No popish recusant, quaker or any who shall not attend duly on his maister at the public ordinances . . . be taken into apprentice on pain of being fined two marks." If John converted to Quakerism after completing his apprenticeship, he could have served his term with a member of the joiners' guild and possibly been a member himself. Widdifield was described as having been a Quaker for a "few years" in 1705.[3]

It is unclear when joiner John Widdifield immigrated to the colonies. On "4 mo. 29, 1705" (June 29, 1705), "John Widowfield" was received by the Philadelphia Monthly Meeting, where he was described as a young man "who has been Conversant amongst a few also Since he came Among friends" and presented a letter of removal from "Mo. Mtg. at Thirsk" (Yorkshire) dated "7 mo. 14, 1703" (September 14, 1703) and a letter dated "4 mo. 12, 1705" (June 12, 1705) certifying that he "was unmarried when he left England".[4]

Widdifield wrote that he "began to contribute to ye writings" of the Philadelphia Monthly Meeting in 1706. The following year, he served as constable in Philadelphia and married Mary Lawrence (1687–1737), whose father, William, was a tailor. Together the couple had seven children: John (1712), Hannah (1716), Sarah (1718/1719), Ann (1714), Elizabeth (1708), Mary (1710/1711), and Peter (1720). John Jr. inherited the notebook, which has numerous genealogical inscriptions made by later generations of his family.[5]

Aside from the information in his notebook, details regarding the elder John's career are scarce. He attained freeman status in 1717 along with joiners Robert Hubbard and Thomas Stappleford and carver Robert Mullard. The following year he witnessed the will of mariner Jacob Warren in which hatter Jacob Warder and brewer Anthony Morris were listed as trustees. Widdifield must have attained a measure of financial success by 1718. On September 10 he took John and Mary Usher as indentured servants, and on September 11 he and Mary paid joiner William Branson £51.10 for two parcels of land on High Street and Strawberry Alley. The deed for that property mentioned a "House & Office now intended to be built . . . by the said Widifield and . . . Branson," which suggests that the joiners may have intended to form a partnership. The following day, Widdifield secured two adjacent lots and sold a lot on which he had built a brick dwelling house.[6]

A few references to Widdifield making furniture survive in addition to those in his notebook. James Logan's account book has an August 7, 1717, debit to "John Widdowfield" for an "Oval Table" valued at £2.5 and a "Walnut Screen &c" at £10. Furniture historian William McPherson Hornor reported that in 1720 Widifield made a "black Pine Screwtore," had half ownership of two parcels of walnut logs (one "Lying near the Draw Bridge in Philadelphia valued at £25" and one "Lying at Perkiomen valued at £3"), and owned a "Cedar Chest of Drawers" and a "Small red Cedar Table". Although Hornor neglected to provide citations, his source for all those references was Widdifield's inventory. Taken on February 2, 1720, the inventory lists all of the "Goods &. chattles" in his shop and house as well as livestock and materials elsewhere:

his Wearing apparel	13.10.0
Cash	20.0.0
Goods in his Shop Amounting in the whole to	209.10.0
One Clock & Case	10.0.0
One black Pine Screwtore	4.0.0
One Chest of Drawers	5.0.0
Two Ovel black Walnut Tables	3.0.0
One Large Looking Glass	3.0.0
One Small Do. & other Glass on the Mantle piece	2.10.0
Seven Rush bottom Chairs & other odd things in the Middle room below	2.10.0
One Bed & bedste[a]d with the furniture	20.0.0
One black Walnut Chest of Drawers	6.0.0
One Small Walnut Table	2.0.0
Two more Looking Glas[s]es	2.10.0
Seven black Chairs & other furniture in the front Chamber	4.10.0
Two other beds & bedste[a]ds with the furniture	20.0.0
One Cedar Chestof Drawers a Small red Cedar Table	6.0.0
One other Chest of Frawers looking Glass Chairs & other furniture in the upper front Chamber	4.0.0
Two black walnut Chest of Drawers	10.0.0
One Large black walnut table & Two Small Do. and a Mahogany Spice Box	6.0.0
One Trunk & 4 old Chairs	0.10.0
Two beds & bedste[a]ds with furniture & Other things in ye Garret	5.0.0
One pair of Mahognay Drawers unfinished	2.0.0
Sundry Joyner's Tools Amounting to	16.0.0
Two work benches	1.0.1
Carrys Over	£393.0.0
Brought Over	£393.0.0
one other black walnut Chest of Drawers	4.0.0
one hogshead of Mallasses & part of Another	9.0.0
Two hogsheads of Tobacco	4.0.0
One barrel of rosin	1.10.0
Sundrey other Lumber in the Cellar	3.10.0
Iron Pots brass Kettle & pewter in The kitchen	8.10.0
One Large Ovel Walnut Table & A Small Do. in the Kitchen	2.0.0
One Couch four Old Chairs	1.0.0
Two Casks of Salt	1.4.1
one Cask of Pipes	2.0.0
a parcel of walnut boards Scantling & Plank in the yard	6.0.0
Four Grind stones	2.0.0
one Cow and Calf	2.10.0

his half part of a parcel of Walnut Loggs Unsawn Lying near the Draw Bridge In Philadelphia	25.0.0
his half of a parcel of Walnut Do. Lying at Perkasmey	3.0.0
	£470.4.0

Presumably Widdifield made much of the furniture listed above, and all of the forms are included in his notebook.[7]

The intent of Widdifield's notebook is unclear, but its descent in his family indicates that he created it for his personal use as well as that of his heirs. A page devoted to sharpening shows that the purpose of the book was instructional, since Widdifield undoubtedly knew how to maintain his tools. His son John inherited the book, but he was born in 1712 and was only eight years old when his father died. It is possible that the elder Widdifield had planned to train his son and pass along the book when young John reached his majority. John Jr. is described as a "joyner" in two 1737 deeds, but his master's identity and the precise nature of his trade remain unknown. Some craftsmen referred to as "joiners" limited their work to architecture. Later generations of the Widdifield family clearly treasured the notebook, as evidenced by their entries of births and other genealogical information more commonly inscribed in Bibles.[8]

The notebook contains entries that appear to have been made before Widdifield immigrated along with annotations and additions made after his arrival. The earliest date in his hand is "ye 26 th ^{d} 1 ^{mo}: 1704" (March 26, 1704), and it occurs on the first page, which states that "this book contains three parts": "the measure of Tables drawers Chaires &c of household furniture maid by joners"; "staining Coloring & Varnishing with several other experienced Recp.^{s} very useful"; and "Recepts in Physicke . . . for ye good of others." The presence of several blank pages at the end of the adjacent "table of pages" and in the notebook itself reveals that Widdifield intended to add information as his career and experiences developed.

The furniture forms measured, described, and, occasionally, sketched in the notebook provide a glimpse of the range of English vernacular designs émigré joiners brought to the colonies during the early eighteenth century. Among those listed are a variety of seating forms (cane and leather chairs, armchairs, chair tables, child's chairs, easy chairs, and stools), bedsteads (conventional as well as closatts [a bed made like a chest with an optional canopy]), tables (pine, oval, dressing, and chair), chests (single, double, on frame, and table), coat cases, presses, writing desks, clock cases, spice boxes, screens, hanging shelves, coffins, and clothes baskets. Most of the entries are not very descriptive, an exception being "A Writing table standing upon one pillar like a stand having two drawers." The notebook also contains sketches of a spice box, a scrutoire, a chest-on-frame, and a "coffin mojaure" (which resembles a cradle) as well as prices Widdifield charged for certain types of objects.

Some of the entries in the notebook were clearly made after Widdifield arrived in Philadelphia. A page with the heading "spice boxes" has a sketch with the notation, "A little Scruetore for Thomas Lyfords" (fig. 3). His patron was probably the same Thomas Lyford who was received by the

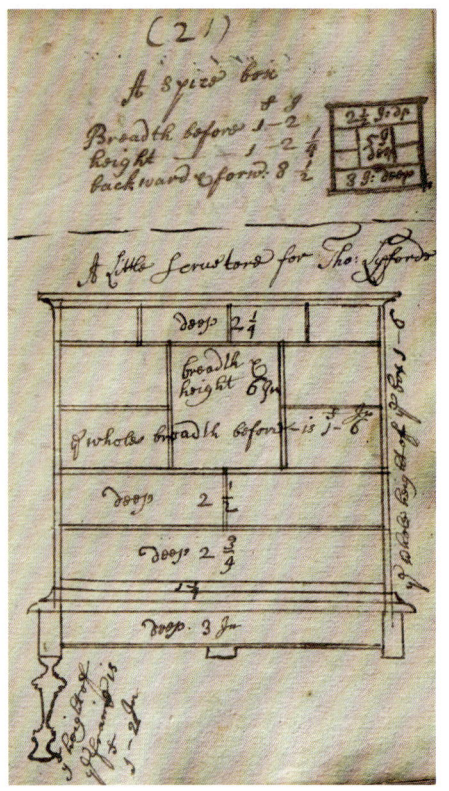

Figure 3 Designs and measurements for a spice box and scrutoire on p. 21 in John Widdifield's notebook. (Photo, Gavin Ashworth.)

Figure 4 Spice box-on-stand, case and frame possibly from the shop of John Widdifield, Philadelphia, Pennsylvania, ca. 1715. Mahogany with white cedar and yellow pine. H. 25½", W. 18⅝", D. 9". (Chipstone Foundation; photo, Gavin Ashworth.) The spice box listed in Widdifield's inventory was made of mahogany.

Figure 5 Spice box-on-stand, case and frame possibly from the shop of John Widdifield, Philadelphia, Pennsylvania, ca. 1715. Mahogany with white cedar, oak, and yellow pine. H. 26", W. 17", D. 9". (Private collection; photo, Gavin Ashworth.)

Philadelphia Monthly Meeting a few days before "John Widowfield" and produced a certificate of removal from the Meeting at Bull and Mouth in London dated "11 mo. 22, 1704" (January 22, 1704). Similarly, David Britnall Jr., for whom Widdifield made a bedstead, became a member of the Philadelphia Monthly Meeting on "12 mo. 27, 1707/8" (February 27, 1707/1708). Other patrons mentioned in the notebook included Mary Lard (oval table), Jonathan Lucan (press), Edward Garmon (press), and William Rob (clock case).[9]

Widdifield's sketch of Lyford's scrutoire resembles two Philadelphia spice boxes (figs. 4, 5), one of which reputedly descended in the Morris family (fig. 4). Although the original owners of the boxes are unknown, brewer Anthony Morris, like Lyford, was a member of the Philadelphia Monthly Meeting. The cases and frames of both boxes are constructed as a single unit, which is the impression given by Widdifield's design. Their legs differ from the one shown in Widdifield's sketch, but joiners often purchased lathe-generated components from different turners. The dimensions and drawer arrangement of Lyford's scrutoire suggest that it was a tabletop form—possibly having a fall front—patterned after a spice box.[10]

The sections on coloring, staining, and varnishing and "Recepts in Physicke" were probably completed before Widdifield immigrated and contain few, if any, subsequent entries. His recipes and instructions for "Coloring Staining & Varnishing According to [his] . . . own Experience" are among the most comprehensive manuscript compendiums surviving from the

Figure 6   Title page of John Stalker and George Parker's *Treatise on Japaning and Varnishing*, Oxford, England, 1688.

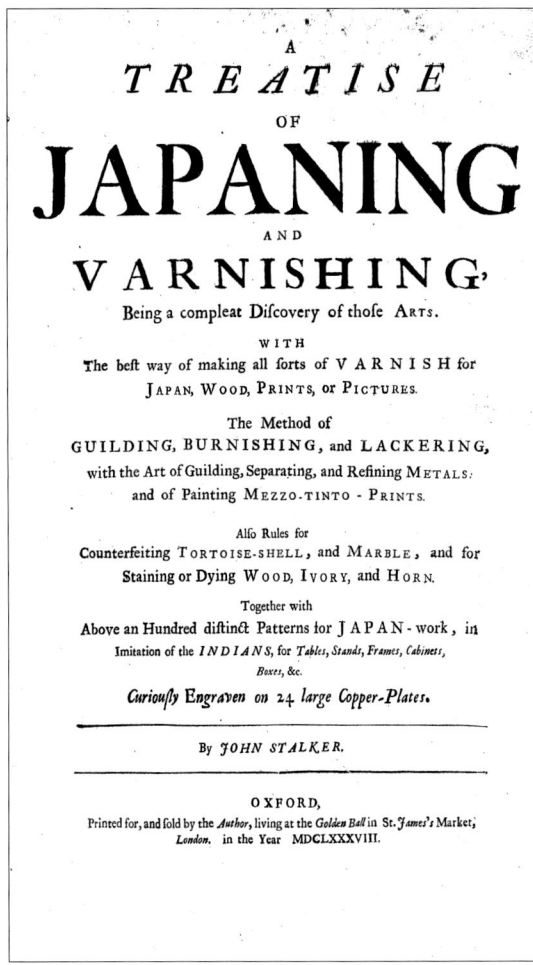

early-eighteenth century. The closest published equivalent is John Stalker and George Parker's *Treatise on Japaning and Varnishing* (1688) (fig. 6). Widdifield's notebook is much more than a collection of recipes, measurements, and prices; it is a deeply personal creation that was a guide and an heirloom for his family and will be a resource for scholars in the years to come.[11]

ACKNOWLEDGMENTS For their assistance with this introduction, the Chipstone Foundation thanks Gavin Ashworth, David Haugard, Alan Miller, Rick Stattler, Jay Stiefel, and Martha Willoughby. The Foundation is particularly grateful to Joseph P. Gromacki for his support of this publication and the digital initiatives associated with it.

1. John Widdifield notebook, last two pages (not numbered), private collection. http://www.myheritage.com/names/john_widdifield is one of several online sources citing John as the first name of Widdifield's father and 1676 as the joiner's birth date. The man who is identified incorrectly as the joiner's father may have been the John Widdiwfield listed in the electoral roll of County Durham in 1675 (Ancestry.com. UK, Poll Books and Electoral Registers, 1538–1893; Provo, UT, USA: Ancestry.com Operations, Inc. 12012. Original data: London, England, UK, and London Poll Books. London Metropolitan Archives and Guildhall Library). Several online sources also note that émigré John Widdifield married Margaret O'Bourne (born in Dublin, Ireland) circa 1704 (http://www.myheritage.com/names/john_widdifield). There-

fore, it is possible that two men by that name arrived in Philadelphia about the same time. Will of John Widdifield, written January 10, 1720, and probated January 21, 1720, Philadelphia County Wills, 1682–1819, Historical Society of Pennsylvania, available at Ancestry.com. Marriages, Darlington District, record no. 452513; www.durhamrecordsonline.com/ViewRecord.php. Peter and Elizabeth were married at St. Andrew's [Anglican] Church. Joiner John Widdifield's firstborn daughter was named Elizabeth, and his second son was named Peter (Widdifield notebook, last two pages). Although those are relatively common names, they support the theory that joiner John Widdifield was the son of Peter and Elizabeth.

2. R. J. Charleton, *A History of Newcastle-on-Tyne* (Newcastle-upon-Tyne: W. H. Robinson, 1887), pp. 188, 191, 421, 425–26.

3. Ibid. pp. 425–426. Quaker Arrivals at Philadelphia, 1682–1750, p. 36, https://archive.org/stream/quakerarrivalsa00myergoog/quakerarrivalsa00myergoog_djvu.txt.

4. Quaker Arrivals at Philadelphia, 1682–1750, p. 36.

5. Widdifield notebook, last two pages, lists six of his seven children and their birthdates. Peter was described as the joiner's unborn child in Will of John Widdifield.

6. http://www.ebooksread.com/authors-eng/j-thomas-john-thomas-scharf/history-of-philadelphia-1609-1884-volume-vi-ahc/page-51-history-of-philadelphia-1609-1884-volume-vi-ahc.shtml. See also Minutes of the Common Council of the City of Philadelphia, 1704–1776, pp. 122–23, available at Ancestry.com. Will of Jacob Warren, Philadelphia County Wills, 1682–1819, Historical Society of Pennsylvania, 1900, vol. D: 78, available at Ancestry.com. For the land transactions and indentures, see Philadelphia County Deed Book H13, p. 86; Philadelphia County Deed Book F1, City Hall, Philadelphia, microfilm, Historical Society of Pennsylvania, pp. 327–30 (new numbering, pp. 361–65).

7. James Logan account book, 1712–1720, Logan Family Papers (collection 379), Historical Society of Pennsylvania, Philadelphia. William Macpherson Hornor, *Blue Book: Philadelphia Furniture, William Penn to George Washington* (Philadelphia: by the author, 1935), pp. 41, 42, 46. The inventory is filed with will of John Widdifield. Chipstone thanks Jay Stiefel for providing the location of the inventory.

8. Philadelphia County Deed Books F9, p. 123; and F10, p. 18.

9. Lyford was received on "4 mo. 29, 1705" (June 29, 1705) and described as "unmarried." Quaker Arrivals at Philadelphia, 1682–1750, pp. 35, 36, https://archive.org/stream/quakerarrivalsa00myergoog/quakerarrivalsa00myergoog_djvu.txt. For David Britnall, see p. 40.

10. https://en.wikipedia.org/wiki/Anthony_Morris_(I).

11. Widdifield's section on finishes also includes directions for finishing, silvering, and soldering brass.

This book contained
three parts

first

the measure of Tables drawers
Chaires &c: of houshold furnitr
maid by Joners

the second

of staining Coloring &
varnishing with
severall other experienced Recp:s
very usefull ye 26th 1mo: 1704

the third

of Receipts in Phisick
whereof ye most has been tryed
& taken from People of Credit benefitt
reced: thereby hath occationed me to
write them for ye good of others
        John Widdifeild

The Table of pages	
The Sizes of plaines	page 1
of drawors	2
Clock case	3
Dressing Tables & dine Table	4
ovial Table	5
Close stooles	6
Squabs	7
Stooles	8
Chaires	9
Childs Chaires	10
Chaire Table	11
Cradles	12
Closatt or drawer like body	13
hanging shelves	14
Screens	15
Spining wheels Knack Reele	16
A writing Table	17
A Coale Case	18
A Chaire of ease Table	19
Chist of Wall & quie Chyst	20
A Spice box	21
A Worsted wheele	22
A Wallnutree Chist of drawers	23
A Coffine	24
A Cradle	25

	41
	42
	43
	44
	45
	46
	47
	48
	49
	50
	51
	52
	53
	54
	55
	56
	57
	58
	59
	60

The 2d Booke: of Coloring p	61
of staineing in Colors divers	62
of varnishing linseed oyl var: gums	63
with tempering varnish & pry of	64
of ye best spirit varnish commar:	65
ye lye of it	66
seedlake varnish	67
of severall Colors	68
of staineing	69
of staineing black: Knotty wood as mapl or other	70
to frames mapps or paper	71
Jappan var: & Jappaning	72
	73
	74

	75
	76
	77
	78
	79
	80
	81
	82
	83
	84
	85
	86
	87
	88
	89
	90
	91
	92
	93
	94

The 3d part Receipts in Physick p	95
	96
dyat drinks	97
Recepts for stoppings of obar breathing by Rumes	98
for salted Colds	99
A Jelly for a Consumption, or Looseness	100
Excelant plasters for strames or syatica	101
for sore eyes Cures warts	102
Pultice for swellings itch boiles venoms	103
A Plaister for ye stomack in Physick	104
Sore leggs or wounds & Cuts	105
for a Consumption scurvey or dropsie	106
	107
	108
Sore breasts & cuts 111	109

(1)   Joynter Length f 2 — I 6 & 3 s

Allthough I maid my tiling plaine serve me for a Joynt whose length was 1—0 and 2½ square for plaine length 1—2 & 2¼ Sq

stritblock Len: 1—1 squar 2½

Smoothing plaine 7½ long

deep 2½ thick 2¼

Moolding tooles Len: 10 deep 3¾
ob

found the eye of each pla.
to be sett ⅓ from ye found
and the Iron laid 1/6 from
mitter

when I say one third or one
sixth itt is to be divided into
3 or 6 parts & one of these is
⅓ or 1/6 therefor ye Iron is to
ly mitter all but one sixth
of ye mitter

(2)

A Chist of drawers or Chist
of drawers there are many sorts
but I shall only sett down 2 or 3 sorts
and first of our old fashond kind
one y^t for sides

 duble drawer
hight f 3—I 7 length f 3—I 6 broadth
backward & forward 1—10 taking
of in ye midle ye top dra: deep 5
ye 2 & low drawers each one foot de
and ye loest but one to deep ye swelling
or raiseings breadth 2 thickness 1¾
ye loer sort of swelings bea: 1½ th ¾

 single drawer
hight f 2—I 9½ ye length ye same
ye eye drawer deep 5½ ye other 2
both of one breadth or rather deep

A Chist of draw: standing on a fram
whole hight f 4—I 2 or 5 ye frame
height 1—7 deep first drawer I 5
& 2^d 6 ye 3^d 7 & ye loest 8 or 12½ each
ye length of ye dra: 2—11 or 3 foot
backward & forward 1—8 if a dra.
in ye frame make itt 4 deep

~~[struck-through lines]~~

first of all to keep all thy edge tools
very sharp for ye attaineing of wch keep
(*nature of grinston*) a grinston of a fine greet not very hard
but very true haueing one ye end of ye Axletree
a torn or crook with a knop or button on itt
let ye turn be about 6 Inces long on itt
fixe a foot of wood to tourn like to
a line wheele by ye foot wch may be easily
done then haueing it very true grind all
thy edge tooles one itt or as many as thou
can when euer they want sharpening then with
a hone sett ye edge of them wch will doe it
very fine keep thy planes Irons and Chysels
very squar sharpe one ye edge oncept ye for pla
(*y{e} Sorts of wood for pla*) and very close cut in ye eye gitt them of very
hard wood as beech holy or old oake of
which Sorts the hardest is best

---

(3) made for John Ward

Clockcases

Whole high 6—9 the balls ½
the hight of ye base 1—8 ¾
the height of ye body of ye base
between the base & subase that is ye
moolding wch ye head slids one is ¾
breadth before 1—0 thickness 6
the dial plate 11 ye sides of ye dial do
are 2 broad the top & bottom 1 ¾ ¼
ye Arkitriue 1¼ ye frise 1¼ ye Cornyes 2
Soo ye hight of ye head is 20 ½ ye top
of subase is ½ I thick

A lesser Clockcase whose dial pla{te}
is 10 ¼ breadth before 10 ½ or 11 fi{ne}

A Clockcase head only
the dial plate being 11 ye body sh{all}
be in breadth before 09 ¾ thick
and ye other members may some
this afore

made for John Ogden

(4)

dressing Tables

ℓeaf Length 3ᶠᵗ breadth 2-00ᶠᵗ
ye frame length 2ᶠᵗ-4ⁱⁿ
breadth 1ᶠᵗ-9ⁱⁿ hight 2ᶠᵗ-6ⁱⁿ
deepness of yᵉ drawer 4ⁱⁿ

A dressing Table
ℓeaf length 2ᶠᵗ-10ⁱⁿ breadth 1ᶠᵗ-10½ⁱⁿ
height 2-5 dra 4ⁱⁿ deepe

A Pine Table in Pen
Leafe length 3ᶠᵗ-6ⁱⁿ Breadth 2ᶠᵗ-9ⁱⁿ
drawer 4ⁱⁿ deep Price 15 Shill

An Ovall Table for Mary Lard
yᵉ Leafe Length 5:09ⁱⁿ breadth 4ᶠᵗ-7ⁱⁿ
frame Length 3:10 breadth 1ᶠᵗ-9ⁱⁿ
height 2:5

Small Ovall Table
Leafe length 4-6 breadth 3-8
frame Length 3-2 broadth 1-5
yᵉ wings brd̄ 1-6

(5)

Ovall Tables

The hight of a Large one
is 2ᶠᵗ-7ⁱⁿ the Length of yᵉ ovile
obout 9 or 10 more then yᵉ brad
the breadth of the standing Leaf
is one third of the length (or
some times more) of the Leaf
and for a little one about
2ⁱⁿ lower

Ovall Tables in Pen

5 foot & 6 foot yᵉ Leafe yᵉ hight
2 foot 5 or 6 Inches price 3£
yᵉ fraime is 9ⁱⁿ shorter then yᵉ Leaf
& 1 In narrower

Ovall Table
Leafe 4 & 5 foot height 2ᶠᵗ5ⁱⁿ
yᵉ Length of yᵉ fraime 3-8ᶠᵗ broadth 1ᶠᵗ-4ⁱⁿ
broadth of yᵉ wings 1-8

(6)

Close Stoole measures
hight 1f–6i breadth before
and behind 1–6 backward
and forward 1–4

A Cabinet ye Stoole
may be ye Same size onely
ye deepness of ye pan: is 10
w:th ye Railes and ye lower part
is thrown haueing a stritching
Raile att bottem

(7)

Squab measure
Length 5f–6i breadth 1f–9i
height 1–6 from ye seat
to ye Top of ye Stiles 2 foot
the Stiles may be very crooked
except the head lett down
wch is done by joyneing the
Top Railes together ye lower
goeing one pins and hier
haueing a Line fastened
to each end of itt goeing
through ye Top of ye Stiles
by wch itt may be raised or
settled as you will

A Couch is ye the same meaning
Length 5f3 breadth 1f10 hight 1f4

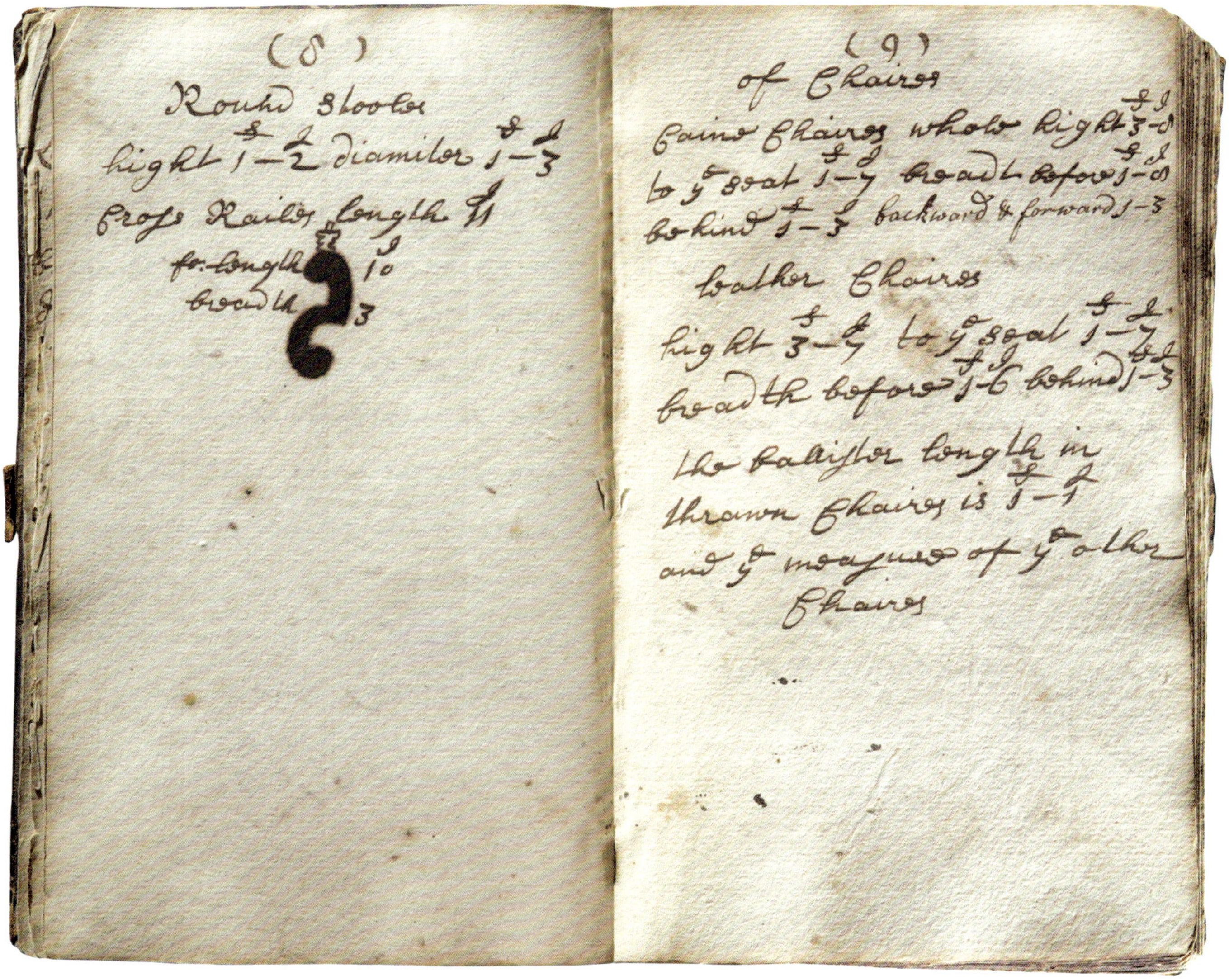

(8)

Round Stools
hight 1–2 diamiter 1–3

Cross Rails length 11
 fo: length 10
 breadth 3

(9)
of Chaires

Caine Chaires whole hight 3–9
to y seat 1–7 breadth before 1–9
behind 1–3 backward & forward 1–3

Leather Chaires
hight 3–4 to y seat 1–7
breadth before 1–6 behind 1–3

the Ballister length in
thrown Chaires is 1–5
and y measures of y other
 Chaires

(10)
Child Chaires Mea.

to sitt att ftable in to ye seat
from ye ground 2^ft—2^in to topp
of ye armes I more breadth
before att ye seat 1^ft—4^in behind 1-2
backward & forw: 11 att y^e
ground backward & forw: 1^ft—4^in
before 1^ft—2^in½ behind 1-6½
from ye seat to ye foot peice 1^in
from ye seat to ye topp 1^ft—4^in

A Childs Chaire

hight 2^ft to ye seat to topp
of ye Armes 3^in br: before 1-2½
behind 1^ft backward: & fore
ward 1^ft 1¼

(11)
Chaire Table

hight 2^ft—6^in breadth before
and behind 2^ft backward
& foreward 2—6½ hight of
ye seat 1^ft—1^in length of ye Leaf
is 3—2 breadth 2—3

(12)

A Cradle
Length ft brea[d]th ft in
   3   1 — 5½
         ft in
deepness 1 — 1

A Childs Close Baskitt
att ye Toppe 15 & 16 Inches
att ye bottom 11 & 12 Inches &
of Pine 3 bitts ye £ 2 — 6
of Wallnt 3 — 6 — —

(13)

A bed like a Chist of drawers
          ft in   ft in
height 3 — 11 breadth 3 — 4 foot
backward & forewards 2 —

Some has these beds
made like Closetts ye foreside
being ye Teaster when turnd up
ye Curtans being fixt one ye in
side the fraime goeing in fold
within

A Canopy Teaster
broadth of ye Rising with ye
Railes allsoe is 11 Inches ye height
of ye Rising is 7 Inches
                        In   In
the Cornich deepness 10 & projector 7

(14)

A hanging shelf
whole height 1—9 ½
length 1—0 breadth 0 8 ½
pillors height 7 ½ ballisters 2 ½

(15)

of Skreens
first for drying Cloaths one
height 6—9 bradth of each
leaf 2—9 with 6 Railes
4 of them are thrawn Round
ye low Raile of ye ground 1—2
ye upper R 2 of ye top being 2 broad
the other equally divided

A screen oual i Pen
ye oual length 1 ft 9 broadth 1 ft
hight of ye stalk 4 foot
thickness of ye stalk ¾ 1/0 In

(16)

of Spin: Wheels

Lyne wheel stoole length 10
diamiter of the Rimm 1-4
length of ye foot 1-0 distance
of ye heads 7 & ye 2 Rimm standards
is length 1-2 cross heads 10½ & ye 2 little
standards 9½ & ye Rock stand: 1-0

Slabb Wheels

Stoole Len: 3-6 br ye Len:
of ye foot 1-0 heads 2 foot long
ye Rimm 3 diamiter spokes 15
Stand: 2 long above ye stoole

Knack Reele ½ ell long
9-4 Circumferance naf 3 spokes 1-3
2-9¼ diamiter Cros heads 5 in number
having to tale 100 & is a score ye Axtree
haveing one wire tooth ye first wheel
20 tooth with 4 on its Axtree the other
wheel 20 tooth which makes up ye
number: rather 2 nogs on ye reele th: 20
in ye 1st wheele 3 in its Ax: & 30 my last wheel
the easer sort is 00 to tale ye Reele 3 about
its 2 nogs 20 ye first sohi 3 in Ax: 24 in last wheele
ye distance between ye standards 7½ in ye stoole is long

(17)

A writing Table

standing upon one piller like
to a stand haveing 2 drawers
one for paper 1d deep and the
other for standish sand box & ye
3d deep screwing fast upon ye
piller the leaf being fixed with
hinges one ye drawers by & soo
when to write one turns up like
a deske ye leaf being foot & long 2-4
and 1-6 broad being cutt in 3
one quarter turning up at each
end & soo covr ye midle part
the hight being 2-7 the dra:
caps being one Inc & less one every
side then the midle leaf w ch is
1-6 one way & 1-2 ye other way

(18)

A Scale Case

whole hight 5 broadth before $\frac{f}{3}$ and behind 2—4 thickness 1—8 haueing a drawer att top 4 deep

---

A Press for Jn:º Lucan

whole height 5—9 broadth before 4=4 thick —1—11 y.e balls 5 Jn Cor 3 Jn aboue the top y.e drawer 8 Jn deep with 2 Shelues a boue y.e drawer

---

A Press for Edward Garmon

whole height 5—6 broadth before 3:3 thick 1—5 drawer 6 Jn deep balls 4 or 2 Jn aboue y.e top ———

(19) n:tº

A Chaire of ease m:r Stackums

whole height 4—4 ssabe height 1—9 Armes aboue y.e ssab 1—0 broadth before 2—4 broadth behind 1—10 haueing retourns or two sides each of y.m bing to rest ones head against 1 foot & 2 Jnsh broad att tope & 4 or 5 Jn: att y.e bottam wch is y.e seale y.e broadth of y.e Chaire backward & forward is 1—8 it may be maid 2 or 3 Jnses higher att y.e toppe: y.e bottam of y.e side peices Nar: nott to exceed 3 or 4 Jn

(20)

of Chist of Wallnutt
length 3-10 brod: 1-9 deep
in all 1-9 dra: deep: 6 In
Prise 2-10 ho: lock & dr

A Pine Chist
length 3-8 brod: 1-5 deep 1-5
prise 15 shill.

A Pine Table
base height 2-4 length 3-6
broadth — 2-8 dra deep -9
prise 15 shill.

A Wallnut Chamb: Table
base length 3 foot broadth 2 foot
frame length 2 f: 6 J broadth 1 fo 8 Jn
height 2-6
prise 1:4:00

(21)

A 8 yrd box
Broadth before 1-2
height 1-2¼
backward & forw: 8½

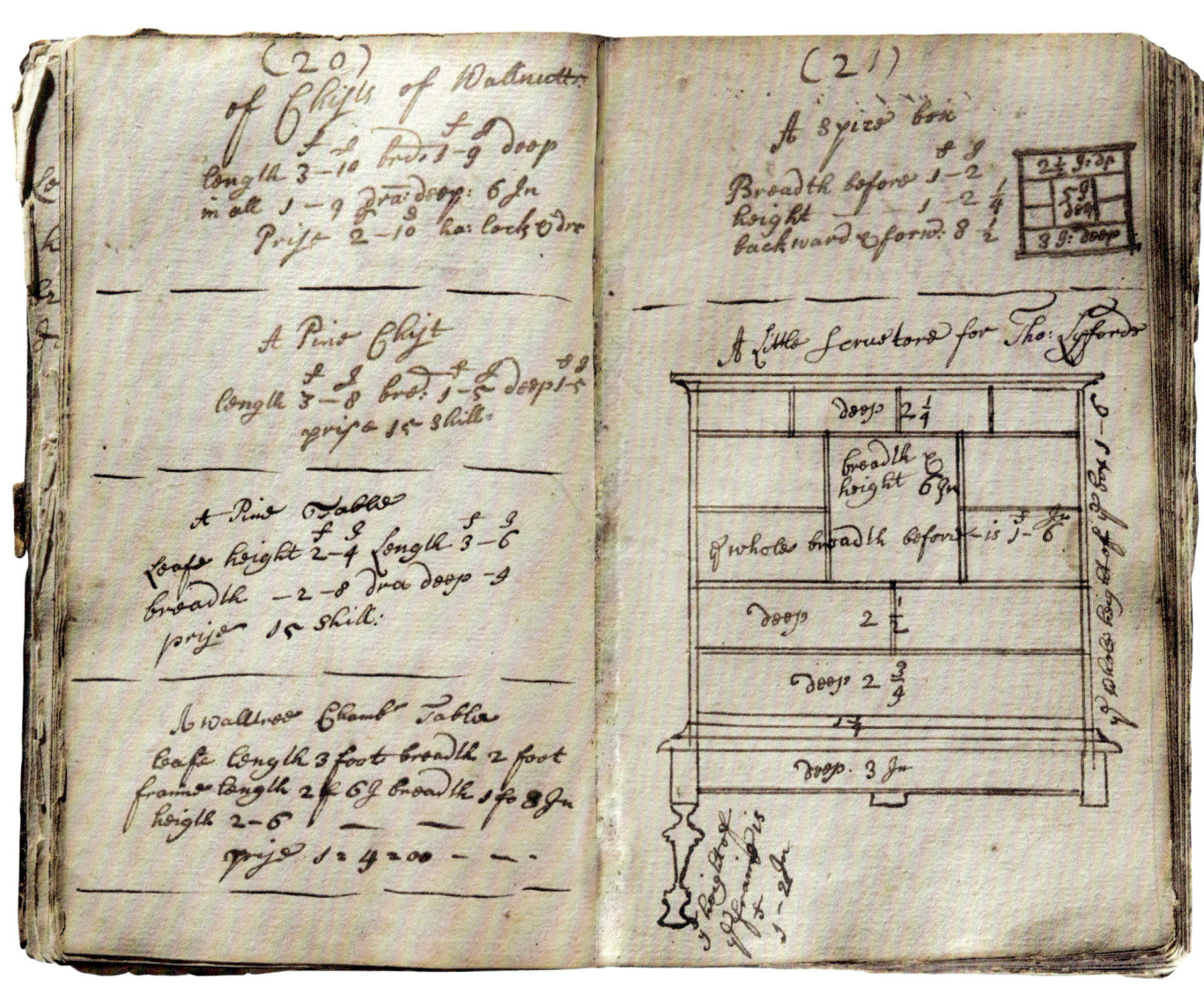

A Little scrutore for Tho: Lyford

(22)

A Worsted Wheele
                    ft In
stools length   3 - 6
hight of ye spindle 3 - 7
diamiter of ye Runne 2 - 3
hight of ye standard
   of ye foot

_____

To one duzen of Leather Chaires
                                    £   s   d
prise of Wallnutree frames
is 6 s p Chaire frame   } 3 : 12 : 00

To ye Covering of ye doz.   1 : 09 : 00

To ye 2 hydes of Read Leather 3 : 00 : 00

To 24 yards of girth webb ―― 0 : 08 : 00

To Groakes for vnder bottoms   0 : 10 : 00

To 3 Thous: small Tacks 3:4 ye Thou : 10 : 00

To Brass nailes

(23) vpon Balls

A Chist of Walb: drawers
prise 4 pound
              ft In   ft In
Height   3 - 6   length 3 - 9
back & forward ――― 1 ― 10
drawers Low 3 deep ye Low
one 9 s next ye 7 s next 6½ ye
hier one 4½

A Chist of Walbutt: Drawers
vpon a fraime prise 6 pounds

[drawing of chest of drawers with annotations:]
deep 4½
5½
6½
ye whole broadth before 3 - 2½
                         ft In
8 Inales
ye hoyght of ye fraime 2
                              small
low
In 2
4½ In deep
broadth ye back Ye forward
is 1 ft 9½

(24)

a Childs Coffin 2 Mo old

within Length 2 b: at shoul: 8½
deep at head 5½ at foot 4½
breadth at head 4 in 3½ foot 3½ [?]
of pine pris'd 4 = 6
black Wallnutt: 10 = 0

A mans Coffin
Length within 6 foot breadth
at yͤ Shoulders 18 Inches
breadth at yͤ head 7½ In:
at yͤ foot 6½ In:
deep 11 Inches
from head to Shoulders is about 16 In:
Price is 15 Shill —

A Childs Coffin measure 1¼ year old
Length 2 = 7 breadth at yͤ Shoulders
is 9½ In at yͤ head 4 In at yͤ foot 3½
deep at yͤ head 7 In at yͤ foot 6 In

(25)

breadth att Top $\frac{f \cdot I}{1-5}$

$\frac{f}{2} - \frac{I}{9\frac{1}{2}}$ 10 In

$\frac{f}{2} - \frac{I}{9}$ in   all

breadth at yͤ bottom 3-2

br: at head $\frac{f \cdot I}{1-8}$
1 foote
6
1 foot
7¼
10 In
19 In
all
3-2

A Bed Stead w͂th short posts
for David Brintnall
Length 6 = 2 breadth 4 = 5
height of yͤ head posts 3 = 6
h: of yͤ feet ditto 1 = 10
prise — 12 Shill

---

the price of yͤ Comon sort 10 S

The Sacking bottom is 18 S
68 for Screws & 256 for fixing
Screws for balls 35 for Rods
to yͤ Sacking 68 —

(26)

Dr Evans Clockcase measure
whole height 8=9   frize br. 1 3/4
to ye dyal — 5"11 base — 2
height of ye base 1"9 Top plints 3
hig: of ye uper Top "11
between Cap & Bay 3"9   old Case
mead one for Wm Rob. price 4=10=00

Samuel Pennock Dr ————
10 m. 3 to Cash lent ——— 0:3:6

Eliz.ᵗʰ Pennock Dr ————
12 m. 17 To Cash lent 1:0:=
   0

(27)

Lent to Philip Kingey
Clarks Introduction to
makeing of Latin August
ye 3d 1754

1814 2 mᵒ. 18 this Day
Remarkable pleasant
19 this Day the frogs
out ——
20 Frogs Singing
Bats flying out
——————————
21 very pleasant
22 very pleasant

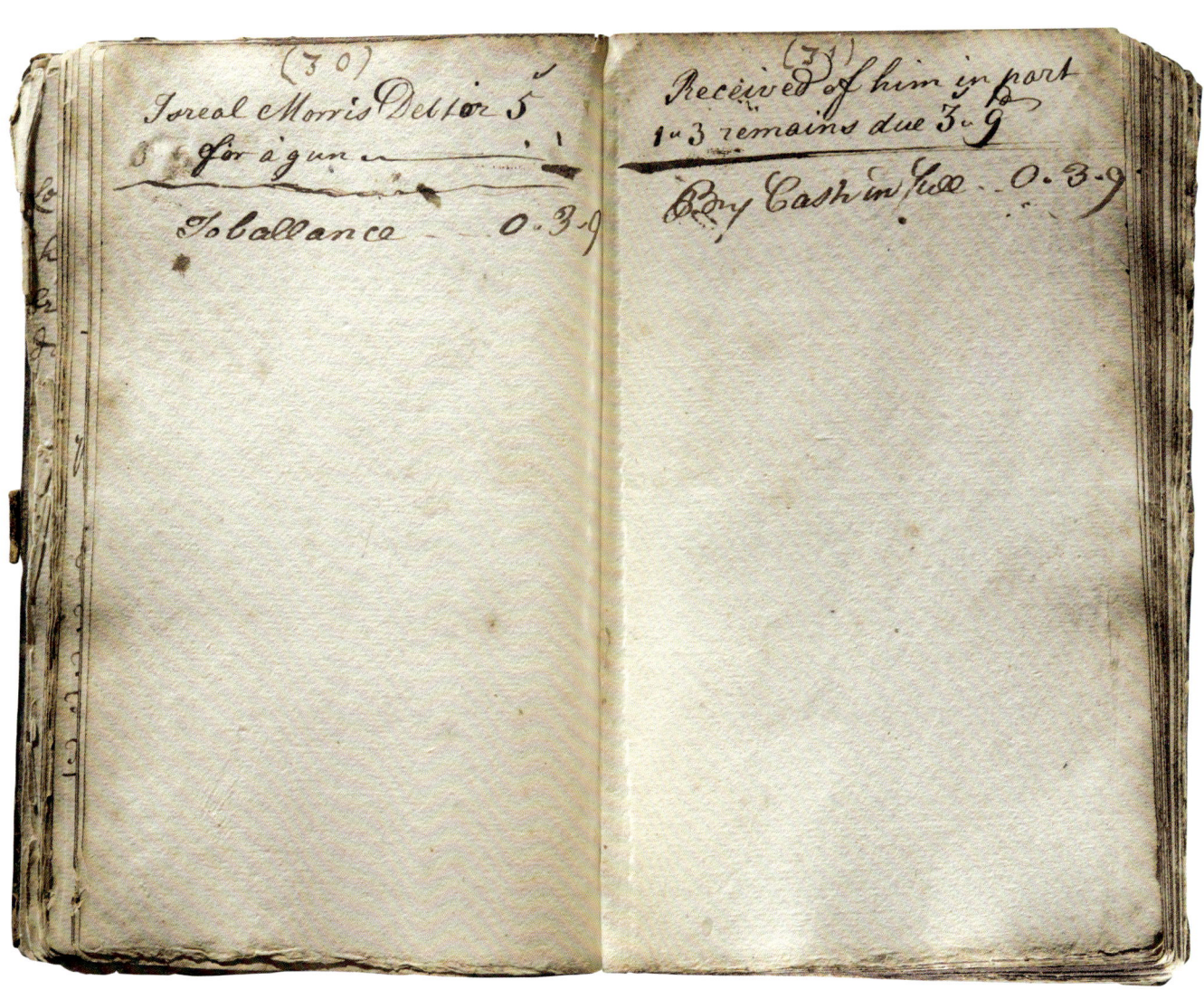

(30)
Isreal Morris Debtor for a gun — 5

To ballance — 0.3.9

(31)
Received of him in part 1..3 remains due 3..9

By Cash in full — 0.3.9

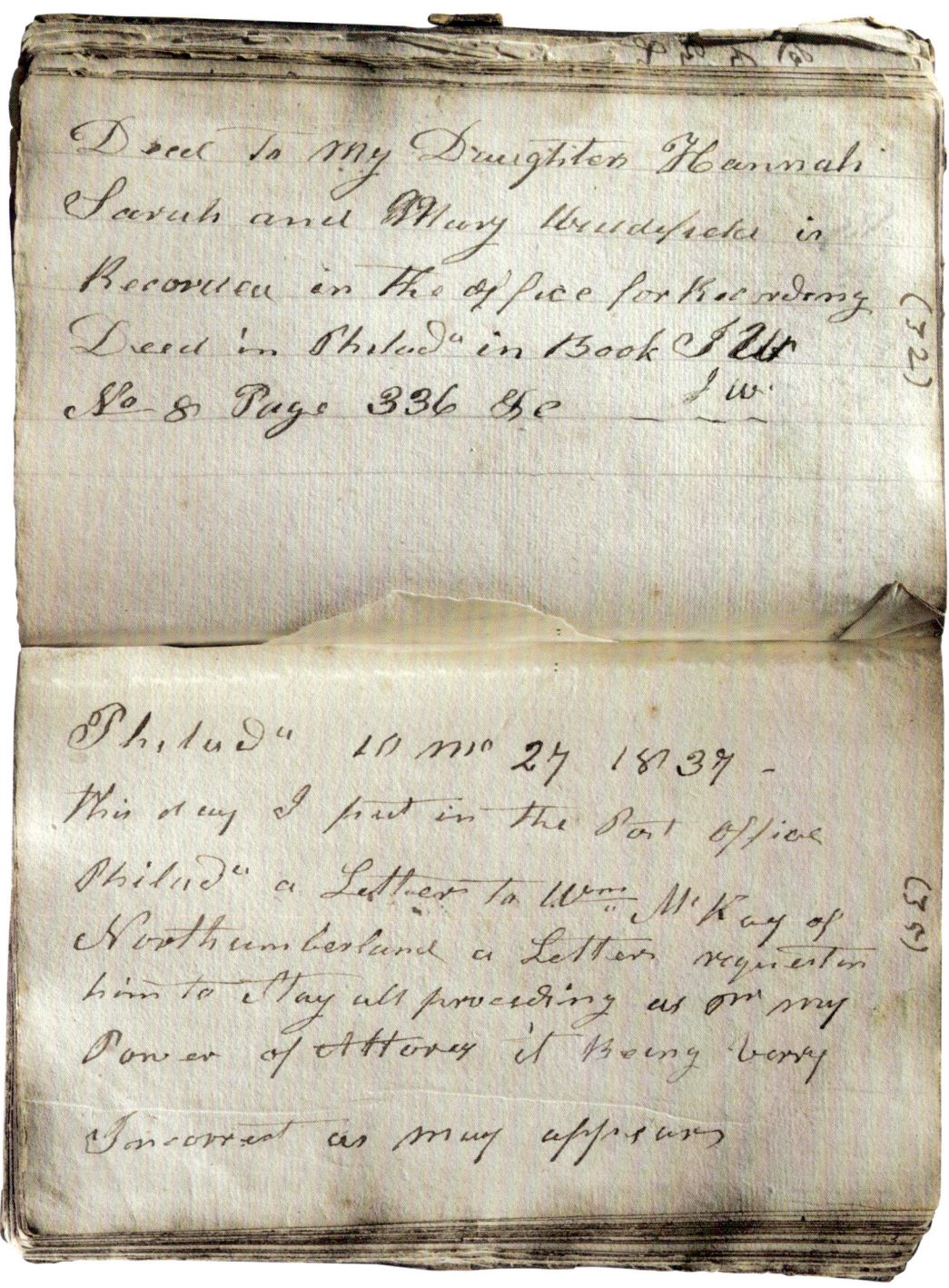

One leaf torn out presumably (33) and (34). Following this spread are twenty-four pages each with the numbers in parenthises at the center top of the page beginning at (36) ending at (59). The numbering is consectutive.

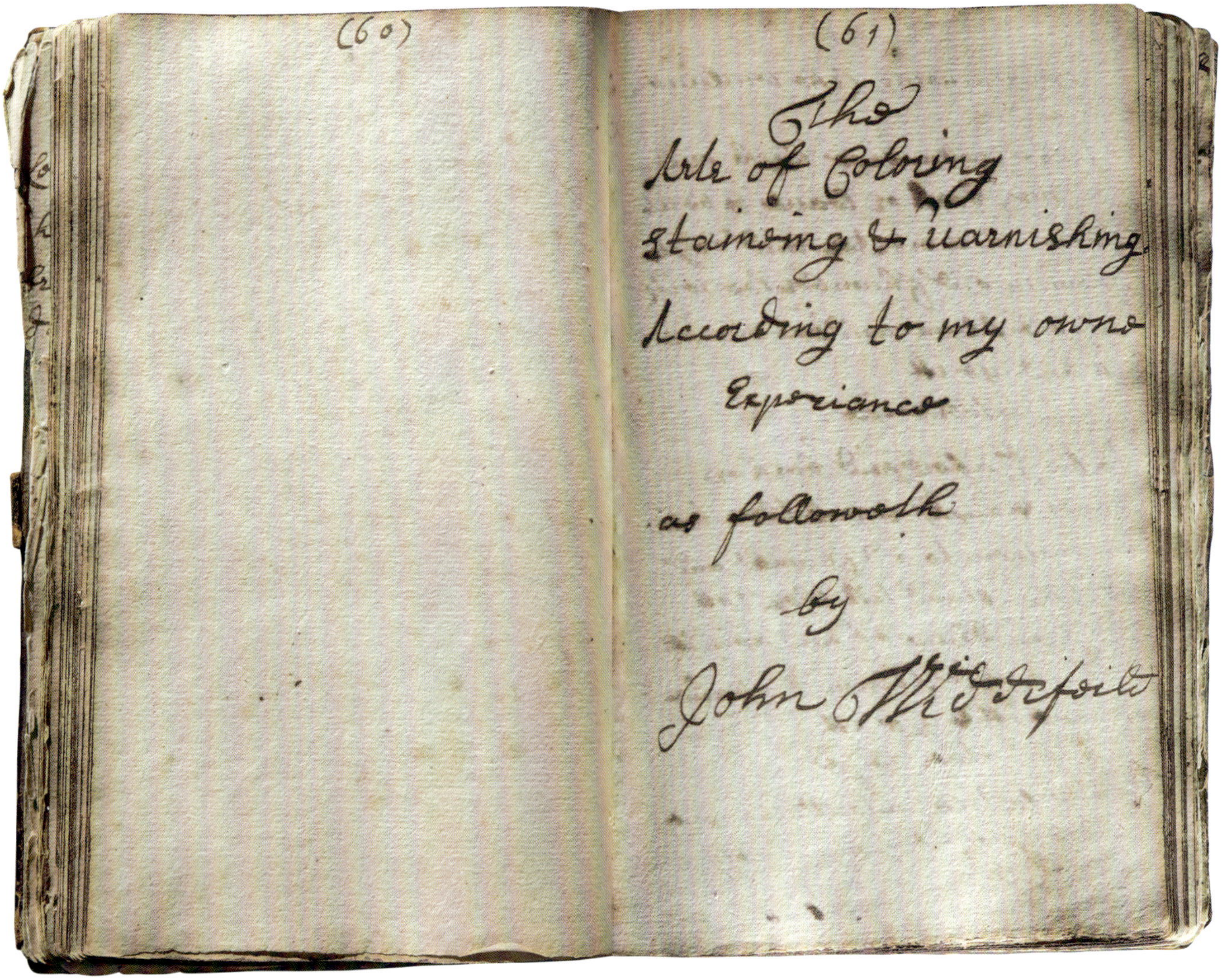

(60) (61)

The
Arte of Coloring
staineing & varnishing

According to my owne
Experiance

as followeth

by

John Widdifeild

(62)

of staineing like wallnuttree

Take wallnuttree huske or leaves
or other bark or leaves & beat
them in a morter and boyle
them in old Chamberlee with
alittle Allum and soe straine
itt and use itt

otherwise

Take ye aforesaid bark or
leaves & huske & put them into
an earthen lo old Chamberℓ and
let them stand till they rott
and then draw of and boil itt
with alittle Allum & straine
straine itt & use itt

otherwise

Aquafortis into which put
alittle steel filings and after it's
done fuming use itt if with your
hands oyle yn wth sallatt oyle

(63)

Shining varnish

Take of ye spirits of wine
1 quart ad to itt 1 lb of ye
Roadest Rosel powdred & 1 spoon
full of venice Turpentine

Another

The common Turpentine
varnice if soft put oyle
of turpentine or spirit varnish to itt as much
as to make itt dry soone

Locker varnice

To 1 quart of ye best spirit add
5 oz of ye best seed Lake &
2 dra of gum buguium with 2 dra
of Aloes in powder

(64)

the price of gums

gum Animes ⅌ pound — 6
Seed Lake ⅌ ℔ 1 - 6
Sandrick ⅌ ℔ 1 - 4 Mastick
⅌ oz 4 dragons blood ⅌ oz 7
gum Araback ⅌ ℔ 6 venice
turpentine ⅌ ℔ 1 - 6 oyle
of turpentine ⅌ ℔ 2 nutt
oyle 1   Sirter 10 trippolo 10

Varnice of Linseed oyle

To one quart of linseed oyle
ad ¼ of a pound of read Lead
& as much of ye whitest Rozen
boile ym well when clear'd is
very usefull any Strong sized
color adding a glass & bedding
coat trobal

(65)

of varnishing with spirit va

To one quart of ye best spirits
add 5 oz of Seed & 1 oz of gum
Animes & ¼ oz of Mastick

black Jappan va

To 1 quart of ye best spirits
add 2 oz of Mastick 3 oz of Sandrick
2 oz of Animes & 1 oz of frankincens

white Jappan va

To 1 quart of spirits add 3 oz
of Mastick 3 oz of white Sandri
& 1½ oz of the whitest gum
Elemes well pict & washt

the common using varnice

To ye comon turpentine varnice ad
¼ of spirit of wine varnice or spirit
of wine it only which will occasion
it to dry ye sooner & will a good gloss

(66)

ye of itt
be for you varnice your
worke lett ye graine be fild
with wax as thus if on flatt
flatt worke then rub your
wax all over itt as much as
you think will fill ye graine
then with a braise or boot brush
rub itt very sore till itt is gon
into ye pores of ye wood then
take itt of with a glass scra
per & rub itt with a woolen clo:
if it be thrown worke polish itt
in ye threw with wax and a cloath
then being smooth lye on your
varnice till itt be att a body
on the worke then wth powderd
tripolo take itt with a peice of
fine hatt flipes veth in water rub itt till sooth
then rub itt of & when dry with
a cloath lightly oyld wth lintseed
or salet oyle take of the dulness
and white of ye tripolo

(67)

good Lake varnice

To one gallon of ye best spirits
add 1½ ye of ye best good Lake
and ½ ye of gum sandrick put
in into a wide moothed bottle
sett itt prety nigh ye fire for 3 dys
be of ten shaking itt least ye gum
Claue to ye bottle then strain
itt through a flanning strainer
and botle itt 2 or 3 dys then skim
itt of into another bottle for
use keeping itt close stopt

all sorts of hard spirits var:
to be polished as aforesaid but
for comon varnished worke
itt need not be poll: but itts
worth your while to fill up
ye graine as aforesaid with wax
before you varnish itt

(68)

but our comon colors are
spanish brown & yallow oaker
of each alike quantity grinded
with size pretty strong for brown
or alittle size & old Chamberlee
when dry rubb them up with
a wast brush or hare rope
and soe for pollishing all
other colors

umber is a dark brown when
burnt itt inclines more to black
for a wallnuttree coloe in gain
burnt umber mitigated with whit
Lead which is y'e comon white and
mixd with burnt umber
y'e cheapest way of painting & readyest
is to goe your work over with strong
size made of specks or glue when dry
your other color ground with lintseed
oyle for your colors I shall refer
to smith art of painting price 1 shill

(69)

To color or staine severaly
first Logwood is a purple with
old Chamberle & Allum but w'th
water & a little Allum is near black
being very good to dress hatts
alittle to black with it for wallnuttree
color
brazeele is a read color Read
wood is a pail Read
Turmarick is yallow with w'ch
mixe Lyntseed oyl to color our
plaines or any such thing
it preserves from wormes & is a
very pretty color like box

or they may be used as
the discription of Logwood is

(70)

To staine mappsell or other *ye* knotty

purple a black staine
tak logwood & boile with water
and staine itt with when dry hawing
this in a bottle ½ a pinte of *ye* best
wine viniker to which put ¼ pound
of steel filings when wrought
together goe itt over with itt
you may heat it if you please
to heten *ye* strength of itt

pollishing or rubing
goe when its dry pollish your
worke with shave grass and *ye* hard
places will appear white & *ye* other
black then you may varnish itt
with spirit varn: as before direct:

linseed oyl varn
or doe often over with linseed oyle

black
for striking or staining
any colors fitting for that purpose
is viniker allum juice of stond hors
dung steel filings Aquafortis
old chamberloe

a Black staine
Another of the same to staine black
Tak *ye* aforesaid Logwood color
goe itt 2 times over with itt then tak
of the same Logwood water put to
it alittle Copperus and vardigras
is a very good Black

(71)

To put on mapps on fraimes or boards

Take wheate meale a handfull or 2
and put to about ½ *ye* pinte of water
boile till itt be of the thickness of
starch (used for Cloats) then spread
it on the bords & with a smoothing Iron
& a paper between smooth it alonge *ye* boards
but if it be to put one a fraime first
take a cloth of liming as large as *ye* paper
dipp it in water then wringe it out
and spread it on *ye* backe of *ye* paper or
mapp wch is to be fraimed and let it
lye till it be damped well then with
ye paste above mentioned put it on *ye*
fraimes & when it comes to drye it will
be at stretch very well probatt

To Blacke lines in scales

Take a little Charkole & grinde with
linseedoyle & Rub it all over *ye* scale
vntil *ye* lines & figures be filled then wash
it of with salat oyle & let it lye
vntil it be dry & then pollish with shaw
grass & oyle it with Yalow oyle
as in page (69) probatt

(72)

A Jappan varnish

Take of gum sandrick & mastick
each 5 oz & gum Enimee 1 oz
in powder To pint Qt of Spirit

In Jappaning observe your
works be very fine smooth'd &
after colord or stain'd pollish
w'th wax & so proceed to varnish

it may doe well to color & pollish
yor mouldings before fit on foot

(73)

Receipt for Thomas Browns &c
½ pt Spirit Wine
1 oz Camphor
1 oz Spt Sal Armoniac
½ oz Laudnum
1 oz Spt Turpentine
¼ oz oil Origanum or thyme

Disolve the Camphor in the Spt
Wine then add the other Ingredients
a very valuable medicine
JW

(74)

5 mo 17 — 1836
This day began to take

(75)

Per lb
Ice of the Philada Co a 25

(90)

Soment for stone

Ta ½ of white pitch & as much Rozel as ¼ of beaswax & a little brimston with Chalke or brickdust & after you have melted ye pitch & Rozel put in ye beas wax then having boild them woll put in ye Chalk or brickdust & brimston & boile them well then pour them into cold water & so worke it well as shoomakers doth their wax & make it into rowles & keep it for use

To make Asthmatick Ellixir

Take Honey   one oz
Liquoris Root   2 Do
Salt of tartar   1 Do   } Drachm
Flowers of Benjamin — one
Camphire   2 Scrupples
Opium   2 Drachms
Oil of Anniseed 1 Scrupples
Spirits one quart then ad all together in a bottle and let it stand too weeks to foment, shake the bottle every day after that let it settle and then pour it of for use

(91)

how to silver brass

Take 2d weight of cuttings of leaf silver desolve it in ½ oz of Aqua fortise before ye fire in a glass then take tartar in pouder stiring it well before ye fire till it be stiff as past with it rub very sore the brass mettall att ye hot fire

To solder brass

After your brass is shapt according to your mind and bound fast with wire then ly your silver sowder cut very small all along ye joynt then wet it a little with your spattle & dust on pouderd borax so ly it on your charcole fired by ye blast of a lamp thus haveing a peice of iron plate about 6 inch long & 2 or 3 inch broad turnd up att ye edges into which put your tallow haveing a peice of tow dipt in itt ly along ye midst & fire it at ye one end then with your blowpipe blow ye low of it on ye charcole and roost till ye solder run & melt into ye joynt ye blowpipe is near afoot long small & taper ing crook att ye small end for want of wch an older fire may doe if clear ye same for silver

(92)

how to worke in silver

first to cast silver take Alliblaster
in fine powder or fine sand
mixt with bole Armanach haveing
a payre of flasks wch is like to
a little squar box takeing of
in ye midst of ye doazness in wch
press down the sand haveing the
figure of your worke in itt soe
takeing out the mood poower in
the mettall melt itt in a Crucible

solder   when the silver is cayten
cold: then draw itt into what form
         thou pleases if itt be for
         hoopes or such like att a squill
it will knill with a hammer but
solder   after sad itt lcast itt harden
dayes   sad as to beake then pay honed
         to solder take silver softned with
         blocktinn cut small laid on ye joynt
         wett itt a little & dust on powderd borax

Boil silver, take argall & alum broken
put into ye water with ye silver boil
them well often takeing ym out & with
a stick wett take up ondry & rub ym

(93)

for quick silvering glass

Take tinne file or blocktinn
according to the measure of the
glass & lay itt one a very levall
bord or marbale stone then
powr one the quick silver one
the leaf of tinn and itt will spread
all over the leaf then oyle the glass
with Linseed oyle and lay itt one
to itt and lay a weight 3 or 4 howrs
one itt and itt will cleave

drink of itt m__
your constant drinke probatt

a diat drinke for changing ye blood

gitt figgs hounds tongue whitelooks grass
of each ½ a handfull roadmint water cresses
sorrell time and savory of each a handfull
roots of allicampaine tormentill hors radish
& gention of each 1 oz for purging add to ym
of sena ½ oz of agrick 1 oz of rubarb ¼ oz
to a gallon of drinke probatt

(94)

Recepts in Physicke

being

Mostly experienced & Approved

by

People of Credit whose commen-
dation of ye same occasioned me
~~~~~~~~~~~~~~~~~~~~~~~~ Fashion
then draw itt into what form
cold: thou pleases if itt be for
hoopes or such like att a smith
itt will
sodder after cold itt least itt harden
hays   so as to break then fashioned
to sodder take silver softned with
blocktinn cutt small laid on ye joynt
wett it a little & dust on powdred brass

boil silver take argall & alum then
put into ye water with ye silver boil
them well often takeing ym out with
a stick well takeing em dry & rub ym

(97)

for a Consumpsion or fulness of blood

to one gallon of table beer wch is 4 quarts
or 2 gallons of Ale ad as followeth
of sage hysopp germander scurvy grass
water cresses brooke-lime elder buds horshound
harts tongue folefoot Agramony dandilion
ground juye hounds tongue maiden haire
liverwort wood sorrell pollipodie dwarf elder
of each a handfull roots of Allicampaine
comphrey horsradish licquorice & gention
of each 2 or 3 slices ye roots and bruise the
herbs then put them into a net with a weight
to sink them put them to ye bruing when
new and let them work together and soe
drink of itt morn & after noone or for
your constant drinke   probatt

a diat drinke for cleansing ye blood

gitt figgs hounds tongue whitelooks grass
of each ½ a handfull readmint water cresses
sweet time and savory of each a handfull
roots of allicampaine tormentill hors radish
& gention of each 1 oz for purging ad to ym
of sena ½ oz of Agrick 1 oz of rubarb ¼ oz
to a gallon of drinke   probatt

(98)

for a stoping of flegm

for a Cough or Feaver
Take Allicampane roots poudered floor of brimston sweet oyle honey & trakle mix them together & take y quantity of a wallnutt morn & night

Another of y Kind

for flegm or stoping or Coughing
Take Allicampaine pouder and English honey and work them together as strong as the party can take itt take y same quantity as before

Another

for a Consump:
Take of Allicampaine & liquoris in pouder of each ½ oz conserve of roses ½ oz balsom of sulfer 6 penyworth mixt them together with honey and take them as before probatt

Allicampaine & Liquoris pouder is 2ᵈ per oz Con: Ros: 4ᵈ ye oz

(99)

for a settled Cold about ye head or stomach

Take of English safron ye weight of one shilling of licquoris 6 penyworth Angilicos roots ½ oz ½ oz Anniseeds 1 oz Allicampaine Roots ½ of nutmegs ¼ oz sliced 2 branches of Rosemary stript steep them all in a pint and halfe of the strongest Aquavitee in a glass stopt very Close 9 days then take 2 spoonfulls morn & night

An Excellant Electuary for a Cough

for a Consump:
Take of germander horehound hysope white maiden haire Agramony buttonye liverwort lungwort and harts tongue of each a handfull put them to nine pints of water and boile yᵐ to three then lett it Coole & straine it then add to it of clarified honey ½ pd fine pouder of licquorie 5 oz of Allicampaine pd 3 oz and boile yⁿ to the thickness of an Electuary take of this att any time but especially in ye mornen fasting and att goeing to bed

(100)

to make a jelley for in a Consumption
or troubled with a Looseness

Take ye 4 feet of a Calfe dress ym Cleane
Slitt ym in ye midst & take a way ye
black vaines and the fat & wash ym
Cleane & put ym in a buckett of faire water
and lett ym ly 24 howers in ye time Shift
ym often then boile ym in 2 gallons
of Cleane water very softly allwayes
takeing of ye scum & fatt yt rises & when
ye liccquor is more then ½ boiled a way
put into itt 1 pint & ½ of ye best wine &
as itt boileth scum itt cleane & when ye
Jelley is boiled enugh you may kno
for your fingers will cleave to ye spoone
then take it from ye fire & take out all
ye bones and flesh & when its almost cold beat
ye whites of six egges & put into itt & sett itt
on the fire again & lett it boile til it be cleare
then straine itt through a Cloth into a bason &
lett it stand all night ye next morn put it in a
skellett & put to it 1 pound of sugar ½ oz of Cinemon
broken 1 oz of nuttmeggs 1 oz of ginger bruised
& a good quantity of large mace boile ym all together
till they tast as much of the spice as you desire & when
its almost cold take ye whites of 6 egges beat ym & put into it
sett it on ye fire & when itt rises work it in ½ a pint of white wine
then straine itt through a Jelley bagg and use itt morn & night

take of this as you find occasion

perhaps morn & night

slice ye nutmeggs

(101)

An excellent playster for a straine

Take gum galbanum gum Amaracum
mirre frankincense mastick & venice
turpentine of each 2 pennyworth of Rozen
white pitch & bees wax of each the quan
tity of a wallnutt, well them all together
and spread ym on sheeps leather mad
fitt for ye place lying itt on warme

Another oft tryed & experienced
worke

for a straine approved

Take of becie Grotia and
perricellis of each 2 pennyworth
well them and spread them
as above mentioned and . pen
Dissolve 1 penyworth of Camphire in 3 of spirits
of wine its a cure for ye itch allso

A oyntment for a strayne

Take 2 penyworth of spike oyle
mix itt with the duble quantity
of brandy & itt one before
the fire

Approved

for ye syatica

Take one pound of black sope & 4 oz
of frankincence & a pint of white wine
vinekor boile ym together gently till itt be
thick and spread it on sheeps leather
if ye paine be very great add to it a little
Aquavitee

an excell: plast:

(102)

for sore eyes

approved — Take of Roman vitriall stone ℈ij you may put into a spoonfull off spring water & it will turn ye water blewish with which wash your eyes before you goe to bed or when you have occasion

approved cure for warts — The same allsoe cureth warts by wetting itt with your spittle and rubing the warts once or twice a day for a weeke or 10 dayes

Another

for sore eyes — Take rayons nid'ye sun take ye stones out beat ym in a clean morter with a little honey to a salue tye on your eyes some of this at nights going to bed

Some has gott good by blistering ye neck some by having an issue in ye arme some by having their head shaven

(103)

for swellings A pultis

boile — boile in old Chamberlee wormewood rue Cammamile & ye lowere leavine of oak ½ handfull shred ym small wh̄t strong thicken oatemeal & wheat after boylings then add to itt of hogs grease the quantity of a hens egg & it on warme

for the Itch an oyntment

cast ye skin away — Take of hoggs grease ye quantity of a hens egg take ye skin of it put to it in a galley pott 6d worth of quicksilver working ym together with a finger until ye quicksilver be all mixed with ye greese yt ye least bitt of it be not to be seen unmixed and rub thee hands & most itchie places with it

Another

Take of Camphire 6d worth desolve it in ℥ worth of spirits of wine good for a straine allsoe

(102)

Doctor Edwards plaster for ye Stomach

Take galbanum ¼ oz spread itt on sheeps leather take 5 graines of Civitt one of musk & y^m on a peice of cotten or any soft thing lying them in ye midst to ye pitt of ye Stom:

Phisicke for purging watry humors

Doctor William

Take of Sena 2½ dra: of Rubarb 1 dra: of diagrodium 15 graines of aromaticum Rosatum ½ dra: Cream of Tartar 1 dra: make this into An Electuary with ye syrop of Buckethorn take ye quantity of a walnutt in the morning fasting 2 or 3 houres after

good inwardly

alsoe taken inwardly Allso

An Excelant plaster for ye Stomack or any paine in ye Sides back or body used with good success laid to ye stomack of Rickoled or liver grown children or Siatica

take of Mitheridate Diascordium & saffron of each 1 peny worth take ½ a spoonfull alittol loaf sugar strain ye saffron in 2 spoonfulls of winiker & boile ye saffron trakel sugar & winiker over a gentil fire til well mixed then put in ye other & boile y^m gently til thick & spread it on sheeps leather

(103)

to Ripen a boile

Take 1^d worth of venis Turpentine a little honey & ye yolke of a hens egge beaten well then mixe them all together with as much wheat meale as will make y^m of a right thicknes for lying on then spread itt on sheeps leather & strew on itt alittle saffron & apply itt

for a venom

Take green wormwoode and with hoggs grees beat itt a morter till itt be well mixt together and apply it to ye place venomed

An Excelant Balsom for wounds or sores

Take of Sallad oyle ½ a pinte fine powdred Read Lead 2 oz or more boile y^m well till blackish to the thicknes of an Electuary and keep itt in a gally pott for use as ye other balmsom

(105)
Sore leggs

for Scorbutick breakings out in ye leggs I have known som to have their leggs to break out in ye winter time and soo continue runing while cold weather lasted to remedy these it is convenient to have an issue in ye legg and to keep the sores shifted twice a day with fresh Cabbage leaves they being good for takeing the anger or paine out of mostly any sore of ye sorte and ye issue that hot and paineing lye ym one they yt allsoe ease

and the diet drink in pag 97 is very good to take spring & fall ye first of weh is for cleansing the blood without purging ye body the latter is for purging ye body use weh occasion may require Som use only water toasts tund up in their constant drinks

or dross hums
or sore issues
diet drink pg 97

for a green wound

Take ½ oz of white lillies, balsom price 3¼ dross ye wound well to ye bottam sometimes wash it with a little brandy then take fallen scraps of a lining cloath make a peice fitt to ye wounde spreading of ... some of ye balmsome on ye ... put it well into ye wounde lyeing a playster of dia palma or dia: accalem to cover all lying or roling it well down

dress ye wound flesh away to come about ye edges

a dyet drink (106)

for clensing the blood of scruy or dropsicall humors wch often cause a consumption

for a Consumption

Take lungwort burrage polopody of ye oake hore hound harts tongue water Cresses Sage germander hysope scruby grass dandelyon germander Agramony wood bettoney Juniper berres lavender pellitory of Spaine plantan Rosmary ground Juse time maidenhaire fole foote Chamomile wormwood Angelica Elder buds wilde marjorom borrage Centaury featherfew fumitory houndstongue marsh mallows mouse Ear nettles pellitory of ye wall plantan scabious woodsorroll wildetime variaians walnutree leaues of each a handfull roots of Allicampaine hors Radish Comphery Lickorus & Gention of each 2 or 3 sliced bruiss ye herbs and put ym into a nett and put ym into 6 or 8 gallons of drinke before it be thorowly barmed yt ye herbs and drinke may worke together & drinke of it morne & Afternoone or att any time

(107)

To open ye Breast & Cleans ye obstructions
of ye liver & spleen wch causeth a dropsey
for A diat drinke

Take ye Juse of Ground Ivy Sweet
Cicely Motherwort Sweet marjoram
masterwort hart trafoile scurvey gras
smallago Lilly of ye valey Angilica
garden Valerian Damshire sweet tansi
Germander sage hisope Time mint
balm Agramony wormwood Elder buds
water Cresses hors Parsley Rosses
marigolds Clove gilliefloors Rosemary
maidenheair harts tongue horehound
southernwood hopp buds walnut tree leaves
Burage & Buglos Caraway Centuary
Dandilion woodbin called honey suckels
wood Bettony Chamomile Doder of
time polopody of ye oake Arch Angel
fennell fumitory Lavender Lovage
madir march malows millolot
mustard Parsley & Rue of each
a hand full ye finest & driest sorts put
in ye bag with ye beries of Juneper
and bay tree & Root of Elicampani
Gentien Licquorice hors Raddyh
monks Rubarb Angilica & Comphry
of each 3 or 2 bruised seeds of Caraway
fennel & mader & Jacob herbs bruis
and strain & put ye Juce & bagg of herbs
wth ye Roots &c: into 5 or 6 gallons of
working drink to drink att any time

the drier herbs put in with Roots seeds & berrys

(108)

for weak stomachs want of digestion

Take of mustard seed a dram
Cinnimon as much: beat ym to powder
& half ye quantity of Mastick in
powder with gum Arabeck disolved
in Rose water make it up into
troches of wch swallow one of half
a dram weight 1 hour or 2 before
meals let old people make
much of this medicine

¼ of gill

for ye Jandice

Take 3 or 4 wood lice called
hobthough lice dry them on a
puter plate before ye fire then
powder them and take it with
honey or trakle att 2 times
if that doo not doe gil more
powder

(109)

ffor digesting Cold humours
falling on ye stomack or Joynts
and dropsey obst: liuer & spleen

in 3 or 4 galls: Tunn up in your Constant drink
Mother-worte Mustard pellitory
of ye wall Burnet Saxifrage
Sage Rose Mary Polipody of oak
Peny Royal Master Wort sweet
Marjorum Maidenhair Louage
liuer wort Lauender hounds Tongue
hore hound hysope Germander
dwarf Elder Dandilion wa: Cresses
Ale hofe Samphire sweet Cicely
Careaway Burnet Burage
Buglos Wood Bettoney Balme
heirb Bonett or ffetwort Arch-
Angel Angillica ground Iuy
and Agramony each a handfull
Roots of horse Raddish Elicampain
Parsley & Comfry Each 2 or 3
use ye method proscribed before
in puting y^m up

John Widdifeild

(110)

for Auenum or poison

Take halfe a pinte of your own
piss to it straine ye Iuce of a
handfull of Rue called heirb of
grace and drinke it at once
it Cures immediatly

for the Kings euill Consumption
it swellen of blood Stops fluxes Running
gout & pissing euill eyes scurvy or
dropsey

To 12 quarts of spring water
hot ad 3 pound of new lime at 24 hours
ond scum it & Clear it of & put
it in a Iron pot & ad to it half
a pound of lignumuited & 2 ounces
of sasafrass let it hang ouer a
gentle fire all night next morning
ad 2 oz of sersaperella of licquoric
2 oz of Raisons · sun stond on pound
of China Root 2 oz of sweet fennell
seeds 2 oz ~~of polopody Agramony
scabious each 1 oz~~ you may ad
of nutmugs mace & Cinamon of each
½ oz boile ye licquor to half ad bottle
it & take 1 pint morn & night and
sweet in ye bed after it

(151)

for womens Sore Breasts
the following Poultice

Take Rice & boile in water
till thick & soft ad to it of ye herb
called tantarabogos cut small
& to a quarter of this ad 2 oz of
good Sugar & apply to ye Sore
12 times in 24 hours it gives
Ease Immediatly

good Sugar will heal cuts
Sores or wounds being applyd
probatt

good Sugar will heal cats
Sores

For Alum

(152)

For thy Constant drink

run up to a gallon one
handfull of Bay leaves & one
handfull of water trefoile & one
ounce wilde Carrot Seeds in hott
weather omitt ye trefoile

For a vomitt
a vomitt
Take tarter
Emittick 4 drams

Take of ye Infution of (Crocus
Metallorum) vj drams of
Oxymell of Squills and Syrop
of Roses Solutive of each
halfe an ounce mix & take
it in an Evining after itt
doth opperate drink plenty
of poset drinke getting a little
fresh meade and broth after
its done working
its to Cleanse ye Stomack of
Cold ~~for~~
~~p doo Midfort~~

(113)

Oct 7 Bullock for my ankle
a bad humor occationed by
a great cold gott in winter
traveling through water, falling
on ye nerves became very painfull
viz Take Philo, oyle of brick
oyle of Eiler Spike &
Turpentine, myrrh mixt
with Oyntment herein
& it on before ye fire

(114)

~~John Widdifield~~
Son of John Widdifield

~~John Widdifield~~

John Widdifield of the
Citty of Philadelphia
House Carpenter and
Grandson to the Auther
of this Book, His and his
famileys ages are
Carefulley Set Down
In the Next Page

(115)

John Widdifield eld. Son of John & Ame Widdifi was Born January the 6th 1735 Between one & two a Clock in the Morning

Was Married to Elizabeth Hoillmon on the 9th of the 7th Mot Called July in the year of our Lord — 1762

Elizabeth Hoillmon was Born the 22 Day of the 3 Mot Called March in the yeare of our Lord 1740

Ame Widdifield Daughter of John and Elizabeth Widdifield was born the 3d of the 8 Mot Called August in the year of our Lord 1763 at ½ past two in the Morning and fourth Day of the week

(116)

James Widdifield Son of John and Elizabeth Widdifield was Born the first Day of the Twelvth Month Called December in the year of our Lord 1765 at a Quarter past two in the Morning and first Day of the Week

David Widdifield Son of John and Elizabeth Widdifield Was Borne the 30 of the 3 Month Calld March in the year of our Lord 1768 at 6:0 Clock in the Afternoon and fourth Day of the Weak

John Widdifield Son of John and Elizabeth Widdifield was borne the 9 Day of the 8 Mot Calld August in the yeare of our Lord 1771 at ½ after Six a Clock in the Morning & 6 Day of the week

William Widdifield Son of John and Elizabeth Widdifield was Born the 29 Day of the first M:o Call:d January in the year of our Lord 1774 Ten Minuets after Ten in the Morning & 7th Day of the Week

Mary Widdifield Daughter of John & Elizabeth Widdifield was Borne the 22 Day of the 9 M:o Call:d September in the year of our Lord 1776 ½ after 6 a Clock in the Morning & first Day of the Week

George Widdifield Son of John & Elizabeth Widdifield was Borne the 13th Day of the 6th M:o Call:d June in the year of our Lord 1779 at half Past Twelve a Clock in the Morning & first Day of the Week

Sarah Widdifield Daughter of John and Elizabeth Widdifield was Borne the 2 Day of the 7th M:o Call:d July in the year of our Lord 1783 at a Quarter Past 7 a Clock in the Evening and Seventh Day of the Week

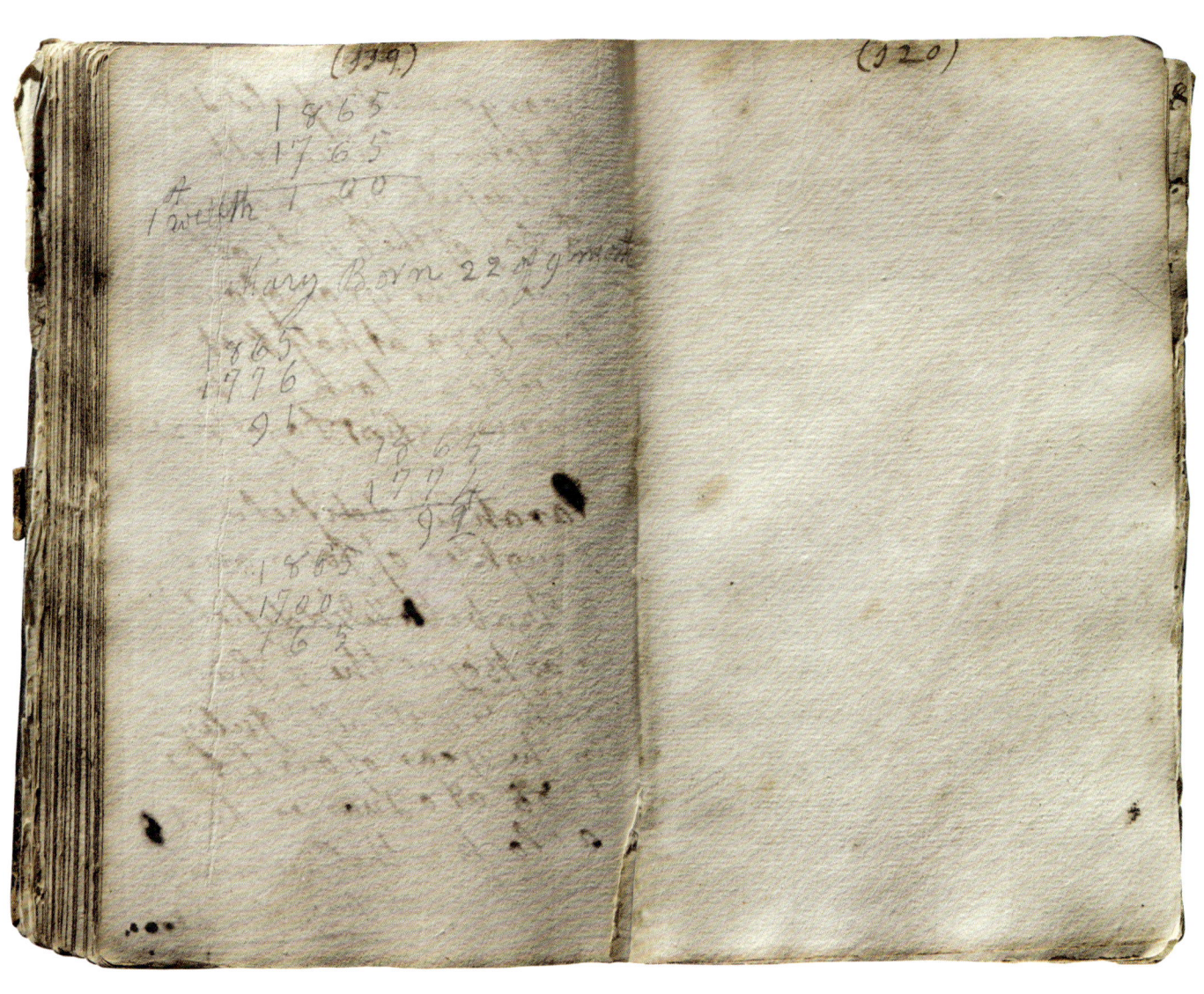

(121)

I James Widdifield
Which was the Son of
John Widdifield Which
was the Son of John
Widdifield Which was
the Son of John Widdifield
= the author of this Book
Who came from England
from Newcastle upon the
River Tyne about the year
Seventeen Hundred 1700
Settled in this citty purchased
a house & Lot on the West
Side of Strawberry Alley and
Market Street Where he
Carried on his Business of
a Cabbinet Maker &. &.
Jn⁰ Widdifield

(122)

Which was the Son of Peter =

Pages (123) and (124) have no notes.

(125)

[126]

ye 2d ye 8 month 1706

A Breife account of my stock trading
$
To England w:th Guy to Cha: Hunt   09:00:00
A Bill p:d Richard Smith p Jn:o Hart 06:00:00
A Bill to Cha: Hunt p Ch: Toyham   5:15:06
Trading to maryland w:th Ch: Toyham 08:00:00
in S:th Hart's hand due to me   07:00:00
to Barbados w:th Jn:o Lowson   08:00:00
Rum in my Seller ½ p:s twice   06:00:00
                    Totall sum in all 49:15:06

in the year 1800 the Locusts was uncommonly
Numerous and Suppos'd will again appear in
the year 1817 — & 1834 & in 1851
this year they had a Singular mark on the wing
of W somewhat in this manner

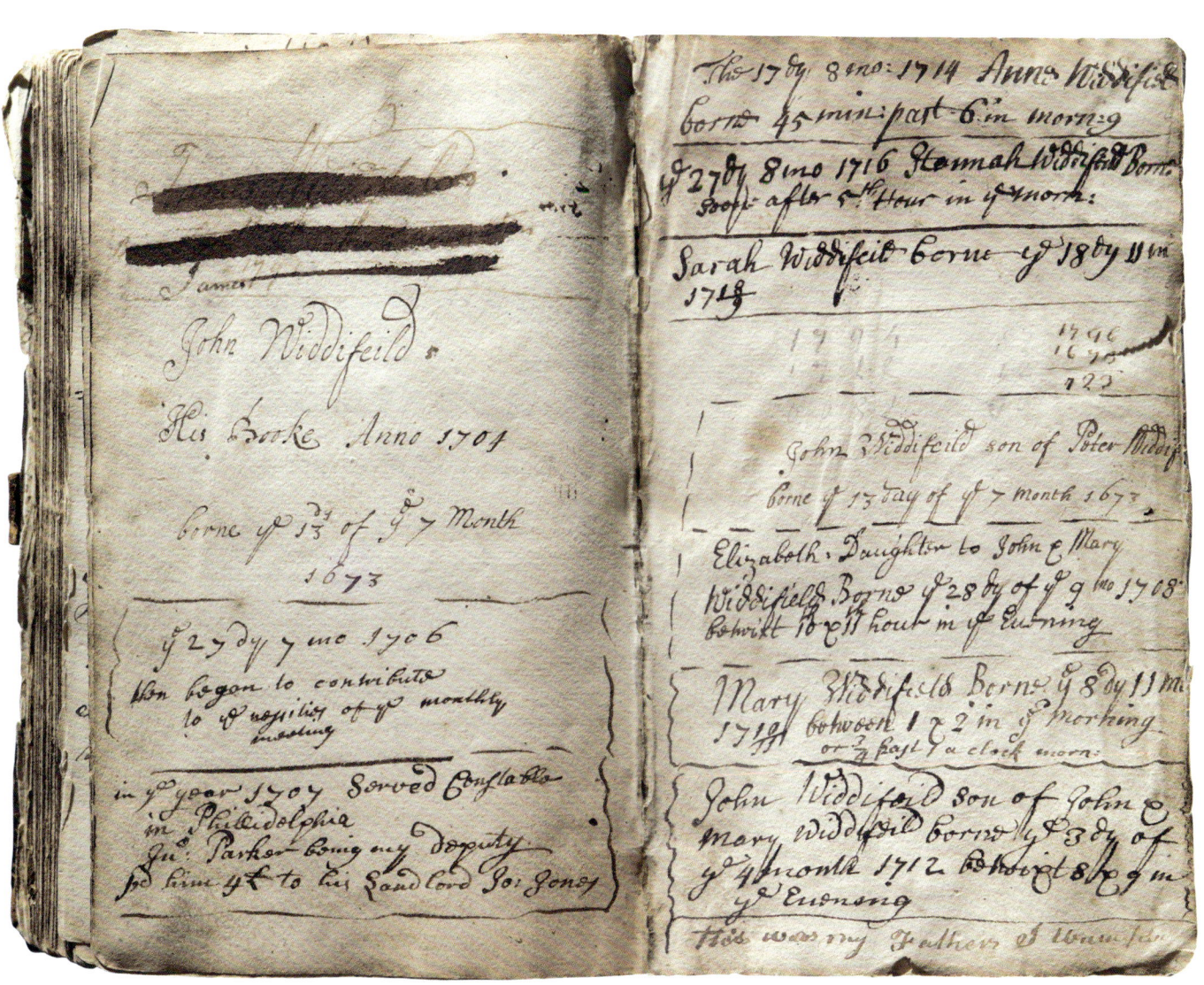

~~[crossed out]~~

John Widdifeild's

His Booke Anno 1704

borne ye 13d of ye 7 Month
1673

ye 27 dy 7 mo 1706
then began to contribute
to ye necesities of ye monthly
meeting

in ye year 1707 Served Constable
in Philadelphia
Jn.o Parker being my deputy
pd him 4£ to his Landlord Jo: Jones

The 17 dy 8 mo: 1714 Anne Widdifeild
borne 45 min past 6 in morn:g

ye 27 dy 8 mo 1716 Hannah Widdifeild Borne
soon after 5th Hour in ye morn:

Sarah Widdifeild borne ye 18 dy 11 m
1718

John Widdifeild son of Peter Widdif[eild]
borne ye 13 day of ye 7 month 1673

Elizabeth Daughter to John & Mary
Widdifeild Borne ye 28 dy of ye 9 mo 1708
betwixt 10 & 11 hour in ye Evening

Mary Widdifeild Borne ye 8 dy 11 m
1710 between 1 & 2 in ye morning
or ½ past 1 a clock morn

John Widdifeild son of John &
Mary Widdifeild borne ye 3 dy of
ye 4 month 1712 betwixt 8 & 9 in
ye Evening

This was my Father I Wm [illegible]

Figure 1 Door panels from a shrank made for Emanuel and Mary Herr, Lancaster County, Pennsylvania, 1768, Walnut with tulip poplar; sulfur. (Courtesy, Winterthur Museum.) The design and execution of the panels show the hand of a highly component craftsman: the inletting is crisp and even, with no knife overruns or visible tool marks. While most of the cartouche is knife-cut, tight curves were set in with specific curved gouges, confirmed by the repeated radii throughout. Most feathers on the birds are in a thumbnail style with two gouge cuts used to form the chip; the smaller feathers on the head of the large bird are punched with a triangular tool. A tracing from the right-hand door cartouche overlaid on the left indicates that the designs were transferred from a full master or half-master template for the major areas of the design. Insignificant variations between the quadrants of the cartouches are accounted for by shifting the pattern during transfer or by variations in cutting the channel.

Mark Anderson, Brenda Hornsby Heindl, and Jennifer Mass

Sulfur-Inlaid Furniture: New Insights on Materials and Techniques

▼ THE TECHNIQUE OF sulfur inlay—most commonly observed on black walnut furniture and likely used as a rapid and attractive alternative to wood inlay—has long been considered a rare type of decoration associated with objects whose production centered on present-day Lancaster, Pennsylvania (fig. 1). However, recent research has identified more than 125 objects with sulfur-inlaid decoration and the names and locations of many original owners. It is now clear that sulfur-inlaid furniture was made in multiple shops throughout southeastern Pennsylvania as well as in Maryland, Virginia, and North Carolina. A schrank dated 1763 is the earliest documented example and a chest dated 1844 the latest object known to these authors.

Sulfur inlay is most often found on chests, schranks, and clocks, although tables, cradles, cupboards, desks, chests of drawers, straightedges, small boxes, a wall pocket, and a looking glass with this enhancement also survive. Most of these pieces are dated, many have initials identifying the owners, and a few have full names. A fragmentary frieze inlaid "Fronica" and "17" is unique in having come, presumably, from a schrank that bore a woman's name alone (fig. 2). Typically schranks have either a man's name or the names of a married couple. Scholars have traditionally assumed that schranks with male and female names were made for their owners' wedding, but the dates on those objects suggest otherwise. Genealogical research does indicate that most of the people who commissioned schranks were the children of immigrants, primarily from Germany and Switzerland. This article will review

Figure 2 Schrank frieze fragment, possibly Pennsylvania, 1750–1799. Walnut; sulfur. (Courtesy, Alan Andersen.) The sulfur inlay, unobscured by later finishes, highlights the color shift in period sulfur inlay from yellow when new, to white when aged. The black specks visible in the white field occur as finish and grime collect in pits formed when water vapor rising out of the wood is captured in the solidifying sulfur. These inclusions are a good indicator that the inlay is sulfur and not paste.

previous scholarship on furniture with sulfur inlay, discuss historic uses and sources of sulfur and its chemical properties, and describe the techniques used to create sulfur and related inlays.

Historiography of Sulfur-Inlaid Furniture

In the November 1958 issue of *Antiques*, Frances Lichten described the decoration on the Huber family schrank illustrated as the article's frontispiece: "the intricate filigree of ornament, executed in an obscure technique known as wax inlay . . . seems to have no early European antecedents, and only a few insignificant nineteenth century descendants on very minor artifacts" (see fig. 79 in Lisa Minardi's article in this volume). Then, in 1960, she described the decoration as *Wachseinlagen*, suggesting that the origin of wax inlay was Germanic. We now know the inlay is sulfur, not wax, but Lichten's error in identifying the ornament on the schrank is understandable because unvarnished aged sulfur inlay is an ivory-white color. Lichten's assertion led other scholars to conclude that the material was wax paste with lead white pigment [$2Pb(CO_3)Pb(OH)_2$] intended to simulate "inlay produced in ivory, holly, and rare imported woods." Monroe Fabian's 1977 *Pennsylvania Folklife* article, "Sulfur Inlay in Pennsylvania German Furniture," was the first publication to identify the technique correctly (fig. 3). Among the objects illustrated were a 1768 schrank that descended in the Herr family, a 1772 hanging cupboard, a 1773 box from the Mosser family (fig. 4), the 1779 Huber schrank, and a 1783 walnut chest. In 1982 Beatrice Garvan and Charles Hummel attributed the Huber schrank to Christian Huber and Peter Holl III of Manheim and Warwick townships, Lancaster County. They also speculated that Holl, who was both a joiner and a pump maker, would have been familiar with sulfur as a repair material. Mark Anderson's 1995 article on sulfur inlay generated new interest in the subject, and in 2003 he and Jennifer Mass began intensive scientific analysis of the materials used for sulfur inlay and other allied techniques.[1]

Figure 3 Cover of *Pennsylvania Folklife* (Fall 1977) featuring the Georg Huber schrank. Monroe Fabian's article, "Sulfur Inlay in Pennsylvania German Furniture," in this issue was the most accurate source of information on sulfur inlay at the time, utilizing analyses carried out at the Smithsonian Institution.

Figure 4 Valuables chest, Lancaster County, Pennsylvania, 1773. Walnut with tulip poplar; sulfur and white composite repairs. H. 7¼", W. 14¾", D. 8⅝". (Courtesy, Winterthur Museum.) The central design for this small box was generated with a compass and straightedge, witnessed by the pivot points. The flower designs, slightly varying because of inletting, are from a template. The yellow tint on the top is due to a thick resin coating and stands in contrast to the chalk-white color on the tulips, which have a sparse and likely original coating.

Figure 5 Splint matches, origin and age undetermined. White cedar; sulfur. L. 4". (Courtesy, Winterthur Museum.) A riven white cedar splint dipped in molten sulfur makes a nonstrikable match that carries a flame once ignited.

Historic Uses and Sources of Sulfur

No direct European antecedents for American sulfur-inlaid furniture are known, but some of the designs on examples from southeastern Pennsylvania are similar to those on South German and Swiss painted furniture forms, which are typically executed with a white pigment and often have foliate motifs, initials or names, and dates. Similarly, no period documents or bills pertaining to the use of sulfur inlay have been identified either in this country or abroad. A yellow hardened paste inlay in Italian Renaissance furniture resembles sulfur inlay, but scientific analysis identifies that material as primarily orpiment (arsenic trisulfide, As_2S_3).[2]

The use of sulfur as a component in decorative arts and trade practice is ancient. The Egyptians are credited with developing niello, a black metallic alloy of sulfur mixed with copper, silver, or lead. Typically used as an inlay for metal, niello spread throughout Europe during the late Iron Age and is common in medieval jewelry and as an inlay on arms and armor. During the Renaissance, collectors of coins and medals used molten sulfur as an alternative to plaster for making detailed molds from originals. The process is described in *Il libro dell' arte* (*The Book of Art* or *The Craftsman's Handbook*), first published in the fifteenth century. Molten sulfur was used to cast three-dimensional forms including castings for determining the bore diameter of gun barrels, a process known as "slugging." Household uses for sulfur included fumigation and bleaching (when burned), and for matches (fig. 5).[3]

Sulfur or sulfur and lampblack mixtures were compounded to create acid-resistant coatings and lutes (adhesives). Molten sulfur mortars were also used to join cast-iron bell and spigot pipe components as an alternative to the more common molten lead joint. Parallel use of molten sulfur and molten lead alloy is significant since the latter also occurs as a poured fill material in southeastern Pennsylvania furniture.

Most of the sulfur used in the colonies and the young republic came from vast deposits in Campania and Sicily. Europeans typically processed sulfur ore in mud-brick structures that were built on slopes around large stacked chunks of the ore and fired with lit sulfur dust. As the ore melted, it ran downhill from the base of the kiln, where it cooled and could be collected. Sulfur melts at 239 degrees Fahrenheit (115 Celsius), cools quickly, and forms a virtual cast of the surface it occupies. These very qualities made sulfur ideal for inlaying wood and stone objects in the eighteenth and nineteenth centuries.[4]

Sulfur was produced in the colonies by 1776, when the Continental Congress requested "all persons . . . in this or any neighboring Colony" to provide speedy intelligence" to the Committee of Sulfur Ore and solicited proposals "from any person or persons that are willing to engage in procuring [sulfur] . . . for the public use." One of the first respondents was Thomas Bedwell, who lived near Philadelphia. The notes of the Committee of Safety indicate that he had access to crude sulfur and was able to process it with public assistance. Several sources in the records also refer to sulfur deposits on the Susquehanna River near York, Pennsylvania. All of this sulfur was intended for the production of gunpowder, but the same sources could have been exploited for other uses including inlay. Newspaper advertisements from southeastern Pennsylvania document the availability of sulfur through merchants and apothecaries.[5]

In addition to being a naturally occurring element, sulfur was a by-product of merchant blast furnaces. Pyrite (iron disulfide, FeS_2), which has a high sulfur content and decomposes into $FeS + S$ at 1022°F, was used for iron production in southeastern Pennsylvania. After visiting a Pennsylvania furnace in 1772, a "Mister Goddard" recommended the addition of a limestone shelf in the upper half of the structure, "the use of which is to absorb and take to itself the crude sulfur from the metal before it falls into the

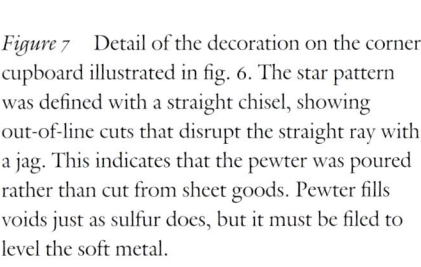

Figure 6 Corner cupboard, possibly Pennsylvania, 1780–1810. Walnut with sulfur inlay and poured pewter decoration. H. 89½", W. 50½", D. 40½". (Courtesy, Skinner, Inc.)

Figure 7 Detail of the decoration on the corner cupboard illustrated in fig. 6. The star pattern was defined with a straight chisel, showing out-of-line cuts that disrupt the straight ray with a jag. This indicates that the pewter was poured rather than cut from sheet goods. Pewter fills voids just as sulfur does, but it must be filed to level the soft metal.

hearth." Since many other reaction pathways could occur during smelting (for example, $2 FeS_2 + 11/2 O_2 \rightarrow Fe_2O_3 + 4 SO_2$, $3 FeS_2 + 8 O_2 \rightarrow Fe_3O_4 + 6 SO_2$, $FeS_2 + 3 O_2 \rightarrow FeSO_4 + SO_2$), additional documentary research will be required to determine if elemental sulfur was collected and sold as a by-product of iron production in Pennsylvania. Sulfur was, however, obtained from pyrite by the Chinese as early as the third century.

Avenues for Technological Transfer

Craftsmen who worked with pewter inlay may have been familiar with the properties of molten sulfur, which has applications in different types of metalworking and gunsmithing. It is worth noting the tradition of inlaid longrifles, tomahawks, and related accoutrements that in some cases feature poured pewter inlay though no arms to date with sulfur inlay are known. An unusual corner cupboard is decorated with both poured pewter and sulfur inlay (figs. 6, 7), and other Pennsylvania objects with only pewter inlay survive. The pewter-inlaid examples are similar in form to those with sulfur and often feature names or initials and dates in the same contexts.

Masonry was an avenue for technological transfer, since molten sulfur fillers were commonly used to set iron hand-rail supports or iron cleats into large stones. The 1858 Oswego, New York, Customs' House was erected with internal iron cramps anchored in poured sulfur, and in other applications molten sulfur socketed lightning rods and the hubs of grinding stones. Further links between stonemasonry and furniture joinery have been established by such scholars as Bradford L. Rauschenberg, who identified a large group of Davidson County, North Carolina, tombstones with carved details matching those on local case pieces. If furniture designs influenced the decoration on tombstones, there is no reason to exclude masonry practices as a source for the technique of sulfur inlay in furniture.[6]

There are numerous surviving tombstones with sulfur inlay in Maryland. Three cemeteries account for the majority of the stones: St. Benjamin's Lutheran Cemetery, St. Luke's Lutheran Cemetery, and St. Mary's Union (Reformed and Lutheran) Cemeteries, all in Carroll County, Maryland. The tombstones are made of black slate, a common stone from the region, and most have epitaphs in German with decorative carving or inlay pattern. Several of the tombstones exhibit designs that mimic those found on sulfur-inlaid furniture (figs. 8–11).

As Garvan and Hummel suggested, the use of sulfur inlay on furniture may represent crossover between the pump-making and cabinetmaking trades. Iron waste pipes were joined with sulfur mortars during the nineteenth century and possibly much earlier, as the following citation indicates: "a long abandoned ancient cast iron main unearthed in the Carolinas . . . the joints poured with sulfur . . . the line laid shortly after the War of the Revolution." If iron fittings for wooden hand reciprocated pumps were joined with sulfur lutes or pure molten sulfur pours, then Christian Huber and Peter Holl III may have been familiar with the use of molten sulfur. Although no exhaustive study of early wooden pumps has been carried out, it is possible that some had metal fittings seated in sulfur or sulfur-based materials.[7]

Figure 8 Tombstone, St. Luke's Lutheran Cemetery, Carroll County, Maryland, 1793. Slate; sulfur. (Photo, Brenda Hornsby Heindl.) Many of the tombstones are sculpted in baroque profile designs with inlaid sulfur highlights. Germanic designs found on sulfur-inlaid furniture are common.

Figure 9   Detail of a tombstone from St. Luke's Lutheran Cemetery, Carroll County, Maryland, 179. Slate; sulfur. (Photo, Brenda Hornsby Heindl.) The deeply cut pinwheel design has sloping sides on the interior. It appears that the molten sulfur fill was intended to stop below the surface of the stone, thereby highlighting the finely crafted edge.

Figure 10   Tombstone from St. Mary's Union Cemeteries, Carroll County, Maryland, 1799. Slate; sulfur. (Photo, Brenda Hornsby Heindl.) German or English inscriptions are found on all of the tombstones in this group.

Figure 11   Tombstone detail from St. Mary's Union Cemeteries, Carroll County, Maryland. Slate; sulfur. (Photo, Brenda Hornsby Heindl.) Sulfur poured into stone tends to level without bubbles.

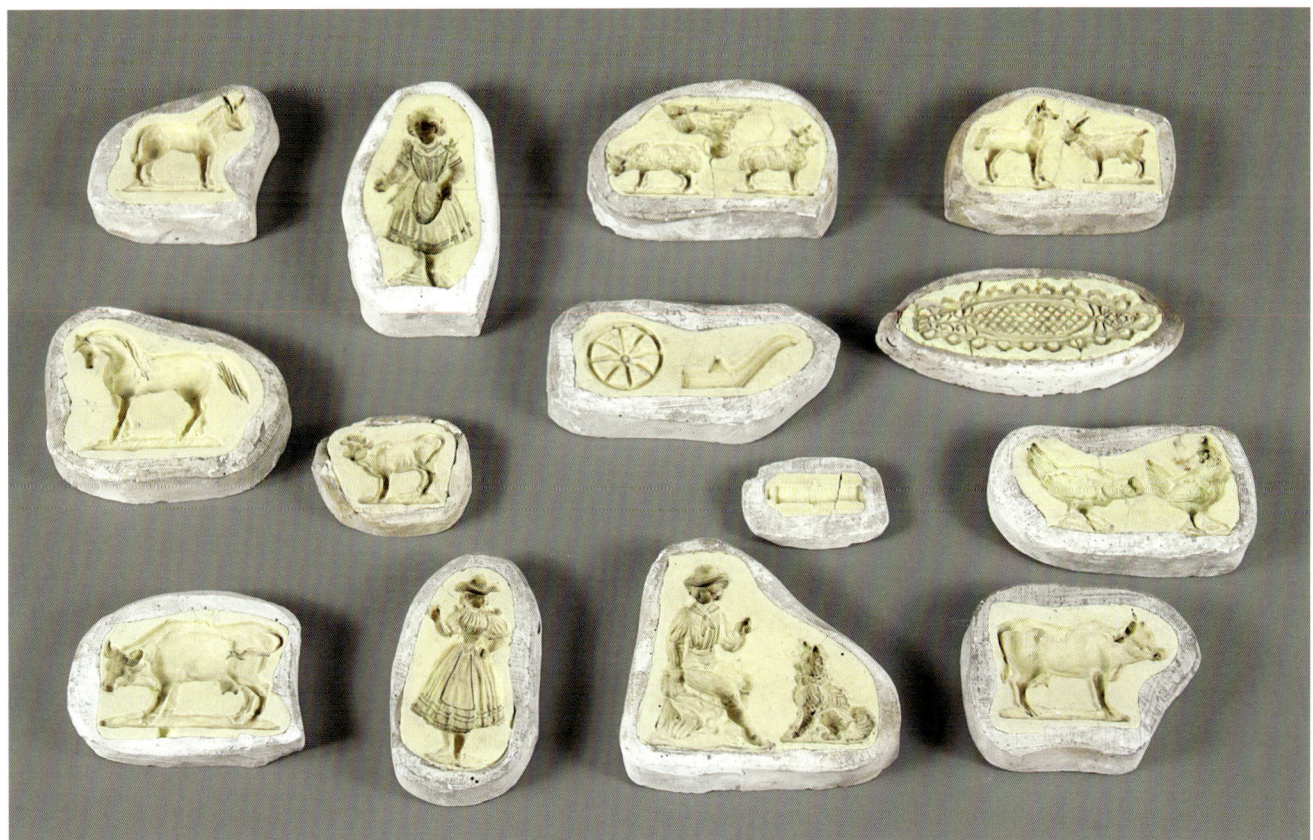

Figure 12 Confection molds, date and origin unknown. Sulfur; plaster. (Courtesy, Mercer Museum.) These molds, which were acquired from the Thomas Mills Company, established in Philadelphia in 1866, are probably European. The brittle sulfur cannot stand up to repeated use or environmental extremes without chipping and cracking.

Figure 13 One of the molds illustrated in fig. 12. This mold illustrates crossover between the carver and the mold maker. Curved gouge cuts define portions of the design.

A seemingly unconnected but very plausible origin for the sulfur inlay technique may be the confectioner's trade. A recently discovered cache of plaster-reinforced sulfur molds for pressing marzipan or barley sugar sweets suggests a link between wood carving and pouring molten sulfur (figs. 12–14). Patterns for sulfur molds were sculpted in pliable materials like wax or clay, but more durable ones were carved from wood, as the brittle sulfur molds could deteriorate with repeated use and require recasting from a hard pattern. Wooden molds for cookies and butter are well known and illustrate the craft of incised carved decoration quite similar to designs found on sulfur-inlaid furniture (fig. 15). Carvers who produced reverse-image wooden molds could easily carve raised relief patterns for sulfur molds. The date

75   SULFUR-INLAID FURNITURE INSIGHTS

Figure 14 One of the molds illustrated in fig. 12. Animal motifs are common on confection molds and decoration on American sulfur-inlaid furniture.

Figure 15 Butter or cookie mold, possibly Pennsylvania, 1813. Conifer. Diam. 4½". (Courtesy, Winterthur Museum.) This reverse-carved mold uses patterns and a letter style common to sulfur-inlaid designs.

Figure 16 Router plane, European or American, date unknown. Lignum vitae; iron. L. 2½". (Courtesy, Winterthur Museum.) Small router planes allowed rapid clearing of waste between the incised borders of larger designs intended to receive molten sulfur.

and provenance for the sulfur confection molds illustrated in figures 12–14. are unknown, but their motifs suggest Germanic or Swiss origin. There is no reason to believe that sulfur confection molds were not produced in the Germanic regions of Pennsylvania and that the crafts of wood-carver, furniture maker, confectioner, and confection mold maker might not have commingled. Instructions for making a sulfur mold are found in the 1820 compendium *The Italian Confectioner*: "oil lightly the articles you intend to mould with a hair pencil; put some sulphur in a glazed earthen pipkin . . . and melt on the fire, when it is melted and clear . . . pour it into your mould . . . the sulphur will find its level softly without blowing."[8]

Similar processes were described in plasterer's handbooks. According to William Millar's *Plastering—Plain and Decorative*:

> The moulds are generally made in sulphur, but some large manufacturers keep metal and box-wood and pear-wood moulds for stock designs. . . . Box-wood and pear-wood moulds require to be carved which only a skilled carver can do, as they have to be cut or sunk in the reverse way to give the given design. Sulphur moulds are made by dissolving the sulphur (which is generally sold in sticks) over a slow fire in an iron pot, continually stirring to prevent burning. When melted it is allowed to stand until sufficiently cool to pour on the original. . . . A good guide to know when it is fit for pouring on is to let it stand until a thin skin has formed on the top then break the skin on the side intended for pouring. . . . Should the sulphur catch fire, remove the pot from the fire and cover it with an old plaster or cement bag to extinguish the flames. It only requires attention to prevent this mishap. Burnt sulphur does not run so freely, and does not take so fine an impression as when pure.

The crafts of sulfur mold making and carving also overlapped in the production of composition ornaments. On May 25, 1805, carver John Doggett charged James Evans $2 for "2 sulphur molds for composition."[9]

The Technique of Sulfur Inlay

Surviving examples of sulfur-inlaid furniture reveal different methods of inletting designs. Some makers formed their channels with a fixed cutter, such as a router plane (fig. 16), whereas others used a knife or chisel (for

Figure 17 Procedures used in the production of a scaled down, replica panel with sulfur inlay. (Courtesy, Winterthur Museum.) The pattern is transferred to the wood using a printed image with carbonized paper. Sooting the reverse of a drawing in period work would produce a similar outline when traced. Pricked patterns using pounce powder could also transfer a design. The initial outline inletting is done freehand with a knife, while two separate curved gouges cut the thumbnail feather motif. A single gouge with an elongated, tapered cutting edge is rolled to incise slightly varying curves.

Figure 18 Detail of the chest façade illustrated in fig. 29. Inletting for this design was made using a knife, possibly in conjunction with a V-shaped gouge. The bottom channel is smooth from the sharp cutting edge. A knife and a straight chisel were likely used for other areas and waste removal.

removing waste) (fig. 17). The excavated channel did not have to be perfectly rectilinear, as with wood inlay, thus a rough bottom or sloping side was perfectly acceptable for the molten sulfur pour (figs. 18–21). The outlines for floral and animal motifs were typically established with a knife. A simple V cut was common for freehand inletting, as the sulfur adheres well even without the benefit of an undercut edge. Gouges with the upper corners sharpened back to create a leading edge at the tip were used for chip

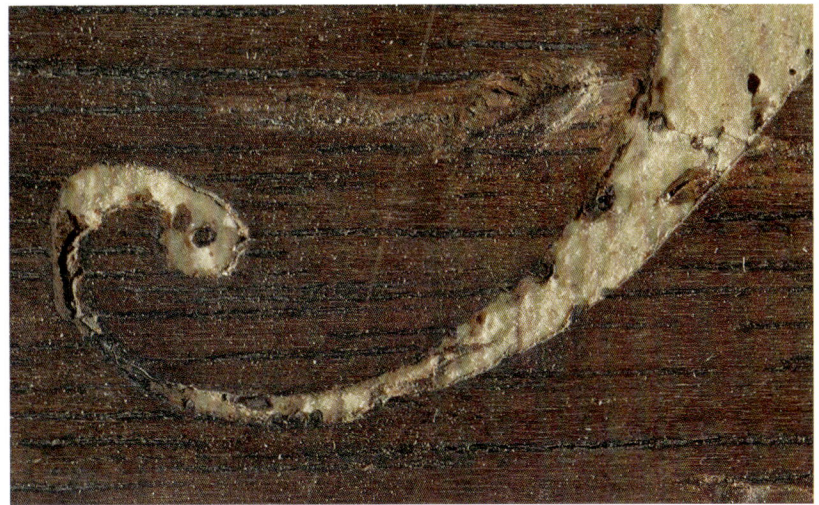

Figure 19 Detail of the Germanic numeral "1" on the chest façade illustrated in fig. 29, showing the knife and gouge work. The chip of walnut embedded in the molten sulfur is probably waste that strayed into the molten sulfur pour. This can occur when pared-off hardened sulfur is remelted.

Figure 20 Detail of the Germanic numeral "8" on the chest façade illustrated in fig. 29, showing knife and chisel work. The aged sulfur is white and does not have bubble pitting. The sulfur may have been near its melting point—only slightly above the boiling point of water—so less water vapor was driven out.

Figure 21 Detail of fig. 17, showing the gouge made "thumbnail" cuts and straight knife cutting.

Figure 22 Overall of fig. 21, showing the knife and gouge carving.

Figure 23 Detail of a lower door panel of a schrank made for Emanuel and Mary Herr, Lancaster County, Pennsylvania, 1768. Walnut with tulip poplar; sulfur. (Courtesy, Winterthur Museum.) The knotwork pattern is compass-generated. A single or double cutter on the end of the compass beam could have described the outline before waste removal.

Figure 24 Detail of figure 17 during the sulfur inlay process. Solidified sulfur must be pared away with an edge tool or scraper. The hardened sulfur is abrasive and quickly dulls the tools. The area of lighter sulfur is due to overpouring. The trail, fully hardened, but still crystallizing, has a deeper color. Small details like the feathers can be "dotted in" with liquid sulfur.

Figure 25 The completed design illustrated in fig. 17, poured and scraped smooth. This image shows the replica panel (with a shellac finish) after cycling in an artificial aging chamber at the Winterthur Museum.

Figure 26 Molten sulfur poured from a ceramic crucible is difficult to control and often overpours.

Figure 27 A slow charcoal fire melts the sulfur with stirring. Careful melting at the lowest possible temperature is important as the sulfur begins to become more viscous above 300 degrees. Away from the heat the sulfur hardens quickly and must be poured without delay.

cuts, and compasses were used to produce geometric patterns (figs. 22, 23). Excess hardened sulfur was pared away with edge tools and scraped smooth before a finish coating was applied (figs. 24, 25).

Replication experiments suggest that makers of sulfur-inlaid furniture could achieve better results with iron rather than stoneware crucibles, which create surface tension at the lip that inhibits smooth pouring. Experimental pours with ceramic vessels were difficult to control and typically produced a large overflow of sulfur (fig. 26). Most texts that give instructions for melting sulfur recommend the use of iron ladles heated over a wood fire, and tests with comparable implements produced an even release of the sulfur (fig. 27).

An initial attempt to replicate period sulfur-inlay produced air bubble inclusions like those observed on the original objects (fig. 28). These bubbles result from water vapor rising out of the wood by action of the hot sulfur and their consequent trapping within the solidifying inlay. The final scraping off of the hardened excess sulfur deposited above the wooden surface reveals the pocked pattern created by the trapped air bubbles. Unlike the period inlays, which generally appear an ivory-white, the replicated inlay

Figure 28 Detail of the chest façade illustrated in fig. 29.

Figure 29 Chest façade, probably southeastern, Pennsylvania, 1784. Walnut; sulfur (yellow cave-sulfur crystals from Mexico). (Courtesy, Winterthur Museum.) The sulfur crystals are formed as a result of bacterial action on organic material leached through the soil and crystallized on limestone from a cave roof. They show the natural bright yellow sulfur color in contrast to the aged sulfur inlay.

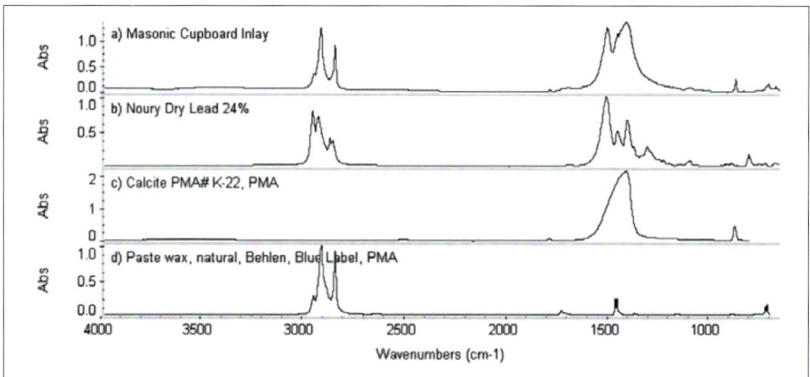

Figure 30 FTIR results for white inlay on the corner cupboard illustrated in fig. 31.

Figure 31 Corner cupboard, Bertie County, North Carolina, ca. 1795. Walnut with cypress; white lead, chalk and linseed oil filler. H. 103¼", W. 50", D. 20½". (Courtesy, Winterthur Museum.) The inlay material for the tympanum cupboard was thought to be sulfur, but analysis indicates that it is white lead putty.

Figure 32 Detail of the putty inlay on the corner cupboard illustrated in fig. 31.

was bright yellow, the color of the most common crystalline form of sulfur (fig. 29). This finding, together with the results of analyses carried out for Fabian's 1977 article, raises several questions about the chemical characteristics of eighteenth- and early nineteenth-century sulfur inlay.

An ivory-colored, sulfur-based inlay could also have been made by adding a minor phase or filler such as calcite (chalk, $CaCO_3$), gypsum (a hydrated calcium sulfate, $CaSO_4 \cdot 2H_2O$), or silica (SiO_2) to the sulfur. In North Carolina, cabinetmakers used two basic formulas for a non-sulfur paste or putty inlay previously identified as sulfur (fig. 30). These mixtures are composed of chalk, rosin, and linseed oil, like composition ornament formulas; or chalk, white lead, and linseed oil, like traditional stopping or glazing putty. An eastern North Carolina corner cupboard utilizes the white lead putty inlay (figs. 31, 32). In contrast, a Reading, Pennsylvania, clock has white and orange paste inlays that are chalk-based with a protein glue binder, as in traditional gesso

Figure 33 Detail of the inlay on a tall case clock, Reading, Pennsylvania, 1801. Birch with pine; white and colored gesso type inlay. H. 95½", W. 21¾", D. 11". (Courtesy, Mabel Brady Garvan Collection, Yale University Art Gallery.) The composite inlay on this case has components similar to gilder's gesso. Previously published as being wax, the inlay is unusual for its multicolor rendering.

(fig. 33). Color alone is not a reliable indicator of sulfur inlay, as non-sulfur substitutes, repair materials, aged sulfur inlay itself, or translucent surface coatings and finishing materials that infuse the inlay body, all complicate visual identification.

To begin answering the questions raised during the replication phase of this study, scientists in Winterthur's scientific research laboratories performed a number of elemental and molecular analyses of the inlays, which involved x-ray diffraction (XRD), Fourier transform infrared spectroscopy (FTIR), scanning electron microscopy (SEM), x-ray fluorescence (XRF), colorimetry, and gas chromatography-mass spectrometry (GC-MS). XRD revealed that all the samples were composed of pure alpha sulfur, the room-temperature-stable, crystalline form of sulfur. XRD, FTIR, and Raman spectroscopy produced no evidence for fillers that could account for the ivory-white color. The minor elements in the inlays identified by SEM and XRF are the commonly observed components of surface dirt (calcium, aluminum, silicon, and iron) and later varnishes (lead driers). The absence of colorless or white fillers such as sand, chalk, or gypsum suggests that there was no original intention to create an ivory-, rather than bright yellow-, colored inlay as has been frequently suggested. Furthermore, FTIR and GC-MS confirmed that no organic binder, which could have been used to create a sulfur-filled mixture, is present in any of the samples (fig. 34). Traces of plant resins and drying oils were found on top of the sulfur, but they relate to finish rather than the composition of the inlay.

Why, then, is sulfur inlay on period objects ivory-white? A factor commonly responsible for changing the value of a mineral's color is fluctuation in particle size. To test this theory, scientists in Winterthur's lab performed non-spinning Debye Scherrer x-ray diffraction on an inlay sample from a 1775 schrank from the Heritage Center Museum (77.71), and a sample of the

Sample Number	Accession Number	Object and Date	EDXRF	XRD	SEM-EDS	μ FTIR	GC-MS
1	Unaccessioned fragment, Winterthur	Blanket chest 1784	S, Ca, Fe	α-S_8	S Ca, Al	ND[a]	NA
2	1965.2256	Mosser box 1773	S, Fe, Pb	α-S_8	S, Ca, Si, Al	ND	NA
3	1965.2256	Mosser box repair	Ca, Pb, S, Fe	$2CaSO_4 \cdot H_2O$ $CaSO_4 \cdot 2H_2O$	Ca, S, Pb, Ni, Fe	PVA $2CaSO_4 \cdot H_2O$	NA
4	Winterthur loan no L02.2635	Candle box 1796	S, Ca, Zn, Pb, Fe, Sr	α-S_8	S, Ca, Si	Trace organic component	NA
5	1964, 1530	Masonic cupboard 1792–96	Pb, Fe, Ca, Zn, Sr	$2PbCO_3 \cdot Pb(OH)_2$ $CaCO_3$ (calcite)	Pb, Ca, Si, S, K	Lead white, drying oil, $CaCO_3$, Behlen Blue Label Paste Wax™	Plant-based drying oil, pine resin
6	Heritage Center Museum 77.71	Reist Schrank 1775	S, Ca, Fe, Pb	α-S_8	S	Venice turpentine or copal varnish	NA

[a] Analysis performed by Kate I Duffy [10].

Figure 34 Instrumental analysis data for eighteenth-century inlays and repairs. Major elements found by EDXRF and SEM-EDS listed in blue. ND indicates no organic compounds were detected. NA indicates not analysed.

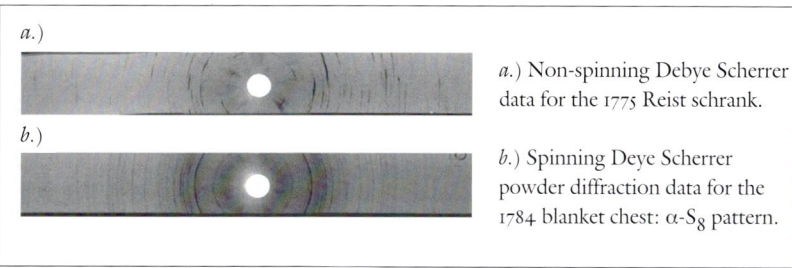

a.) Non-spinning Debye Scherrer data for the 1775 Reist schrank.

b.) Spinning Deye Scherrer powder diffraction data for the 1784 blanket chest: α-S_8 pattern.

Figure 35 XRD diffraction patterns used to identify smaller crystal domains found in aged sulfur inlay.

replica sulfur illustrated in illustrated figure 26. The modern inlay displayed an x-ray diffraction pattern made up of individual points or diffraction peaks, the data expected for a sample with relatively large crystallites. The same experiment on the schrank inlay revealed partial diffraction rings, consistent with the data one would obtain from a powder of finely ground particles (fig. 35). The decreased particle size observed in the schrank inlay suggests that over time the large crystals present after the molten sulfur is poured are replaced with smaller and more randomly oriented sulfur crystals.

On the macro level, sulfur crystal specimens are so temperature sensitive that they can crack from the heat of a person's hand alone. Damage caused to sulfur crystals due to their poor heat conductivity and the resulting thermal expansion has been observed when handling sulfur crystals in natural history collections. Minerals with low thermal conductivity, like sulfur, will spall and flake off fragments, conditions that are also frequently observed on period sulfur-inlaid objects.

To further investigate this phenomenon, one of the reproduction panels was artificially aged in the labs at Winterthur. Repeated light and temperature cycling shifted the yellow color of the reproduction panel toward the ivory-white color seen in period sulfur inlays (figs. 36, 37). Additionally surface checking and minor spalling occurred as a result of the exposure cycles. The artificial aging instrument was not capable of cycling through temperatures that a piece of furniture would have experienced in an eighteenth-century household, where low to freezing temperatures, at times, would have prevailed. Low temperature cycling would further contribute to the color shift.

Figure 36 Close-ups of the replica panel illustrated in fig. 25, showing spalling and color shift as a result of artificial aging.

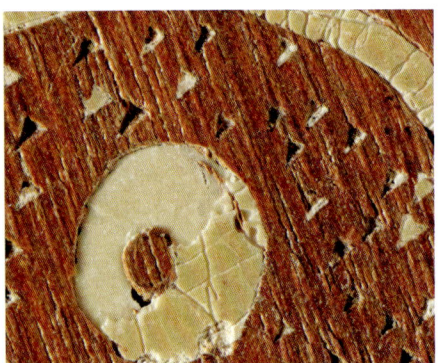

Figure 37 Close-up of the replica panel illustrated in fig. 25, showing spalling and color shift as a result of artificial aging.

In summary, the mechanism that creates ivory-white sulfur inlay is repeated thermal shock over time and the repeated compressive action of the wood as it expands and contracts with humidity changes. As the inlay is subjected to these forces, the natural yellow color of the sulfur begins to appear ivory-white in color as the particle size decreases. Light exposure may play a part, but the color shift is a physical, rather than a chemical, change. Surprisingly, despite the particle size reduction, the inlay does not become powdery.

Much remains to be known about the shop-craft and aging mechanisms of sulfur inlay and the characteristics of other paste inlays, but continued research into the makers themselves may illuminate this decorative technique. Original citations in the form of bills or workshop notebooks may turn up in the future, and genealogies of cabinetmakers or allied craftsmen may shed light on sulfur-inlaid furniture. However, fifty-five years after Frances Lichten's reference to wax inlay or *Wachseinlagen*, we can now identify inlays of pure alpha sulfur as well as other inlays of varying components. The origin of this short-lived decorative technique is still not known nor is the cause for its demise as a craft process. Melting sulfur can certainly be dangerous, and it gives off noxious fumes. Working with sulfur produces fine dust that workers can inhale, and workspaces and clothing become saturated with it. Perhaps craftsmen working with sulfur became annoyed by the tendency of ingested sulfur to be excreted through the skin, leading to, as one period source describes, "silvers being blackened in the pockets of those who take sulfur."[10]

1. Frances Lichten, quoted in Alice Winchester's editor's statement, *Antiques*, no. 5 (November 1958): 416–7. Frances Lichten, "A Masterpiece of Pennsylvania-German Furniture," *Antiques*, no. 2 (February 1960): 176–8. Monroe Fabian, "Sulfur Inlay in Pennsylvania German Furniture," *Pennsylvania Folklife* 27, no. 1 (Fall 1977): 2–9. See also Monroe Fabian, *The Pennsylvania-German Decorated Chest* (Lancaster, Pa.: Heritage Center of Lancaster County and the Pennsylvania-German Society, 1978), pp. 38, 51. Beatrice Garvan and Charles F. Hummel, *The Pennsylvania Germans: A Celebration of Their Arts, 1683–1850* (Philadelphia, Pa.: Philadelphia Museum of Art, 1982), p. 31. The cupboard, box, schrank, and chest are illustrated in Lisa Minardi's article in this volume. Mark Anderson, *Sulfur Inlay*, Chester County Historical Society Antiques Show Catalogue (West Chester, Pa.: Chester County Historical Society, 1995), pp. 36–40. Jennifer L. Mass and Mark J. Anderson, "Pennsylvania German Sulfur-Inlaid Furniture: Characterization, Reproduction, and Aging Phenomena of the Inlays," *Measurement, Science, and Technology* 14, no. 9 (September 2003): 1598–1607.

2. Bernard Demay and Christine Demay, *Meubles polychromes alsaciens*. (Saragossa, Editions du Bastberg: 2002), p. 33. Gislind Ritz, *Alte geschnitzte Bauernmöbiel* (Munich: Georg D. W. Callwey, 1974), p. 157. Heinrich Kriesel, *Die Kunst des deutschen Möbels* (Munich: C. H. Beck, 1970), p. 37. Siegfried Seidl, *Riederbanrische Bauernmöbel* (Munich, Germany: Callwey, 1973), p. 27.

3. Cennino d'Andrea Cennini, *Il libro dell'arte*, translated by Daniel V. Thompson (New York: Dover Publications, 1933), pp. 101, 130.

4. http://en.wikipedia.org/wiki/sulfur (accessed September 2015).

5. State of Pennsylvania, *Minutes of the Provincial Council of Pennsylvania from the Organization to the Termination of the Proprietary Government* (Philadelphia, Pa.: Jo. Severns & Co., 1852), p. 519. It is unclear where Bedwell built his operation. One congressman noted that Bedwell was in Middletown, but not whether that was Pennsylvania or New Jersey. Ibid., p. 514. *Pennsylvania Evening Post*, December 21, 1775. *Pennsylvania Chronicle*, April 13, 1772.

6. Martin E. Weaver, *Conserving Buildings and Materials: A Manual of Techniques and Materials* (New York: Wiley, 1997), pp. 64–66. Bradford L. Rauschenberg, "A Study of Baroque and Gothic-Style Gravestones in Davidson County, North Carolina," *Journal of Early Southern Decorative Arts* 3, no. 2 (November 1977): 24–50.

7. Walter Lee Sheppard, *Corrosion and Chemical Resistant Masonry Materials Handbook* (Norwich, Conn.: W. M. Andrews Publications, 1986), pp. 222, 226, 228.

8. G. A. Jarrin, *The Italian Confectioner: or Complete Economy of Desserts, Containing the Elements of the Art According to the Most Modern and Approved Practice, Full and Explicit Directions Respecting Distillation, Decoration and Modeling* (London: Harding, 1820), p. 120.

9. William Millar, *Plastering—Plain and Decorative: A Practical Treatise on the Art & Craft of Plastering and Modeling . . . Together with an Account of Historical Plastering in England, Scotland and Ireland, Accompanied by Numerous Examples* (London: B. T. Batsford, 1899), pp. 398-99. John Doggett daybook notation for James Evans, May 25, 1805, 64x10, Collection 330, Joseph Downs Collection of Manuscripts and Printed Ephemera, Winterthur Library.

10. Abraham Rees, *The Cyclopedia; or Universal Dictionary of Arts, Sciences, and Literature* (Philadelphia: Samuel F. Bradford and Murray; Fairman and Co., 1802-1819), 36: S. V. "sulphur" in *Materia Medica* entry.

Figure 1 Miniature chest, made for Johannes Mosser, Lancaster County, Pennsylvania, 1773. Walnut and sulfur inlay with tulip poplar; iron. H. 7¼", W. 14¾", D. 8⅝". (Courtesy, Winterthur Museum; photo, Laszlo Bodo.)

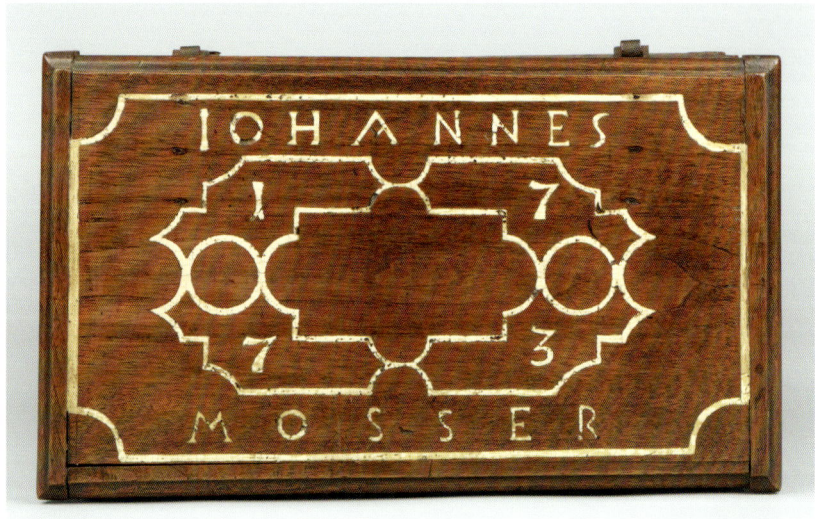

Figure 2 Lid of the miniature chest illustrated in fig. 1.

Lisa Minardi

Sulfur Inlay in
Pennsylvania
German Furniture:
New Discoveries

▼ IN DECEMBER 1929 ANTIQUES dealer Hattie Brunner of Reinholds, Lancaster County, Pennsylvania, wrote to Henry Francis du Pont offering an enticing object for sale:

> Am enclosing photo of a miniature chest which I bought last week, out of the original family, who had cherished it all these years, always kept it stored in a large chest, is in wonderful condition for the age. A unique piece. Dated 1773 made by Johannes Mosser who was one of the first settlers in this section. Was a shoe maker by trade. The old lady that owned it gave me the whole history of the piece.... It was inlaid with the same old putty as that walnut Kass [schrank] I sold you this spring. Will send it on approval if interested.

Du Pont complained about the $1,000 asking price but bought the chest anyway (figs. 1, 2). What neither he nor Brunner realized was that the "putty" inlay on the chest and schrank (see fig. 34) was in fact sulfur—a material used by Pennsylvania German craftsmen in southeastern Pennsylvania from at least 1763 to 1801 and for several decades later in the South. For years this inlay was described as putty or wax, as Frances Lichten claimed in 1960 when she wrote that it was made of "humble substances: powdered white lead and beeswax" and referred to the technique as *Wachseinlegen* or wax inlay. It was not until analytical work was undertaken in the 1970s at the behest of Smithsonian curator Monroe Fabian that the inlay was correctly identified as sulfur. In Fabian's 1977 article on the subject, he claimed to have located twenty-two examples of sulfur-inlaid furniture. Subsequent work by Clarke Hess later identified many more pieces owned by Mennonite families in Lancaster County. Analytical work by Mark Anderson and Jennifer Mass at Winterthur Museum has also yielded new insights into the materials and techniques of making sulfur inlay. More than 125 examples of sulfur-inlaid furniture can now be documented from Pennsylvania, as well as from Maryland, Virginia, and North Carolina; they range in date from 1763 to 1844. The majority are chests, tall clocks, and schranks; other known forms include slide-lid boxes, miniature chests, corner cupboards, hanging cupboards, kitchen cupboards, tables, a slant-front desk, and even a straightedge.[1]

Brunner's letter typifies some of the other challenges that have plagued efforts to research sulfur-inlaid furniture. Although she claimed to have acquired the miniature chest out of the "original family" and to have its "whole history," no further information was ever provided to du Pont. Like so many other objects, the chest lost its provenance once it was removed from the family in which it had descended. Thankfully, many pieces of sulfur-inlaid furniture include the owners' names, or at least initials, and dates that offer clues as to their points of origin. Based on this information, sulfur inlay can now be documented in Lancaster, Lebanon, Dauphin, and York counties, Pennsylvania (fig. 3). The following article is an attempt to reconstruct the origins of the various major groups as well as individual examples of Pennsylvania German sulfur-inlaid furniture. In many cases, the owners' names are unique or sufficiently unusual that they can be identified with certainty. In other cases, especially for those pieces bearing only initials, educated guesswork must be used to make tentative identifications. Depending on the level of certainty, this article will use the modifiers "probably" or "possibly" to indicate when attributions of ownership or maker are less than certain.

Figure 3 Map of Pennsylvania. (Courtesy, Winterthur Museum.)

In the case of the miniature chest acquired by du Pont, the presence of an owner's name, "Johannes Mosser," and the date 1773 inlaid on the lid provide a starting point for investigation. Brunner's letter also claims that Mosser was "one of the first settlers in this section," implying that he lived somewhere near her antiques shop in Reinholds, located in West Cocalico Township, Lancaster County, near the Lebanon County border. Armed with this information, a search of local church records offers some promising leads. A Johannes Mosser/Moser is mentioned numerous times in the baptismal records of John Waldschmidt, a German Reformed minister who served in the Cocalico region from 1752 to 1786. In 1780 and 1782 Johannes Moser and his wife, Anna Elisabeth, served as baptismal sponsors; on both occasions she is identified as the daughter of Christian Eschelman. In 1785 Johannes and Anna Elisabeth had a son, Johannes Jr., baptized by Waldschmidt. Waldschmidt also confirmed a Johannes Mosser (possibly the same one) in 1775 at the Cocalico church "at Michael Amweg's" (the German Reformed congregation also known as Little Cocalico or Swamp, located in what is now West Cocalico Township). Given the close proximity of this church to the Reinholds area in which Brunner's shop was located and her claim that Mosser had lived locally, it is probable that this Johannes Mosser was the original owner of the box.[2]

European Origins: Ivory, Orpiment, and Metallurgy

Before turning to examine the use of sulfur inlay in Pennsylvania German furniture, some investigation of the European origins of this decorative technique is needed. The contrast of light and dark was one of the foremost design concepts of the baroque era. At the same time, exotic materials such as ebony and ivory were becoming increasingly accessible to Europeans. During the seventeenth and eighteenth centuries, elaborate furniture in which light-colored inlay was used in contrast with dark woods became fashionable. Possibly as a less expensive alternative to such precious materials, arsenic sulfide, or orpiment, was also used to achieve a similar visual effect. Although highly toxic, orpiment was used for medicinal purposes, to remove hair from hides as part of the tanning process, and as a gold-colored pigment for paint and sealing wax. Formed by the crystallization of sulfurous gases emitted from volcanic fumaroles, orpiment was especially prevalent in Italy, home to the only active volcanoes in mainland Europe. Several examples of Italian furniture inlaid with orpiment have been identified, including a Venetian prayer bench and a small Bolognese chest dating

Figure 4 Chest, Bologna, Italy, ca. 1550. Walnut and probable orpiment inlay. H. 16⅛", W. 32¼", D. 14½". (Courtesy, Museum Angewandte Kunst, Frankfurt am Main; photo, Ute Kunze.)

Figure 5 Detail of the inlay on the front of the chest illustrated in fig. 4.

to the mid-1500s (figs. 4, 5). Mining sulfur ore was once very common in Italy, especially in Sicily, but also in places such as Naples, Campania, Formignano near Cesena (mined for nearly 500 years), and Perticara near Novafeltria (mined from about 1741 to 1964). In 1864 it was estimated that there were 615 sulfur mines in Italy, of which 237 were abandoned because their ore was already extracted. During that time Sicily's mines alone produced more than 157,000 tons of sulfur per year.[3]

Sulfur has long been used in a variety of trades, especially metalworking. Its properties of melting at a relatively low temperature (about 240°F) and hardening to a solid, yellowish material would have been widely known to craftsmen. Sulfur was also used for bleaching wool, silk, and even hair and was an essential ingredient in gunpowder. Numerous references to sulfur in newspaper advertisements, diaries, and probate inventories reveal that the mineral was commonly available in southeastern Pennsylvania during the 1700s. In 1746 the *Pennsylvania Gazette* ran an advertisement from two

Figure 6 Title page of *De la pirotechnia*, written by Vannoccio Biringuccio, 4th edition, printed by P. Gironimo Giglio, Venice, Italy, 1559. (Courtesy, Bayerische Staatsbibliothek, Munich.)

Figure 7 Detail of a relief carved fleur-de-lis on the schrank illustrated in fig. 38. (Photo, Gavin Ashworth.)

Figure 8 Detail of a sulfur-inlaid fleur-de-lis on the schrank illustrated in fig. 27. (Photo, Gavin Ashworth.)

Philadelphia merchants offering for sale "just imported" fabrics, buttons, sewing supplies, pigments and dyestuffs including "red lead, white lead, Spanish brown, Spanish whiting, madder, ground redwood, allom, copperas, brimstone, sulphur, saltpetre, hammers, augers, files, gimlets" and various types of locks. In 1769 weaver George Michael Kettner of Tulpehocken Township, Berks County, had "brimstone" or sulfur listed in his estate inventory. Daniel Hiester Sr. of Berks County owned a "half Barrel with a quantity of Brimstone" valued at £3 when he died in 1795. Sulfur is also mentioned several times in the journals of Lutheran minister Henry Muhlenberg of Philadelphia and Montgomery County, Pennsylvania. In 1777, Muhlenberg reported with skepticism that his wife Anna Maria took a "mixture of molten sulphur and steel" in an attempt to treat her epileptic condition. "One takes a piece of raw sulphur and a piece of glowing steel," Muhlenberg noted, "the two are held over a pan of water and allowed to drip in; afterwards it is made into a fine powder. Now and then an amount that can be placed on the point of a knife is taken with honey or molasses." He also recorded purchases of sulfur, paying 3s. 9d. in 1777 for a half-pound of sulfur and 1s. 3d. "for steel to strike fire and for sulphur sticks." In all likelihood, Pennsylvania German cabinetmakers turned to sulfur inlay as a less expensive and more readily available substitute for ivory or orpiment. Once the sulfur was inlaid into a native wood such as black walnut or cherry, it provided a similar light and dark effect. Given that it was inlaid in a molten state with the excess simply scraped away after it cooled, sulfur inlay also saved time. And unlike orpiment, sulfur inlay was not toxic.[4]

The technical process for using molten sulfur as an inlay is rooted in metalworking. A brief survey of early metallurgical publications reveals numerous German and Italian sources. Studies by German scholars were especially prominent due in part to the prevalence of ore deposits and mining in Germany; there was also significant pressure to develop new metalworking techniques due to the influx of metals from South American mines after 1492. One such early metallurgical manual, *Das Bergbüchlein* (Augsburg, 1505), explains how to locate and work veins of ore. A 1556 study by Georg Bauer (also known as Georgius Agricola), *De re metallica (On the Nature of Metals)*, focused on mining, assaying, and smelting; it also includes a section on purifying sulfur that was derived in large part from the earlier and highly influential book *De la pirotechnia*, first published in Venice in 1540 and illustrated with dozens of woodcuts depicting various aspects of metalworking. A direct link between Pennsylvania German sulfur inlay and European metallurgy can also be established through the *Pirotechnia*, which very likely served as the design source for the fleur-de-lis motif that is a particular hallmark of the earliest known examples of sulfur-inlaid furniture, made during the 1760s and 1770s in Lancaster County, Pennsylvania. Although the fleur-de-lis motif is often associated with the French, leading some to speculate that the furniture's owners or makers were French Huguenots, most of the owners were in fact of Swiss-German Mennonite heritage. However, the fleur-de-lis was also a popular motif in Italy. Best known as the symbol of the city of Florence, the fleur-de-lis was also used in papal crowns and by the doges of Venice and dukes of Parma. The title page of the 1559 edition of *De la pirotechnia*—which was printed in Venice—features three large fleur-de-lis motifs nearly identical to those inlaid in sulfur and carved on Lancaster County furniture more than 200 years later (figs. 6–8).[5]

The earliest known European manual on metallurgy, the *Pirotechnia* was written by Vannoccio Biringuccio (1480–ca. 1539), who is often considered the father of the foundry industry. A native of Siena, Biringuccio was appointed head of the papal foundry and director of munitions in 1538. The treatise is divided into ten books on topics such as minerals, assaying, smelting, separating gold from silver, alchemy, and the art of casting metals. Book 2 contains a chapter on sulfur, which begins with the statement "Sulfur is a very well-known mineral" and then describes how to purify sulfur ore by heating it in ceramic vessels with a spout near the top, through which the sulfur is distilled by means of ceramic tubes into a second vessel. After applying a "good and powerful flaming fire" to the vessels containing the crude ore, Biringuccio writes that the "substance that is in the ore . . . passes like a smoke through the tubes, thickens there and becomes sulphur; when it becomes like melted wax, it falls to the bottom. If the master wishes, he causes it to run out as it forms . . . to form a cake or else it is poured into tubes of cane, wood, or terra cotta." He ends the chapter: "To conclude: As I told you, sulphur melts and by means of its fusion one can mould any desired object from it as if it were plaster of Paris, wax, or melted metal." There is also a short chapter on arsenic and orpiment that describes them as a "most powerful poison to the life of all things" and advises against using them "except by force of necessity." Although it is not certain exactly how Lancaster County craftsmen would have accessed this manual, it is possible that a copy was in the collection of the Lancaster Library Company, established in 1759 and renamed the Juliana Library Company in 1763. In 1766, the library moved to the home of the Moravian gunsmith William Henry (1729–1786). As a gunsmith, inventor, patron of the arts (including the painter Benjamin West), and member of the American Philosophical Society, Henry is a likely person to have owned a copy of the *Pirotechnia* (fig. 9). He is known to have had an extensive personal library at the time of his death in 1786. Even if Henry could not read Italian, the dozens of woodcuts showing various aspects of metalworking would no doubt have been useful.[6]

Figure 9 Portrait of William Henry, attributed to Benjamin West, Lancaster, Pennsylvania, ca. 1754. Oil on canvas. 36¾" x 30½". (Courtesy, Philadelphia History Museum at the Atwater Kent, Historical Society of Pennsylvania Collection.)

Lancaster County
The use of sulfur-inlaid decoration on Pennsylvania German furniture appears to have originated in Lancaster County. The earliest known dated example is a schrank made in 1763 for Christian and Veronica Herr; the latest known is a chest dated 1801 (see figs. 19, 98). The majority of Lancaster County sulfur-inlaid furniture can be divided into one of three major groups. The earliest group, dating to the 1760s and 1770s, includes at least fifteen tall clocks, schranks, and chests decorated with varying combinations of sulfur, mixed wood, pewter, and even bone inlay. Common design elements include fleur-de-lis motifs and heart-shape, foliate cartouches that frame the owners' names or initials and dates; some pieces also have crossbanded wood inlay in geometric shapes. Highly sophisticated in their design and execution, these pieces were probably made in the county seat of Lancaster, although the original owners lived throughout central Lancaster County. Additional sulfur-inlaid furniture was owned by some of the same families but appears to be the work of various other makers. The second group consists of a pair of chests made in or near Manheim Township in the early 1780s. The third group ranges in date from 1781 to 1801 and includes three full-size chests and a miniature chest, tall clock, stretcher-base table, and straightedge ornamented with floral and bird motifs, dates, and initials.

The Pequea and Conestoga Settlements
One of the earliest settlements in what is now Lancaster County was founded by a small group of Swiss-German Mennonite families about 1710, when some 10,000 acres was warranted to Hans Herr, Christian Herr, Martin Kindig, Jacob Miller, Martin Oberholtzer, John Funk, Hans Graff, Wendell Bauman, Martin Mylin, Christopher Franciscus, and Michael Oberholtzer. The land was located in the Pequea Valley of what was then western Chester County. In 1719 Christian Herr, a Mennonite bishop, built a substantial stone house that also served as a meetinghouse until 1849 (fig. 10). The Conestoga settlement soon grew to such an extent that in 1729

Figure 10 House of Christian Herr, East Lampeter Township, Lancaster County, Pennsylvania, 1719. (Courtesy, 1719 Hans Herr House & Museum; photo, Winterthur Museum, Laszlo Bodo.) The stone lintel above the door is inscribed "17 CH HR 19."

Figure 11 Benjamin Henry Latrobe, view of the Lancaster County Courthouse (built 1787), Lancaster, Pennsylvania, ca. 1801. Watercolor, pencil, pen and ink on laid paper. 8" x 12¾". (Courtesy, Maryland Historical Society, 1960.108.1.8.8.)

the inhabitants successfully petitioned the legislature to establish a new county. The county seat, also known as Lancaster, was laid out in 1730 some ten miles east of the Susquehanna River, near the Conestoga Creek. In 1742 the town of Lancaster was officially incorporated as a borough; it did not assume the legal status of a city until 1818 (this article will use the term "Lancaster" to denote the town/borough). Despite its English name, Lancaster was a predominantly German-speaking locale from the very start. Seventy-five percent of the lot holders in 1740 were Germans; in 1759 about 67 percent of the town's population was German and in 1789 about 63 percent was German. Within twenty years of Lancaster's founding there were 311 taxpayers, and by 1775 its population was approximately 3,288—making Lancaster the largest inland town in America at the time. As the town prospered, its architectural landscape also became increasingly sophisticated. From 1761 to 1766 the Lutheran congregation built a large brick church, Trinity Lutheran, and in 1794 they added a steeple tower adorned with statues of the four evangelists. In 1787 a new brick courthouse was completed, which also served as the Pennsylvania State House when Lancaster was the state capital from 1799 to 1812 (fig. 11).[7]

Early Lancaster Furniture
Lancaster's German-speaking inhabitants included many talented woodworkers as well as affluent consumers who demanded furniture of the best sort. One of the earliest known dated objects associated with Lancaster is an

Figure 12   Tall clock, made for Andreas and Catharina Beierle, probably Lancaster, Lancaster County, Pennsylvania, 1745. Black walnut with tulip poplar. H. 91¼", W. 21¾", D. 12¼". (Private collection; photo, Winterthur Museum, Laszlo Bodo.) The base molding is replaced and the movement is not original to the case.

Figure 13   Detail of the carving on the tall clock illustrated in fig. 12.

extraordinary tall clock made in 1745 for Andreas Beierle (Andrew Beyerle) and his wife Catharina (figs. 12–14). Adorning the hood are two finials in the shape of reclining *putti* or cherubs, while the pendulum door is carved with a baroque floral design and symbols representing Beierle's trade as a baker: a pretzel and loaves of bread. Born in Rohrbach im Kraichgau, Germany, in 1713, Andreas immigrated in 1738 and settled in Lancaster by 1743, when he and his wife served as the sponsors for two baptisms at Trinity Lutheran Church. His training as a master baker in Europe would have included mold carving (necessary for making gingerbread, marzipan, and various fancy pastries), and thus it is possible that Andreas did some of the carving on the clock case himself. In 1754 Andreas and his family moved to Westmoreland County, Pennsylvania; he served as a baker for the army during the French and Indian War and died in 1781. The same person who carved the floral designs on the clock case probably also executed the ornament on an undated paneled walnut chest and a fireplace mantel with a central plaque dated 1746, flanked by rampant lions (fig. 15).[8]

Another early and impressive example of Lancaster-made furniture is a schrank with the pewter inlaid inscription "MF AMF ANNO 1758" (fig. 16). The original owners were probably Michael Fordney (Fortineux) and his wife Anna Margaretha Freuler of Lancaster. Of French Huguenot heritage, Fordney was born in 1714 in Landstuhl in the Palatinate. He immigrated in

Figure 14 Pendulum door of the clock illustrated in fig. 12.

Figure 15 Mantel, probably Lancaster, Lancaster County, Pennsylvania, 1746. (Whereabouts unknown; photo, Raymond J. Brunner.) This photograph was taken in the shop of antiques dealer Hattie Brunner in Reinholds, Lancaster County.

Figure 16 Schrank, probably made for Michael and Anna Margaretha Fordney, Lancaster, Lancaster County, Pennsylvania, 1758. Walnut and pewter inlay with pine and tulip poplar; brass, iron. H. 84", W. 78", D. 21¾". (Courtesy, Clint and Cindy McCauley; photo, Pook & Pook.) The feet are a later addition.

Figure 17 Schrank, made for Johannes and Anna Maria Spohr, Lancaster, Lancaster County, Pennsylvania, 1760. Walnut and mixed-wood inlay with tulip poplar; brass. H. 85", W. 71½", D. 26". (Courtesy, Philadelphia Museum of Art; photo, Pook & Pook.)

1737 together with two of his brothers; their parents and several more siblings joined them by 1742. Michael was a butcher by trade and rented a stall in the Lancaster market house during the 1750s. His father-in-law, Jost Freuler, was Swiss and a gunsmith by trade. Freuler, his wife, and seven children emigrated from Germany to Pennsylvania in 1738, and by 1740 he was an active member of Lancaster's First Reformed Church. Between 1754 and 1762 four of Michael and Anna Margaretha Fordney's children were baptized at First Reformed Church, and in 1769 Michael became a trustee. In his will, Michael left detailed instructions for the distribution of his two town houses, several plots of land, and a brick house and property in Manheim. Michael died in 1778, survived by his widow and three children: Casper, Henry, and John. A great-nephew, Melchior Fordney (1781–1846), was a famous gunsmith in Lancaster prior to his grisly murder at the hands of an axe-wielding religious fanatic. Two years after the Fordneys' pewter inlaid schrank was made, Johannes and Anna Maria Spohr of Lancaster received a schrank of similar form but embellished with relief-carved floral decoration and baroque inlay on the two doors (fig. 17). Born in 1725, Johannes was thirty-five years old when the schrank was made. His oldest child, John George Spohr, was born in 1749 and baptized at First Reformed Church in Lancaster.[9]

Figure 18 High chest, made for Matthias Slough, Lancaster, Lancaster County, Pennsylvania, 1770–1785. Mahogany with tulip poplar; brass. H. 96", W. 42", D. 24". (Courtesy, LancasterHistory.org, Heritage Center Collection, bequest of the estate of George J. Finney; photo, Winterthur Museum, Laszlo Bodo.)

During the 1770s and 1780s Lancaster woodcarvers also produced some of the most sophisticated carved rococo furniture made outside of Philadelphia. One of the most elaborate pieces is a mahogany high chest that was owned by Matthias Slough of Lancaster (fig. 18). A wealthy tavernkeeper and elder

Figure 19 Schrank, made for Christian and Veronica Herr, Lancaster County, Pennsylvania, 1763. Walnut and sulfur inlay with tulip poplar and oak; brass, iron. H. 86", W. 84½", D. 30¼". (Private collection; photo, Gavin Ashworth.)

at Trinity Lutheran Church, Slough also served as the Lancaster County coroner (1754–1769), and as a member of the Pennsylvania Assembly (1773–1776 and 1783–1784). He was also the largest slaveholder in the borough, with five enslaved servants in his possession in 1782. Profuse, relief-carved foliate designs cover the tympanum and skirt of Slough's high chest,

carved from the solid wood in the Germanic manner rather than made separately and applied. During the 1760s and 1770s several of Lancaster County's iron furnaces also cast five- and six-plate stoves using rococo patterns carved by Philadelphia artisans. These and other objects provide a broader context for the study of Lancaster County furniture, especially the earliest group of sulfur inlay, which in all likelihood was made in the borough of Lancaster.[10]

Early Lancaster County Sulfur-Inlay Group

The earliest and largest group of sulfur- and related inlaid furniture made in Lancaster County includes more than twenty objects, consisting of schranks, chests, and clocks. Variations within the group—such as the occasional use of pewter inlay, bone inlay, and crossbanded geometric designs—suggest that several craftsmen or workshops may have been involved in the production of this furniture. The following survey of this group is arranged primarily by form and then chronologically within each category to facilitate comparisons among like types of furniture.

Figure 20 Detail of the sulfur inlay on the schrank illustrated in fig. 19. (Photo, Gavin Ashworth.)

Figure 21 Detail of the sulfur inlay on the schrank illustrated in fig. 19. (Photo, Gavin Ashworth.)

Schranks

During the 1760s and 1770s at least five walnut schranks with sulfur inlay and carved fleur-de-lis motifs were made by the same unknown craftsman for couples living in central Lancaster County (figs. 19–21). A sixth example is neither inlaid nor dated but has carved fleur-de-lis motifs and is otherwise nearly identical (fig. 22). As discussed above, the design source for this motif is almost certainly the title page of the 1559 edition of *De la pirotechnia* (see fig. 6). The maker of the schranks used a small, star-shape punch to mat the ground surrounding the relief-carved fleur-de-lis motifs (fig. 23). A

Figure 22 Schrank, Lancaster County, Pennsylvania, ca. 1765. Walnut; brass, iron. H. 85½", W. 71½", D. 26". (Private collection; photo, copyright 1995 Christie's Limited.)

Figure 23 Detail of the carved fleur-de-lis on the schrank illustrated in fig. 19. (Photo, Gavin Ashworth.)

Figure 24 Detail of the carving on the door of a building in Hildesheim, Germany, ca. 1730. (Photo, Lisa Minardi.)

similar technique was used on both German furniture and architectural woodwork, as seen in the paneled door of a 1730s building in Hildesheim, Germany (fig. 24). Many of the schranks' original owners lived in Manor or Hempfield townships (the latter divided into West and East Hempfield townships in 1817), where a log meetinghouse was constructed in about 1740 by the local Mennonite community (fig. 25). Although the Mennonites are known for their use of plain clothing, humble speech, and spare meetinghouses rather than ornate churches, their furniture was often quite elaborate—especially the fine walnut schranks embellished with sulfur-inlaid decoration.[11]

Like most Pennsylvania German schranks, the examples in this group were made to disassemble into pieces. A distinctive feature of this group is that the sections are held together by wrought iron hooks rather than wedged tenons (fig. 26). Otherwise the schranks display typical Germanic construction techniques, including the use of pegged up drawer bottoms and wedged dovetails. On the interior, shelves for storing folded linens are usually located on the left and wooden pegs for hanging clothing on the right. Some of the schranks also have secret compartments hidden between the drawers. On occasion, one of the drawers is divided into smaller com-

Figure 25 Landisville Mennonite Meetinghouse, East Hempfield Township, Lancaster County, Pennsylvania, ca. 1740. (Photo, Lisa Minardi.)

Figure 26 Detail of a wrought iron hook inside the schrank illustrated in fig. 34. (Photo, Winterthur Museum, James Schneck.)

partments. The drawers are constructed of hefty stock, often a full inch in thickness, and some use walnut for the drawer sides. The schrank doors hang on castle-type hinges, made of either iron or brass. On all of the schranks, the husband's name or initials is inlaid on the upper left door panel and the wife's name or initials on the upper right. The inscriptions also include an exact date (month, day, and year), although the placement of the dates varies; on some schranks the year is on the left and the month and day on the right, and on others just the opposite occurs. Contrary to popular misconceptions, schranks were usually not made for newlyweds but rather for well-established couples. The inlaid dates do not correspond to marriage dates but in all likelihood are the dates of the schranks' completion or presentation. The amount of inlaid and carved decoration varies from piece to piece, with some examples being significantly more elaborate than others. Another variable is the presence of a center foot; the earliest schrank, dated 1763, never had one (see fig. 19) but the other four do.

The earliest known example of sulfur-inlaid furniture made in America is the schrank dated April 7, 1763, and inscribed for Christian and Veronica Herr (see fig. 19). The upper left panel bears Christian's name and the year 1763 framed within a foliate cartouche; the upper right panel contains Veronica's name, the date April 7, and a pair of small birds and a winged angel head above and below the cartouche. This schrank was probably made for Christian Herr (d. 1811) and his first wife, Veronica Bachman; after her death Christian married Catharine Eyeman (d. 1831). Christian Herr lived in Manor Township and owned a sawmill; in his will of 1811, he bequeathed "one wild cherry clothespress with all the contents thereof" to Catharine as well as three feather beds, a chest, a kitchen dresser and its contents, and £1,000 in gold or silver specie. In an earlier will, written in 1796 but never recorded, he bequeathed to Catharine "my Cloths Press standing in the upper story of my House" along with three beds, a kitchen dresser, and a house clock. Of particular note is that he also bequeathed "unto the said Emanuel Herr Junior my Clothes Press standing in my chamber" along with a ten-plate stove and a dining table of cherry wood. Given that Christian Herr owned a sawmill and identified certain pieces of furniture as being made of cherrywood, it is unlikely that he would have confused the wood of the schrank. Thus, the schrank he bequeathed in the 1796 will to Emanuel Herr Jr. (his nephew) was in all likelihood the sulfur-inlaid walnut schrank, which was transferred to Emanuel prior to Christian's death in 1811 and thus not mentioned in his last will and testament. It remains in the possession of Herr family members to this day.[12]

The next schrank in the group bears the date March 1, 1766, and the names "IH KAUFFMANN" and "AN KAUFFMANNIN" (figs. 27–29). In all likelihood, the original owners were Johannes and Anna Kauffmann; the "–in" at the end of Anna's surname is a German feminine suffix used on

Figure 27   Schrank, made for Johannes and Anna Kauffmann, Lancaster County, Pennsylvania, 1766. Walnut and sulfur inlay with tulip poplar and oak; brass, iron. H. 89", W. 84", D. 30". (Courtesy, Pennsylvania Historical and Museum Commission, State Museum of Pennsylvania; photo, Gavin Ashworth.)

women's surnames, both married and unmarried. The schrank also bears the name of a later owner, "C. L. Nissly," and the date 1949 on the top, as well as the inscription "C.L. Nissly, 255 Marietta Pk., Mt. Joy PA." written on the side of a drawer. Closely related in overall form and decoration to the 1763 Herr schrank, the Kauffmann schrank is further embellished with inlaid geometric designs on the lower door panels (fig. 30). John Kauffmann married Anna Shwahr/Schwar, who was probably the daughter of Christian Shwahr Sr. (d. ca. 1784) of East Hempfield Township. Either Christian Sr. or his son Christian Jr. (d. 1807) was the original owner of a sulfur-inlaid tall clock, dated January 18, 1766—a little over a month before the date on the schrank (see fig. 63). In 1775 John Kauffmann and Abraham

102   LISA MINARDI

Figure 28   Detail of the inlay on the schrank illustrated in fig. 27. (Photo, Gavin Ashworth.)

Figure 29   Detail of the inlay on the schrank illustrated in fig. 27. (Photo, Gavin Ashworth.)

Figure 30   Detail of the inlay on the schrank illustrated in fig. 27. (Photo, Gavin Ashworth.)

Figure 31 Schrank, probably made for Peter and Maria Bachmann, Lancaster County, Pennsylvania, 1767. Walnut and sulfur inlay with tulip poplar and oak; brass, iron. H. 89", W. 84¼", D. 30". (Private collection; photo, Gavin Ashworth.) The feet are replaced.

Figure 32 Detail of the inlay on the schrank illustrated in fig. 31. (Photo, Gavin Ashworth.)

Figure 33 Detail of the inlay on the schrank illustrated in fig. 31. (Photo, Gavin Ashworth.)

Figure 34   Schrank, made for Emanuel and Mary Herr, Lancaster County, Pennsylvania, 1768. Walnut and sulfur inlay with tulip poplar. H. 89½", W. 85¾", D. 30½". (Courtesy, Winterthur Museum; photo, Laszlo Bodo.)

Figures 35   Detail of the inlay on the schrank illustrated in fig. 34. (Photo, Winterthur Museum, James Schneck.)

Figure 36   Detail of the inlay on the schrank illustrated in fig. 34. (Photo, Winterthur Museum, James Schneck.)

Reist (owner of the schrank illustrated in fig. 38) served as co-executors of the estate of Jonas Nolt of Hempfield Township. Various John Kauffmanns were named as sons in the wills of Christian Kauffmann (d. 1798), Christian Kauffmann (d. 1806), and Jacob Kauffmann (d. 1812), all of Manor Township, and of Christian Kauffmann (d. 1816) of Hempfield Township.[13]

The third schrank is more restrained in its ornament. It retains the fleur-de-lis carving in the corners of the raised panel doors but lacks the sulfur-inlaid cartouches and bears only the date—February 27, 1767—and the initials "P BM" and "M BM" (figs. 31–33). The original owners have been identified as Peter Bachmann (1725–1782) and his wife Maria of Manheim Township, Lancaster County; a walnut schrank was listed in the inventory taken at Peter's death. Of Swiss Mennonite heritage, Peter married Maria/Mary Kauffman (ca. 1736–1805), daughter of Jacob Kauffman Sr. of Hempfield Township. In 1781, Peter Bachmann and his brother-in-law, Jacob Kauffman Jr., served as co-executors for the estate of Benjamin Eshelman (brother of Jacob's wife, Barbara Eshelman) of Hempfield Township.[14]

The fourth and most elaborate of the schranks in this group is dated February 17, 1768, and inscribed for Emanuel and Mary Herr (figs. 34–36). Like the 1766 Kauffmann schrank, it has sulfur-inlaid geometric designs in the lower door panels. The inlay in the upper door panels is slightly different, however, as the cartouche framing Emanuel Herr's name is topped by a figure of a large parrot eating a tulip. This schrank is also the only one of the group that has an interrupted cornice—a more sophisticated architectural treatment—and relief-carved medallions flanked by turned, engaged columns in the base (fig. 37). The original owners were Emanuel Herr (1745–1828) and his wife Mary. Although most schranks were made for well-established couples rather than newlyweds, this one is an exception since Emanuel Herr was only twenty-three when it was made. Family circumstances likely explain this anomaly, as Emanuel's father Christian Herr (1720–1763) died when he was only forty-three, and his children consequently received their inheritance at a younger-than-normal age. Emanuel Herr's sister, Maria, married John Bachmann, brother of the Peter Bachmann for whom the schrank illustrated in figure 31 was made.[15]

Following the 1768 Herr schrank, there is a gap of seven years before the manufacture of the schrank dated March 8, 1775, and inscribed for Abraham and Elisabeth Reist of Warwick (now Penn) Township, Lancaster County (figs. 38–42). Of similar overall form to the previous examples, the Reist

Figure 37 Detail of the carving at the base of the schrank illustrated in fig. 34. (Photo, Winterthur Museum, James Schneck.)

Figure 38 Schrank, made for Abraham and Elisabeth Reist, Lancaster County, Pennsylvania, 1775. Walnut and sulfur inlay with pine; iron, brass. H. 91", W. 86", D. 31". (Courtesy, LancasterHistory.org, Heritage Center Collection, acquired through the generosity of the James Hale Steinman Foundation; photo, Gavin Ashworth.)

Figures 39 Detail of the inlay on the schrank illustrated in fig. 38. (Photo, Gavin Ashworth.)

Figure 40 Detail of the inlay on the schrank illustrated in fig. 38. (Photo, Gavin Ashworth.)

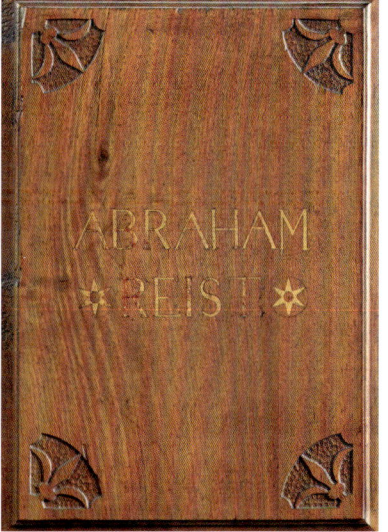
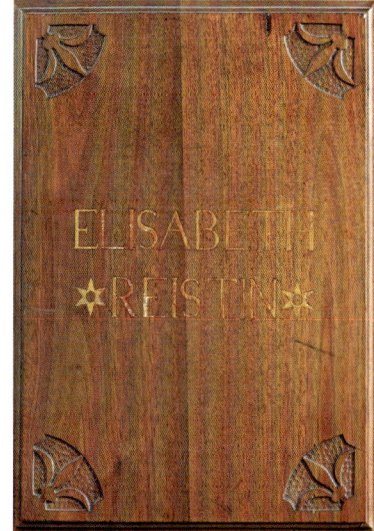

Figure 41 Detail of the inlay on the schrank illustrated in fig. 38. (Photo, Gavin Ashworth.)

Figure 42 Detail of the inlay on the schrank illustrated in fig. 38. (Photo, Gavin Ashworth.)

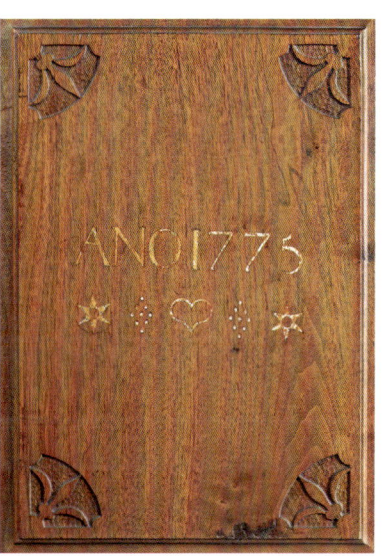

schrank has the fleur-de-lis carving but the sulfur inlay is greatly simplified, consisting of small six-point stars, diamonds, and hearts rather than the foliate cartouches, parrots, and winged angel heads. The schrank was commissioned by the Reists to furnish their new home, a large stone house built in 1774 on what is now Fruitville Pike. Abraham Reist (1737–1813) married Elisabeth Kauffman (1739–ca. 1780); her brother John Kauffman owned a sulfur-inlaid schrank made in 1764 (see fig. 99). His second wife was Elisabeth Metz (1739–1810). Abraham lived on the upper tract of his father Peter Reist's farm in Lancaster County, where Abraham became a wealthy farmer and distiller. He also acquired extensive landholdings in Waterloo Township, Ontario, where the couple's eldest son, John Reist, later settled. In 1786 Abraham and Elisabeth's daughter, Elisabeth Reist (1769–1847), received a painted chest prior to her marriage to John Schwar; the vertical dividers between the two drawers echoes the so-called linen fold panel common on many Lancaster County schranks.[16]

Figure 43 Chest, Lancaster County, Pennsylvania, ca. 1765. White pine; paint; iron. H. 25½", W. 52", D. 24½". (Courtesy, Clarke Hess; photo, Gavin Ashworth.) The paint is restored.

Figure 44 Detail of the chest illustrated in fig. 43. (Photo, Gavin Ashworth.)

Figure 45 Chest, Lancaster County, Pennsylvania, ca. 1765. White pine; paint; brass, iron. H. 26¼", W. 53¼", D. 27⅛". (Private collection; photo, David Bohl.) The paint is restored.

Chests

Two painted chests and three sulfur-inlaid chests are related to this group of schranks. The painted chests, which are built out of pine, have engaged quarter columns and carved fleur-de-lis motifs in the corners of the raised panels on the façade and, in the example built over drawers, on the ends (figs. 43–45). Although both chests have been repainted, traces of the original red, white, and blue palette remained on both examples prior to restoration. The chest over drawers also has elaborate wrought iron hinges with pierced terminals (fig. 46). On the three sulfur-inlaid chests, fleur-de-lis

Figure 46 Detail of a hinge inside the chest illustrated in fig. 45.

Figure 47 Chest, probably made for Michael Kauffman, Lancaster County, Pennsylvania, 1765. Walnut and sulfur inlay; iron. H. 25⅝", W. 51½", D. 24¾". (Courtesy, Rocky Hill Collection; photo, Gavin Ashworth.) The feet are replaced.

Figure 48 Detail of the inlay on the chest illustrated in fig. 47. (Photo, Gavin Ashworth.)

motifs project from both sides of the cartouches, echoing the carved versions on the schranks. The earliest example is dated 1765 and bears the initials "M K" (figs. 47, 48). The owner has been identified as Michael Kauffman (1745–1816), youngest child of John Kauffman (ca. 1700–1759) and Anna

Bamberger, whose farm lay adjacent to the Landisville Mennonite Meetinghouse in East Hempfield Township (see fig. 25). The year after he received the chest, Michael Kauffman married Veronica Berg (1746–1813), daughter of Mennonite émigré Andrew Berg. Michael inherited a 220-acre plantation at the age of twelve; he became a farmer and also a physician.[17]

The next chest, which is virtually identical, is dated 1766 and bears the initials "D W" (figs. 49, 50). It is constructed almost entirely of walnut, includ-

Figure 49   Chest, possibly made for Daniel Wolf, Lancaster County, Pennsylvania, 1766. Walnut and sulfur inlay with white pine; iron. H. 27¼", W. 52", D. 24". (Private collection; photo, Gavin Ashworth.) The feet are replaced.

Figure 50   Detail of the inlay on the chest illustrated in fig. 49. (Photo, Gavin Ashworth.)

ing all visible parts of the till compartment. The till has a false bottom; by pulling up on the front board of the till, a shallow compartment with drawer is revealed. Written on the bottom of the drawer is the name of a later owner: "John C. Sadler Hopewell Township York Co. Pa." A probable candidate for the original owner is Daniel Wolf; his father John Nicholas Wolf emigrated from Germany in 1738, married Anna Maria Bower, and settled in what is now East Hempfield Township, where he died in 1771. Daniel Wolf was born on August 25, 1752, and baptized on September 22 at First Reformed Church in Lancaster; five of his siblings were also baptized there between 1754 and 1769. A store- and tavernkeeper, Daniel Wolf founded the town of East Petersburg, Lancaster County, in 1812. Other surnames beginning with W listed on the 1758 tax assessment for Hempfield Township include Weller, Whitman, Welty, Walter, Whitmore, Wagoner, Wright, Weaver, Waltz, and Weldy.[18]

The third chest is the most elaborate example of the 1760s group. It is dated 1768 and inscribed with the initials "I D" (figs. 51, 52). The only surnames beginning with D on the 1758 Hempfield Township tax list are Dowenbark (probably Dowbenberger), Deyeman, and Davis. In Manor Township in 1780, the surnames include Derstler, Dercher, Domini, Dunckle, and Dundore. A Johannes Dunckel, born in 1747 to Swiss émigré

Figure 51 Chest, made for "I D," Lancaster County, Pennsylvania, 1768. Walnut and sulfur inlay; iron. H. 25⅛", W. 51⅞", D. 24⅞". (Private collection; photo, Gavin Ashworth.)

Figure 52 Detail of the inlay on the chest illustrated in fig. 51. (Photo, Gavin Ashworth.)

Figure 53 Detail of the inlay on the chest illustrated in fig. 51. (Photo, Gavin Ashworth.)

Figure 54 Detail of a foot on the chest illustrated in fig. 51. (Photo, Gavin Ashworth.)

Melchior Dunckel (1701–1769) and his wife Anna Barbara, is one possible candidate whose initials and life dates correspond to the chest. A unique feature of this chest is the pair of mirror-image foliate framing devices that flank the central cartouche (fig. 53). The large ogee bracket feet (fig. 54) are also not found on any of the other chests or schranks, but they relate closely to the original, albeit more diminutive, ogee feet on a sulfur-inlaid tall clock made in 1765 (see fig. 61).[19]

Clocks

At least eight tall clocks are known with closely related cases (several built of cherry rather than walnut) and inlaid ornament including sulfur, pewter, and wood. The earliest example is dated 1762 and has the initials "FR ST" inlaid in pewter in the hood; bands of pewter also encircle two of the finials and additional pewter inlay is on the plinth blocks (figs. 55, 56). Within the arcs of the inlay are clearly visible compass points made by the craftsman as he laid out the design. The pewter was poured into the wood in a molten state, as evidenced by tiny areas in which it leaked beyond the confines of the incised channels. Pewter inlay is extremely rare in Pennsylvania German furniture. Other than this clock, two other clock cases (see fig. 65), and the 1758 schrank (see fig. 16), there are only two or three known examples with pewter inlay. Both pewter and sulfur have a relatively low melting point

Figure 55   Tall clock, probably made for Frederick Stone, movement signed by Rudolph Stoner, Lancaster, Lancaster County, Pennsylvania, 1762. Cherry, mixed-wood inlay, and pewter inlay with tulip poplar. H. 101½", W. 21", D. 11½". (Chipstone Foundation; photo, Gavin Ashworth.) The feet are replaced and a board has been added between the cornice and sarcophagus.

Figure 56   Hood of the clock illustrated in fig. 55. (Photo, Gavin Ashworth.)

Figure 57 Pendulum door of the clock illustrated in fig. 55. (Photo, Gavin Ashworth.)

(depending on its composition, pewter melts between 338–446°F; sulfur melts at about 240°F), enabling them to be poured directly into the wood as an inlay material. The clock case (fig. 57) is inlaid with crossbanded wood strapwork in geometric designs, outlined in pewter stringing; it houses an eight-day, arched dial movement signed by Rudolph "Rudy" Stoner (1728–1769) of Lancaster. A Moravian, Stoner is one of the first documented clockmakers in Lancaster County, where he appears in the borough tax lists by 1754. He purchased a brick house just north of Center (now Penn) Square by 1760, but his life was cut short at the age of forty. The inventory of his estate, valued at £604.19.2, includes fine furniture, a clavichord and two violins, and a workshop full of highly specialized equipment—including clock- and watchmaking tools, a "Cutting Engine for Watch work," polishing and fusee engines, clock and watch parts, and lead patterns.[20]

The pewter inlay on the clock case may have been provided by Johann Christoph Heyne (1715–1781), who, like Stoner, was a Moravian. A talented pewterer, Heyne immigrated to Pennsylvania in 1742 and worked in Lancaster from 1752 to 1781. After the death of his first wife in 1764, Heyne married Anna Regina Steinman, herself a widow who had moved from Bethlehem to Lititz in 1756 with her first husband, Christian Frederick Steinman (d. 1760). Her son John Frederick Steinman (1752–1823) likely apprenticed with Heyne; he was one of the administrators of Heyne's estate and afterwards took over management of the metalworking business, which he developed into a successful hardware store. At the time of his death in 1781, Heyne owned dozens of pewter spoons, plates, basins, and other wares (including three "Church cups" or chalices), as well as household furnishings such as a spinet, window curtains, a twenty-four hour clock, a desk and bookcase, and several looking glasses. Heyne's pewter shows a great deal of ingenuity and skillful craftsmanship; he made ecclesiastical vessels for Lutheran, Reformed, and Brethren congregations, for the Moravian churches in Lititz and Bethlehem, as well as a set of altar sticks for a Catholic church. The baroque style of the pewter inlay on the tall clock was an aesthetic in which Heyne was well-versed, as evidenced by the baroque form altar sticks he made for the Most Blessed Sacrament Catholic Church in Bally, Berks County (fig. 58).[21]

The original owner of this impressive clock was probably Frederick Stone (1734–1792) of Lancaster. He was born on November 4, 1734, to Ludwig and Maria Catharina Stein/Stone and baptized at Trinity Lutheran Church in Lancaster. In the year the clock was made, 1762, Frederick married Anna Maria Hambrecht/Hambright on April 12 at St. James Anglican Church in Lancaster. The clock may have been a wedding present, as Ludwig Stein went to great lengths to help his son Frederick get established. In Ludwig's will of June 4, 1782, he left to Frederick only two English guineas because Frederick had previously received "a handsome Estate consisting of a House & other valuable Effects." Frederick and Anna Maria had at least five children: Frederick Jr.; Ludwig, born in 1770 and baptized at Trinity Lutheran; Catharine; Susanna; and Anna Maria, who died in 1775 at age seven. From at least 1766 to 1773 Frederick rented a pew at Trinity Lutheran.

His father Ludwig Stein was a wealthy innkeeper, land speculator, and staunch Lutheran. Ludwig also made business trips to Germany and on one occasion brought back a silver chalice and bowl, which he presented to Trinity Lutheran. When the Lutheran minister, Laurentius Nyberg, became a Moravian sympathizer, Ludwig led the opposition against Nyberg's efforts to unite the congregation with the Moravians. During a heated confrontation and attempted lock-out in 1745, he shoved the pastor into the sacristy and broke down the church door. Nyberg and his supporters withdrew from the Lutheran church and established their own Moravian congregation in 1746. Despite this turmoil, Ludwig was one of the town's leading citizens and from 1750–1751 served as the burgess of Lancaster. In 1758, Ludwig was made captain of an all-German militia company. He was also an active member of Lancaster's Union Fire Company together with some of the town's wealthiest residents, including Jewish merchant Joseph Simon. The detailed inventory taken after Ludwig's death in 1782 lists an impressive assortment of fine clothing, several sets of bed curtains, two pairs of brass-topped andirons, fourteen glazed pictures, a clothes press, a walnut desk, a gilded German bible and silver-mounted psalm book, and extensive china, delft, and Queensware.[22]

Frederick Stone followed in his father's footsteps and became a tavern-keeper and leading citizen of Lancaster. He helped to found both the Lancaster Library Company (est. 1759) and Friendship Fire Company (est. 1763). Frederick served as Lancaster County coroner from 1761 to 1762 and, in December 1763, was one of fourteen jurors selected by then-coroner

Figure 58 Pair of candlesticks, marked by Johann Christoph Heyne, Lancaster, Lancaster County, Pennsylvania, 1755–80. Pewter. H. 22, W. 7¾", D. 8⅝". (Courtesy, Winterthur Museum; photo, Gavin Ashworth.)

Figure 59 Tall clock, made for the Eaby family, movement signed by Christian Forrer, Lampeter, Lancaster County, Pennsylvania, ca. 1765. Walnut and mixed-wood inlay with walnut; brass. H. 92½", W. 19¾", D. 13". (Courtesy, Carolyn C. Wenger; photo, Gavin Ashworth.) The feet are replaced; the broken scroll pediment is a later addition.

Matthias Slough for an inquest regarding the brutal murder of six Indians on December 14, 1763, by the so-called Paxton Boys, a tragedy known as the Conestoga Massacre. From 1767 to 1773 Frederick served as sheriff of Lancaster County; he was succeeded in this position by John Ferree. Although he was of Lutheran heritage, Frederick Stone was one of several leading Germans in Lancaster who at least nominally joined St. James Anglican (later Episcopal) Church. Other prominent English-speaking members of St. James included George Ross, an attorney and iron forge owner, and Edward Shippen, former mayor of Philadelphia. Frederick Stone was buried at Trinity Lutheran, however, following his death on December 19, 1792.[23]

How did Frederick Stein, whose father had so zealously opposed the Lancaster Moravians, come to own a clock with a movement made by a Moravian clockmaker and a case with pewter inlay possibly supplied by a Moravian pewtersmith? Put simply, much had changed in Lancaster in the twenty years since the 1745 controversy. Under the leadership of Lutheran patriarch Henry Melchior Muhlenberg, head of the Pennsylvania Ministerium, the Lutheran church was thriving while the Moravians' influence was on the decline following the death of leader Nicholas Ludwig von Zinzendorf in 1760. As Lancaster grew, civic organizations also arose that provided opportunities for people of different faiths to interact. A prime example of this was the Juliana Library Company (est. in 1759 as the Lancaster Library Company). Its 1763 charter includes the names of both Frederick Stone and Rudy Stoner as founding members. Matthias Slough is also listed, as is the Moravian gunsmith William Henry (see fig. 9), into whose house the library's books were moved in 1766. As proof of how far Lutheran-Moravian relations had improved by 1782, William Henry even served as a witness to Ludwig Stein's will.

Figure 60 Hood of the clock illustrated in fig. 59. (Photo, Gavin Ashworth.)

Figure 61 Tall clock, made for Peter Ferree, movement signed by Rudolph Stoner, Lancaster, Lancaster County, Pennsylvania, 1765. Cherry and sulfur inlay with tulip poplar. H. 107¼", W. 21", D. 11½". (Courtesy, Rocky Hill Collection; photo, Winterthur Museum, Laszlo Bodo.)

Closely related strapwork inlay appears on a tall clock with an eight-day movement signed by Christian Forrer (1737–1783) of Lampeter, Lancaster County (figs. 59, 60). Although the case is undated, it is stylistically early and was probably made between 1754—when Christian Forrer and his brother Daniel, also a clockmaker, emigrated from Switzerland—and 1774, when Christian moved to York County. The inlaid panels on the sides of the hood mimic the approximate size and location of sidelights; the inlay on the pendulum door is a smaller version of that on the sides of the case. Whereas the Stoner clock used pewter to outline the strapwork inlay, this clock uses lightwood stringing. The clock descended in the Eaby family of Leacock Township, Lancaster County; the pendulum is engraved "Jacob Eaby 1799 / Jason K. Eaby 1907." The first name probably refers to Jacob Eaby (1776–1842), who married Susanna Miller in 1799. He was the youngest son of Jacob Eby (1728–1794) and Hannah Laeder (1733–1810), who were probably the first owners of the clock. Jason K. Eaby was born in 1845 to Moses Eaby (son of Jacob Eaby) and Susanna Kurtz.[24]

The next known dated clock was made in 1765 and houses an elaborate eight-day movement that is signed on the face "Rd^{lph} Stoner / Lancaster" and includes a moon-phase dial, a second-hand dial, and a date aperture (figs. 61, 62). The ogee feet, turned finials, and pierced valance of this monumental tall clock are entirely original. The hood is ornamented with a bold, triple interrupted cornice and relief-carved tulips at either side—executed from the solid

Figure 62 Hood of the clock illustrated in fig. 61. (Photo, Laszlo Bodo.)

wood in the Germanic style rather than carved separately and applied—and a central carved rosette identical to that on the 1768 Herr Schrank (see fig. 37). The date and the name of the original owner, Peter Ferree (b. ca. 1730) of East Lampeter Township, Lancaster County, are inlaid in sulfur. Of French Huguenot ancestry, Peter was the great-grandson of Mary Ferree, a widow who in 1712 became one of the first settlers in the Pequea Valley. When Peter Ferree died in 1795, his "eight-day Clock and Case," valued at £8, was the most expensive object in the inventory of his estate. At his estate sale, the clock sold for £18.2.0 to his fourth son, Jacob, who had also inherited Peter's plantation in Lampeter Township.[25]

A nearly identical clock case was made in 1766 for Christian Schwar/Shwahr/Swarr. Like the Ferree case, it is inlaid in sulfur with the owner's name, but rather than bearing just the year it has an exact date: January 18,

Figure 63   Tall clock, made for Christian Schwar, movement attributed to George Hoff, Lancaster, Lancaster County, Pennsylvania, 1766. Walnut and sulfur inlay with tulip poplar. H. 107", W. 19¼", D. 11". (Courtesy, Rock Ford Plantation, bequest of John J. Snyder Jr.; photo, Gavin Ashworth.) The feet, finials, and valance are replaced.

Figure 64   Hood of the clock illustrated in fig. 63. (Photo, Gavin Ashworth.)

118   LISA MINARDI

Figure 65 Tall clock, made for Daniel Besore, movement signed by George Hoff, Lancaster, Lancaster County, Pennsylvania, 1768. Cherry, red mulberry, and walnut with pewter and mixed-wood inlay and tulip poplar. H. 105", W. 19¾", D. 11". (Courtesy, Dietrich American Foundation.) The finials and valance are replaced.

Figure 66 Hood of the clock illustrated in fig. 65. (Photo, Dietrich American Foundation.)

1766 (figs. 63, 64). The movement of the Schwar clock is unsigned but has been attributed to George Hoff (1733–1816). One of the most influential clockmakers in Lancaster, Hoff was trained in Germany and immigrated to Pennsylvania in 1765. He settled in the borough by 1766, when his son Michael was baptized at Trinity Lutheran Church. Hoff held numerous public offices and served as a warden and elder at Trinity Lutheran. The original owner of this clock was either Christian Schwar/Shwahr Sr. of East Hempfield Township, who died about 1784, or his son Christian Jr., who died in 1807. Christian Jr. married Elisabeth Hiestand; she died in 1819 and in her will of 1809 names children John, Barbara (wife of John Steman), Elizabeth (wife of John Gissy), and Anna (wife of John Kauffman). The latter couple was probably too young to be the Johannes and Anna Kauffmann who owned the sulfur-inlaid schrank dated 1766 (see fig. 27), but they were likely related. Peter Schwar, brother of Christian Schwar Sr., also owned a sulfur-inlaid schrank (see fig. 103).[26]

A fifth clock in a closely related case is dated "1768" in pewter inlay and has a movement signed by George Hoff—one of the earliest known examples of his work (figs. 65, 66). The pendulum door of the clock is elaborately inlaid with a compass star and geometric strapwork—all outlined in pewter stringing—and the panel on the base is inlaid with cross-banded wood in a geometric motif similar to the sulfur inlaid design on the lower door panels of the 1766 and 1768 schranks (see figs. 27, 34). According to family tradition, this clock was made for Daniel Besore (Beshar, Boshaar, Bessieur). Of French Huguenot ancestry, he was born on July 31, 1732, to John Boshaar (1710–1747) and Anna Maria Kunigunda (1710–1753). Daniel married Catharine Rudy (1734–1814; daughter of Rudolph Rudy) on March 30, 1756, in Lancaster County. About 1767 Daniel received a patent for land in Franklin County, Pennsylvania, where he and his family later moved to an area known as Irishtown, located in Washington Township. There, in 1786, Daniel helped found the Salem German Reformed Church, and for years the congregation was known simply as Besore's. He died on January 24, 1811, and was buried in the Salem Church cemetery. The clock was valued at $50 in his estate inventory and was kept by his widow. On her death in 1814 it was sold at auction to Joseph Snively but was later acquired by Daniel's son David Besore (1760–1844); it is listed in David's estate inventory as "1 Eight day Clock" valued at $10. A colorful birth and baptismal certificate made for David Besore's son Jacob (b. 1804) testifies to the family's long retention of their Germanic heritage (fig. 67).[27]

Figure 67 Birth and baptismal certificate for Jacob Boshaar, attributed to Joseph Lochbaum, Washington Township, Franklin County, Pennsylvania, ca. 1805. Watercolor and ink on laid paper. 13" x 15½". (Courtesy, Philadelphia Museum of Art, promised gift of Joan and Victor Johnson; photo, Graydon Wood.)

At least three additional related clock cases are known, but all lack personalization in the form of names or dates. One has three sulfur-inlaid plaques in the hood and an eight-day movement attributed to Samuel Meyli/Meily (figs. 68, 69). Meyli was probably trained by Jacob Graff of Lebanon; his father was Martin Meily (d. 1770) of Lebanon Township. Another clock, with an unsigned thirty-hour, square dial movement, has a closely related case with three plaques of similar shape, but they are outlined in sulfur rather than solidly infilled. The third clock, with an eight-day English movement that sits on two horizontal supports that span the width of the clock, has plaques carved into the hood but no evidence that they were ever filled with sulfur

Figure 68 Tall clock, movement attributed to Samuel Meyli, Lancaster County, Pennsylvania, ca. 1770. Walnut and sulfur inlay with tulip poplar; brass. H. 102", W. 20½, D. 11½". (Courtesy, Virginia A. and Edward F. LaFond Jr.; photo, Gavin Ashworth.) The feet, finials and plinths, and valance are restored.

Figure 69 Hood of the clock illustrated in fig. 68. (Photo, Gavin Ashworth.)

inlay (figs. 70, 71). The horizontal supports also appear in an earlier clock case with a movement signed by Jacob Graff (1729–1778) of Lebanon.[28]

The geometric strapwork inlay that appears on three of the clock cases (the 1762 Stone clock, undated Eaby family clock, and 1768 Besore clock) is also found on a schrank and two chests. The schrank, the present where-

Figure 70 Tall clock, movement signed by Benjamin Lamb of London, case made in Lancaster County, Pennsylvania, ca. 1765. Walnut with tulip poplar. H. 96½", W. 22⅛", D. 12½". (Courtesy, Rock Ford Plantation, bequest of John J. Snyder Jr.; photo, Gavin Ashworth.)

Figure 71 Hood of the clock illustrated in fig. 70. (Photo, Gavin Ashworth.)

abouts of which are unknown, has doors inlaid like the pendulum doors of the clock cases. It does not appear to have any initials or date and descended in the family of Judge Henry Long of Lancaster County. The first of the two chests is undated but bears the initials "I K" on the façade, believed to stand

122   LISA MINARDI

Figure 72 Chest, possibly made for Johannes Kilheffer, Lancaster County, Pennsylvania, ca. 1765. Walnut and mixed-wood inlay with white pine; iron, brass. H. 23", W. 42½", D. 19¼". (Courtesy, Lancaster Mennonite Historical Society, bequest of John J. Snyder Jr.; photo, Gavin Ashworth.)

Figure 73 Lid of the chest illustrated in fig. 72. (Photo, Gavin Ashworth).

Figure 74 Detail of the façade of the chest illustrated in fig. 72. (Photo, Gavin Ashworth.)

for Johannes Kilheffer (ca. 1738–1797), a Mennonite farmer in Manor Township, Lancaster County (figs. 72–74). The chest is constructed with half-blind dovetails and the lid is mitered at the front corners. In the center of the lid is an inlaid geometric design closely related to that on the base of the 1762 clock (see fig. 55). The other chest, which has exposed dovetails but is otherwise very similar, is inlaid in bone with the date 1767 and initials "IB GN," probably for Jacob Gochnauer Jr. (1742–1817) of Conestoga Township (figs. 75, 76). The Gochnauers were of Swiss Mennonite heritage, hail-

Figure 75 Chest, probably made for Jacob Gochnauer, Lancaster County, Pennsylvania, 1767. Walnut, mixed-wood inlay, and bone inlay; iron. H. 24¼", W. 50", D. 23½". (Private collection; photo, Gavin Ashworth.)

Figure 76 Detail of the façade of the chest illustrated in fig. 75. (Photo, Gavin Ashworth.)

ing from the village of Grüningen about ten miles southeast of Zurich. Jacob Gochnauer Sr. had emigrated in 1732 at the age of twenty on the *Samuel* together with his siblings Christian, aged seventeen, and Catharine, aged eighteen.[29]

Pewter inlay also occurs on two more pieces of furniture probably made in Lancaster County, although by different woodworkers. The first is a tall clock with walnut case inlaid in pewter with the inscription "17 MO 63." The clock has an eight-day, arched dial movement signed by Jacob Graff. The initials are those of Michael Oberlin/Oberle; two men of that name both lived in southeastern Pennsylvania at the time. One Michael Oberle immigrated in 1751 and settled in the area of Schaefferstown, now part of Lebanon County. The other Michael Oberle was born in 1717 in Germany and immigrated with his father Johann Martin Oberle and older brother Johann Adam Oberle; the latter two men were named on a 1743 list of members of Emanuel Lutheran Church near Brickerville in Elizabeth Township, Lancaster County. This Michael Oberle married Christina Barbara Zwecker/Swecker (1723–1791) on November 15, 1741, at Trinity Lutheran Church in

Figure 77 Chest, made for "EL S," Pennsylvania, 1769. Walnut, pewter inlay, and sulfur inlay with pine and oak; iron, brass. H. 24¼", W. 53¾", D. 22⅜". (Private collection; photo, Gavin Ashworth.)

Figure 78 Detail of a drawer from the chest illustrated in fig. 77. (Photo, Gavin Ashworth.)

New Holland, Lancaster County, and four of their children were baptized there between 1743 and 1754. The church records show that at the baptism of their son Georg Friedrich on January 13, 1754, Georg and Magdalena Jundt were the baptismal sponsors. Jundt was a prominent member of Bergstrasse Lutheran Church near Ephrata and owned a tall clock inlaid with his name, a pair of parrots, and the date 1755. Michael Oberle later became active in the Bergstrasse Lutheran Church, where he was buried in 1788. The second object makes an even more direct connection between sulfur and pewter inlay by incorporating both materials on the drawer fronts, which are inlaid with the date 1769 and the initials "EL S" (figs. 77, 78). A walnut corner cupboard is also known which includes both sulfur and pewter inlay (see p. 72, fig. 6 in this volume).[30]

Possible Makers

Although the owners of this group of furniture can be well-documented to central Lancaster County, they resided in varying locales and were not of the same religious faith. Questions remain as to who made this group of furniture and whether or not it was all produced within the same workshop. Many details appear to be nearly identical even when found on disparate forms, such as the relief-carved rosettes at the center of the hoods on the Ferree and Schwar clocks and the rosette at the bottom center of the 1768 Herr schrank (see figs. 34, 61, 63), suggesting that these pieces are

125   SULFUR INLAY IN PENNSYLVANIA

from the same shop. Many of the clocks have movements that were made in Lancaster. The sophistication and overall similarity of the cases strongly suggests that the principal cabinetmaking workshop responsible for this group of furniture was also located in Lancaster. Unfortunately, narrowing down the list of possible makers is made difficult by the fact that more than 160 joiners, cabinetmakers, and carpenters worked in Lancaster between 1760 and 1810. In 1759 alone, there were twenty-seven carpenters and joiners in Lancaster; twenty-two in 1770; and twenty-five in 1788. The 1780 Lancaster directory lists only eight men under the category of joiners: George Burkhard, Peter Brotzman, Gottlieb Blimler, Jacob Flubaker, William Hensel, Robert Sence, John Shortel, and Philip Thomas. Nine carpenters are also identified: Joseph Algier, Theodore and Nicholas Bartholomew, Christopher Franciscus, Michael Lind, Frederick Mann, Francis Morrow, Cornelius Switzer, and Matthias Zahneiser.[31]

Several likely names can be gleaned from the records as strong possibilities. One is joiner George Burkhard/Burkhart/Burkert (1721–1783), who in 1763 was a charter member of the Juliana Library Company (along with Frederick Stone, Rudy Stoner, and others). Born in 1721, Burkhard would have been at the height of his career during the 1760s and 1770s when the furniture was made. He may be the "Hans Jurig Burghart" who emigrated from Germany in 1739. Burkhard is known to have been in Lancaster by 1750 when he bought a lot on the corner of Duke and Orange streets, where he erected a house and workshop. In 1753 he married Mary Doll and in 1764 built a large stone house. Burkhard was probably the most prosperous of Lancaster's joiners prior to the Revolution. The earliest documented extant example of his work is the case of the organ at Lancaster's First Reformed Church (where Burkhard was a member), which he built between 1769 and 1770 at a cost of £50. At his death in 1783, Burkhard owned £20 of mahogany boards, £5 of walnut boards, and £30 in "tools and other work not finished." The administration papers of his estate include the names of many prominent men, including attorney Jasper Yeates of Lancaster and Michael Withers of East Lampeter Township, who owned a cherry desk-and-bookcase ornamented with elaborate relief carving from the solid wood.[32]

Joiner Gottlieb Sehner/Sener Sr. (d. 1788), who emigrated from Germany in 1749, is another strong possibility. He married Maria Barbara Kline in 1750 and settled in Lancaster, where he became an active member of Trinity Lutheran Church. The couple had five children baptized there between 1751 and 1765, including their son Johann Gottlieb Sehner Jr. (1751–1802), who was also a joiner and carpenter. In the late 1780s Gottlieb Jr. built an elegant brick townhouse in Lancaster with elaborate architectural ornament—including wainscot paneling and windows topped with pulvinated friezes and double cornices with Greek key moldings. From 1801 to 1813 the house was rented by Andrew Ellicott, first surveyor-general of the United States. The Sehners also built Lancaster's Masonic Hall in 1795.[33]

Another strong candidate is Michael Lind Sr. (1725–1807), who immigrated to Pennsylvania in 1752 and within a year had established a shop in Lancaster on Orange Street. He married a woman named Juliana; six of their children were baptized at First Reformed Church between 1753 and 1766. Michael is identified as a carpenter in the 1780 directory, and three of his sons became joiners, namely: Conrad (1753–1834), Michael Jr. (1763–1840), and John. Michael Sr. also had a brother named Conrad, who with his wife, Anna Maria, had several children baptized at First Reformed between 1760 and 1765. Michael evidently knew the Stein/Stone family well, since in 1782 Lind was among several leading Lancaster citizens (including gunsmith William Henry and Henry Muhlenberg Jr., minister of Trinity Lutheran Church) who testified as to the validity of Ludwig Stein's will. In the 1790 U.S. Census, Michael Lind Sr. and Jr. and Conrad Lind are also listed in close proximity to Frederick Stone, owner of the pewter inlaid clock made in 1762 (see fig. 55). A small walnut lift-top chest and slant-front desk signed by Conrad Lind are known, as is a high chest with ornate carving signed by a member of the Lind family.[34]

Other joiners worked in early Lancaster but can be excluded as probable candidates. The records of Trinity Lutheran Church reveal that in 1743, joiner Ludwig Heinich Dettenborn/Tetteborne donated a baptismal table and boards for the church pews under the pulpit, but he died in 1753. Joiner Conrad Doll (b. 1739) emigrated from Germany in 1741 with his parents, Johannes and Catharina (Hartmann) Doll, and settled in Lancaster by 1747, when his brother Joseph was baptized at First Reformed Church. Conrad was a cabinetmaker and Joseph a carpenter and occasional cabinetmaker, but both men moved to Frederick, Maryland, by the mid-1760s. Their sister, Mary Doll (1731–1812), married joiner George Burkhard. Their older brother, Johannes Doll Jr., who was the schoolmaster at First Reformed Church in Lancaster, had a son named Conrad Doll (1772–1819) who became a joiner. He is the only member of the Doll family for whom documented work is known to survive—an ornately carved organ case built in 1807 for the Peace Church in Cumberland County, Pennsylvania. But given both the departure of Conrad and Joseph Doll from Lancaster by the mid-1760s and their nephew's age, none of these men would have been able to build this group of furniture. The joiner Peter Frick (1743–1822), who built the organ case for Trinity Lutheran Church from 1771 to 1774, can also be excluded due to his not moving to Lancaster from Germantown until the late 1760s.[35]

Previous scholars have proposed other possible makers for the furniture in this early Lancaster group. An erroneous attribution was put forth in 1987 due to the mistaken interpretation of the inscription "D. 1 Mertz" (a German abbreviation for "*Den 1 Mertz*," or the first of March) on the 1766 Kauffmann schrank as the name "D. I. Mertz" (see fig. 27). In 1982 it was postulated that woodturner Peter Holl II (d. 1784) of Manor Township, Lancaster County, and his alleged nephew Peter Holl III (1745–1825), a turner, joiner, and pumpmaker who lived in Warwick Township, were the makers. Peter Holl I (d. 1775), who was said to be a joiner, emigrated from Switzerland to Augusta County, Virginia, before moving to Lampeter Township, Lancaster County, by 1754 and later to Manor Township, Lancaster County, where he lived next to Christian Kauffman and Abraham

Herr. Because sulfur is used to repair metals, it was speculated that Peter Holl III would have been familiar with its properties from his work as a pumpmaker. The Holl attributions, however, have fallen into doubt for lack of evidence. Peter Holl III was however clearly a woodworker. The inventory taken at the time of his death in 1825 includes "Boards and other Joiner Wood" valued at $8.60; two planing benches and a lathe; "134 Planes of every Description"; fourteen saws; seventy-four chisels; two braces with thirty-three bits and "some Punches;" squares, hammers, augers, compasses, gimlets, and files; and a chest of unspecified "small tools." New genealogy research also shows that this Peter Holl was not a nephew of Peter Holl II of Manor Township and may not even have been directly related. He was the son of Johannes Holl (d. 1752), who immigrated about 1730 and settled in Earl Township, Lancaster County. As noted above, sulfur was a common material used in a wide variety of trades, so it was by no means limited to pumpmakers. Given both the sophistication of the furniture and many of the owners' ties to Lancaster, it is far more likely that this group of furniture was made by a cabinetmaker or workshop also based in the borough.[36]

Huber Schrank and Related Chests
Heralded as a "masterpiece of Pennsylvania-German furniture" by Frances Lichten when she published it in 1960, the sulfur-inlaid schrank made in 1779 for Georg/George Huber has long been admired as a pinnacle of Pennsylvania German cabinetmaking (fig. 79). A profusion of sulfur-inlaid decoration covers the façade: flowering vines emanate from vases and trail up the stiles of the doors while fylfots, stars, and crowns adorn the rails; large crowns topped by pairs of birds adorn the doors' upper panels, with swastikas below. The cornice is embellished with architectural details including mutules, guttae, and a Greek key design. Carved fleur-de-lis motifs are in each corner of the doors as well as on the raised panels on the sides—the latter detail is not seen on any of the earlier schranks. Because of the fleur-de-lis motif, the Huber schrank has usually been assigned to the same group as the earlier 1760s and 1770s schranks. Yet aside from this detail and the common use of sulfur inlay, there is little or no similarity between the Huber schrank and those in the earlier group with respect to overall composition, proportions, or molding profiles. Even the hardware is different, with the Huber schrank employing rattail hinges and the other schranks castle-type hinges. Thus the Huber schrank is in all likelihood the product of a different maker or workshop.[37]

Who was George Huber and why did he own such a spectacular schrank? Although it has been speculated that his brother Christian Huber, a joiner, made this schrank as an end-of-apprenticeship masterpiece under the guidance of Peter Holl III (who is no longer thought to be a probable maker, as noted above), there is little evidence to support such claims. There were two John/Johannes Hubers and three Christian Hubers in Lancaster County at this time, and they have often been conflated in previous studies. George Huber (ca. 1749–ca. 1785), owner of the schrank, was the son of Johannes

Figure 79 Schrank, made for Georg Huber, Lancaster County, Pennsylvania, 1779. Walnut and sulfur inlay with tulip poplar, pine, and oak; brass and iron. H. 83⅛", W. 78", D. 27½". (Courtesy, Philadelphia Museum of Art, 1957-30-1.) The feet are replaced.

Huber (1704–1784), a farmer in Manheim Township who emigrated from Germany in about 1742. Of Swiss-German Mennonite heritage, Johannes Huber was never a miller as has sometimes been claimed. The miller was John Huber (1737–1803), who lived at the Oberholtzer mill in East Hempfield Township. George Huber had two brothers who were at least briefly involved with woodworking: Jonas Huber (ca. 1765–1792), a joiner and

Figure 80 Chest, Lancaster County, Pennsylvania, 1783. Walnut and sulfur inlay with pine; brass, iron. H. 29¼", W. 54½", D. 26½". (Courtesy, National Museum of American History, Smithsonian Institution; photo, Winterthur Museum, Laszlo Bodo.) The feet are replaced.

Figure 81 End of the chest illustrated in fig. 80.

Figure 82 Till compartment of the chest illustrated in fig. 80.

wheelwright in Hempfield Township, and Christian Huber (ca. 1752–1804), who is described as a joiner in a 1779 tax list but soon gave that up for farming. The year after George Huber received the schrank in 1779, he married Barbara Oberholtzer (d. 1803) on November 8, 1780, at First Reformed Church in Lancaster. She was the daughter of Magdalena and Christian Oberholtzer (d. 1789) of Hempfield Township. George died intestate and without issue in about 1789, and it has been suggested that the schrank then passed to his brother Christian Huber—but this is uncertain.[38]

The unknown craftsman who built the Huber schrank is also thought to have made a sulfur-inlaid chest in 1783 (fig. 80). Its drawers are inlaid in the same manner as the drawers of the schrank, and the stippled treatment within the foliate cartouches is very similar to that on the schrank. The maker also adorned the chest with four inlaid, fluted columns, echoing the architectural nature of the Huber schrank. The ends of the chest are also inlaid, with additional columns and a lower panel that imitates the inlaid drawer fronts but uses floral inlay in place of the brasses (fig. 81). On the inside of the chest, there is a removable panel beneath the till compartment that is inlaid in sulfur with two stars and the inscription "ANNO 1783" (fig. 82). Although the style of the numerals is much plainer than those on the schrank, their basic shape—especially the curved foot of the "7"—is the same.

Unfortunately, the original owner of this chest remains unknown, although several clues have been discovered. On the underside of the lid is a pencil inscription: "D. W. Dietrich 1876." When the chest was sold in 1910 by the antiques dealer W. H. Spangler of Ephrata, Lancaster County, he noted in a letter to the purchaser that it "was a bridal gift to the owner (Mrs. Dietrich) when she was 17. I bought it from her son who was an old man. Mrs. Dietrich lived in the country about 9 or 10 miles from here and is dead many years ago." The D. W. Dietrich of the inscription can now be identified as schoolmaster Daniel Webster Dietrich (1855–1941) of Lititz, Lancaster County, Pennsylvania. His parents were George Sanderson Dietrich (1795–1886) and Elizabeth Stager (1812–1897), who were married in 1831 at Trinity Lutheran Church in New Holland and lived in Earl Township, Lancaster County. They are buried at the Groffdale Mennonite Cemetery in Leola. Elizabeth Stager Dietrich would have been the "Mrs. Dietrich" to whom Spangler referred; the original owner was probably one of her two grandmothers.[39]

A chest inscribed "Henrich Kaufman" and dated April 12, 1779, shares a number of features with the Huber schrank (fig. 83). Although the inlay is not nearly as elaborate as that on the schrank, the fylfot motif that appears at the bottom of each of the two hearts on the chest's façade is also found on the bottom rail of the schrank's doors. Flanking each fylfot is a pair of six-pointed stars with hollow centers, the same motif that appears on the till

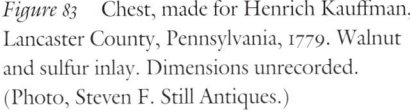

Figure 83 Chest, made for Henrich Kauffman, Lancaster County, Pennsylvania, 1779. Walnut and sulfur inlay. Dimensions unrecorded. (Photo, Steven F. Still Antiques.)

compartment of the 1783 chest (see fig. 82). The shape of the lettering and numerals on the Henrich Kauffman chest is also quite similar, albeit without the extra embellishments used on the Huber schrank. It thus seems possible that this chest was a less ornate product of the same workshop. Henrich Kauffman is probably the son of Jacob Kauffman (d. 1812) of Manor Township. The son of German immigrant Andrew Kauffman (d. 1743), Jacob married Magdalena Hiestand. Her father, John Hiestand, was a wealthy Mennonite farmer in Manor Township.[40]

Manheim Township Chests
Another distinctive Lancaster County group consists of two closely related chests with sulfur-inlaid panels on the front. The earlier chest was made for

Figure 84 Chest, made for Barbara Lang, Manheim Township area, Lancaster County, Pennsylvania, 1782. Walnut and sulfur inlay with pine and tulip poplar; iron. H. 26⅛", W. 52", D. 26½". (Courtesy, Philadelphia Museum of Art, gift of Mr. and Mrs. Robert L. Raley, 1978-101-1; photo, Gavin Ashworth.)

Figure 85 Detail of the inlay on the chest illustrated in fig. 84. (Photo, Gavin Ashworth.)

Figure 86 Detail of the inlay on the chest illustrated in fig. 84. (Photo, Gavin Ashworth.)

Barbara Lang and is dated January 12, 1782 (figs. 84–86). There are at least two viable candidates for the original owner of this chest, both the granddaughters of John Lang/Long (1693–1767). One lived from 1762 to 1852 and was the daughter of John Lang (1730–1817) and Mary Hershey of Manheim Township; she married Charles Rudy (1761–1845). The other lived from circa 1765 to circa 1840 and was the daughter of Christian Lang (1736–?) of Rapho Township; she married Daniel Rudy (ca. 1760–ca. 1835) on November 19, 1782. A third Barbara Lang/Long of Rapho Township

Figure 87 Chest, made for Maria Bachman, Manheim Township area, Lancaster County, Pennsylvania, 1784. Walnut and sulfur inlay with tulip poplar; iron, brass. H. 26¾", W. 52", D. 25½". (Courtesy, Joan and Victor Johnson; photo, Gavin Ashworth.)

Figure 88 Detail of the inlay on the chest illustrated in fig. 87. (Photo, Gavin Ashworth.)

Figure 89 Detail of the inlay on the chest illustrated in fig. 87. (Photo, Gavin Ashworth.)

married Peter Summy, son of John and Elisabeth (Shirk) Summy, and lived in East Hempfield Township. Given the Manheim Township association of the second chest, however, it seems more likely that one of the two Barbara Langs who lived in Manheim Township owned this chest.[41]

The second chest is dated January 8, 1784, and was made for Maria Bachman (figs. 87–89). She was probably the daughter of Peter Bachman (ca. 1730–1782) of Manheim Township and his wife Mary Kauffman (ca. 1735–1805; daughter of Jacob and Eva [Sneveley] Kauffman). Peter Bachman's father, Michael, was one of the first settlers in Manheim Township. The chest's owner, Maria Bachman, lived from 1764 to 1799. She was married sometime before April of 1785 to Jacob Hostetter, when he was appointed guardian of her two brothers following her father's death in 1782. Inscribed on the bottom of a small drawer in the till compartment is the name of a later owner, "Jacob Ebersole."[42]

A possible maker of the Lang and Bachman chests is joiner John Hühn/Huhn/Hun, who resided in Manheim Township between the Lang/Long and Rudy families. He was born on February 1, 1749, and baptized at First Reformed Church in Lancaster on January 25, 1756, together with his siblings Anna Maria (b. 1751) and John Nicholas (b. 1754). John was the son of Johann Valentin Hühn (1723–1808), who emigrated from Germany in 1744, and his wife, Anna Maria. Johann Valentin is buried at the Lehn Cemetery

Figure 90 Detail of the inlay on a chest, Lancaster County, Pennsylvania, 1784. Walnut and sulfur inlay. (Courtesy, Winterthur Museum; photo, James Schneck.)

in Manheim Township. John Hühn is listed as a joiner in the 1780 tax list for Manheim Township. It is also possible that some connection may exist between these two chests and the 1779 Huber schrank, as the six-pointed stars flanking Maria Bachman's name are virtually identical to those within the fylfots on the lower panels of the schrank's doors. The diamonds that flank Barbara Lang's surname are also very similar to the diamonds at the

Figure 91 Table, made for "I R," Lancaster County, Pennsylvania, 1788. Walnut and sulfur inlay with white pine; brass. H. 28⅝", W. 52¾", D. 31". (Courtesy, Chester County Historical Society; photo, Gavin Ashworth.) The stretchers are replaced.

Figure 92 Detail of the inlay on the table illustrated in fig. 91. (Photo, Gavin Ashworth.)

Figure 93   Tall clock, movement by George Hoff, Lancaster County, Pennsylvania, 1790. Walnut and sulfur inlay with tulip poplar, pine, and oak. H. 89½", W. 20½", D. 16". (Courtesy, Joan and Victor Johnson; photo, Winterthur Museum, Laszlo Bodo.)

base of the crowns on the upper panels of the schrank's doors (see fig. 79).[43]

Late Sulfur Inlaid Group from Lancaster County

Sulfur-inlaid furniture was made in Lancaster County as late as 1801, although the ornate decoration used in the 1760s and 1770s was replaced with simpler designs. A distinctive later group of sulfur-inlaid furniture, ranging in date from 1784 to 1801, features images of three-leaf clovers, flowers, and birds as well as an elongated, j-shaped numeral 1 in the dates. Many of the leaves and letters are infilled with diagonal striping. The earliest two examples in the group are a pair of chests with closely related inlay consisting of a pair of initials flanking a flower, below which is the date, flanking a flower or three-leaf clover. The chests were probably made for siblings, since both objects are dated 1784 and the owners, represented by the initials "HN" and "MN," have surnames beginning with the same letter (fig. 90). Four years later, the same unknown maker used sulfur inlay to ornament the drawers of a stretcher-base table with the date "1788" and initials "I R" (figs. 91, 92). Although the drawers are constructed with walnut secondary wood in a hefty, three-quarter-inch stock, this did not protect them from damage when they were shut too hard—breaking off some of the molded edges at the dovetail pins.[44]

The next object in the group is a tall clock case inlaid on the pendulum door with a bird motif and the date "1790;" above this on the waist are the initials "IO SC" flanking a three-leaf clover (figs. 93, 94). The initials are undoubtedly an abbreviation of the first and last name of the owner, such as Johannes Schneider. No provenance has survived with the clock, but the

Figure 94   Detail of the inlay on the clock illustrated in fig. 93.

presence of a thirty-hour movement signed by George Hoff points to a Lancaster County origin.[45]

A miniature chest, dated 1799, is the next known piece of this group (figs. 95, 96). It is inlaid on the façade with a spread-wing eagle and the initials "BA RI." The shape of the R is nearly identical to the R on the drawer of the table (see fig. 91). On the interior of the chest, there is a diminutive

Figure 95   Miniature chest, made for "BA RI," Lancaster County, Pennsylvania, 1799. Walnut and sulfur inlay with tulip poplar; iron. H. 8½", W. 17¾", D. 9½". (Courtesy, Kelly Kinzle Antiques; photo, Gavin Ashworth.)

Figure 96   Detail of the inlay on the chest illustrated in fig. 95. (Photo, Gavin Ashworth.)

Figure 97   Straightedge, Lancaster County, Pennsylvania, 1800. Walnut and sulfur inlay. H. 1⅞", W. 22½", D. ¼". (Courtesy, Stephen and Dolores Smith; photo, Winterthur Museum, Laszlo Bodo.)

Figure 98 Chest, made for Cadarina Moser, Lancaster County, Pennsylvania, 1801. Walnut and sulfur inlay with white pine; iron. H. 23", W. 48¼", D. 20". (Photo, Pook & Pook.)

till compartment constructed of walnut at the left side. The next object is a straightedge, dated 1800, inlaid with flowers, stars, a bird, and the initials "I S" (fig. 97). A chest made in 1801 for Cadarina Moser is the latest known example of this workshop (fig. 98). Given that many Pennsylvania Germans received chests in their late teenage years or early twenties, it is quite possible that she is the Catharina Moser who was born on May 24, 1779, to Weyerich and Margaretha Moser. Pastor John Waldschmidt, who served in the Cocalico region of northern Lancaster County, baptized that Catharina on June 6, 1779. Weyerich Moser was a brother of the Johannes Moser who probably owned the 1773 sulfur-inlaid chest (see figs. 1, 2).[46]

Other Sulfur-Inlaid Furniture from Lancaster County
Many pieces of sulfur-inlaid furniture do not fit within one of the above-named groups and are probably the work of multiple craftsmen. Several of the earliest known examples were made for descendants of Christian and Maria Bamberger, who together with their eight children immigrated to Pennsylvania in 1722. After a short stay in the Pequea area of Lancaster County, the Bambergers moved north to Warwick Township, where Christian died in 1742. The Bambergers' eldest daughter, Anna, married farmer John Kauffman (ca. 1700–1759) of East Hempfield Township. Their youngest son, Michael, was probably the original owner of the sulfur-inlaid chest made in 1765 (see fig. 47). Another son, John Kauffman Jr. (1728–1776), married Anna Elisabeth Long in 1764, and they were probably the original owners of a schrank dated 1764, which is the second-earliest known dated example of sulfur inlaid furniture (fig. 99). The frieze is inlaid in sulfur with the date and an abbreviated form of their names: "J[o]h[annes] K[auffman]" and "A[nna] L[is]B[eth] K[auffman]." John Kauffman Jr. was thirty-seven years old and the father of six children when he commissioned this schrank for his one-story log house, dispelling the myth that newlyweds acquired schranks.[47]

In 1768 another Kauffman sibling, Anna (1726–ca. 1780), and her husband

Figure 99 Schrank, probably made for Johannes and Anna Elisabeth Kauffman, East Hempfield Township, Lancaster County, Pennsylvania, 1764. Walnut and sulfur inlay with tulip poplar and oak; brass, iron. H. 80½", W. 73¾", D. 35". (Private collection; photo, Philip H. Bradley Co.)

Figure 100 Schrank, made for David and Anna Mumma, West Hempfield Township, Lancaster County, Pennsylvania, 1768. Walnut and sulfur inlay; iron, brass. H. 84½", W. 74½", D. 27¼". (Courtesy, Lancaster Mennonite Historical Society, bequest of John J. Snyder Jr.; photo, Gavin Ashworth.)

Figure 101 Tall clock, probably Lancaster County, Pennsylvania, 1767. Walnut, sulfur inlay, and mixed-wood inlay with tulip poplar. H. 89 1/8", W. 19 1/4", D. 10 3/4". (Courtesy, Barnes Foundation, Philadelphia, 01.24.25.)

David Mumma (ca. 1728–1791) of West Hempfield Township commissioned a sulfur-inlaid schrank embellished with their names and the date flanking an eight-pointed star (fig. 100). In or about 1775, the Mummas sold their farm to their son John and moved to Baltimore County, Maryland. Decades later, in 1854, a traveler saw the schrank in his hotel in York, Pennsylvania, and "found exercise in examining an old oaken wardrobe which graced the old hall. It bore the following inscription . . . 17 DAVID MUMA ANAMUMAIN 68—the characters it will be observed resemble the old Roman."[48]

A tall clock with the date "1767" inlaid in sulfur on the hood is also known (figs. 101, 102). Although it has no provenance or inlaid names/initials, the case was likely made in Lancaster County since it houses a thirty-hour movement attributed to George Hoff of Lancaster. Made by an unknown Germanic craftsman, judging by its overall form and the ample use of wooden pegs, the case also has six-point stars inlaid in wood on the pendu-

Figure 102 Hood of the clock illustrated in fig. 101.

139   SULFUR INLAY IN PENNSYLVANIA

Figure 103 Schrank, probably made for Peter and Ada Schwar, Lancaster County, Pennsylvania, 1769. Walnut and sulfur inlay with tulip poplar and white pine; iron, brass. H. 82", W. 87", D. 27½". (Courtesy, Clarke Hess; photo, Gavin Ashworth.) The five ball feet are missing.

Figure 104 Detail of the inlay on the schrank illustrated in fig. 103. (Photo, Gavin Ashworth.)

lum door and base. Its arched top echoes the arched molding that surmounts the pendulum door.

Another singular and early sulfur-inlaid object is the massive paneled schrank made in 1769 for Peter Schwar Jr. and his wife Ada (figs. 103, 104). The frieze bears the inscription "I M I 17 PS A SN 69 M," which may be interpreted as "Im J[ahr] 17 P[eter] S[chwarr] A[da] S[chwari[N] 69 M[acht] (translation: Made in the year 1769 [for] Peter Schwar and Ada

140   LISA MINARDI

Schwarin). At the center is a large six-point compass star or rosette, also inlaid in sulfur. Peter Schwar Jr. married Ada Long, daughter of Hermann Long, and owned land near what is now Long's Park several miles north of the city of Lancaster. His father, Peter Sr., immigrated in 1717 and died in 1767 in East Hempfield Township, leaving a widow, Adaline, and children Maria, Elisabeth, Anna, Peter Jr., John, Catharine, and Christian. This Christian Schwar (d. ca. 1784) or his son Christian Jr. (d. 1807) was the original owner of the sulfur-inlaid clock dated 1766 (see fig. 63). Peter Schwar Jr.'s only son, John Schwar, married Elisabeth Reist, daughter of Abraham and Elisabeth (Kauffman) Reist of Warwick (now Penn) Township; the latter couple owned a sulfur-inlaid schrank dated 1775 (see fig. 38).

A final sulfur-inlaid object that may be associated with the Schwars is a cradle that bears the date 1770 on the headboard and the initials "A S" on

Figure 105 Cradle, possibly made for Anna (Schwar) Shenk, Lancaster County, Pennsylvania, 1770. Walnut and sulfur inlay with tulip poplar. H. 28", W. 30", D. 38". (Courtesy, Clarke Hess; photo, Gavin Ashworth.) One of the pillow panels is missing.

Figure 106 Detail of the inlay on the headboard of the cradle illustrated in fig. 105. (Photo, Gavin Ashworth.)

the footboard, possibly for Peter Schwar Jr.'s daughter Anna (1750–1798), who married John Shenk of Hempfield Township in 1770 (figs. 105, 106). The cradle is further embellished with heart-shape cutouts in the headboard and footboard. The inclusion of a date and initials on this cradle is highly unusual, since cradles were rarely personalized—probably because of their anticipated use by many children rather than any one infant. Cradles were often part of the household furnishings presented to daughters as part of their *Austeier*, or dowry. In 1782, for example, Lutheran minister Henry

Figure 107 Miniature chest, made for Andreas Bartruff, Manheim, Lancaster County, Pennsylvania, ca. 1775. Walnut and sulfur inlay with tulip poplar; iron. H. 7⅝", W. 16⅛", D. 8⅝". (Private collection; photo, Gavin Ashworth.)

Figure 108 Detail of the inlay on the chest illustrated in fig. 107. (Photo, Gavin Ashworth.)

Muhlenberg paid $3 for a cradle "to be given to Salome Reichard [his youngest daughter] toward her dowry."[49]

An undated miniature chest with German *Fraktur* lettering inlaid in sulfur for Andreas Bartruff is another singular object (figs. 107, 108). It is constructed with mitered dovetail joinery at all four corners and a mitered bracket base; the moldings are attached with sizeable wooden pegs. The Bartruffs lived in Manheim, Lancaster County, which was founded in 1762 by ironmaster and glassmaker Henry William Stiegel. Andreas Bartruff Sr. was one of the town's first settlers, a storekeeper, and a founding member of Zion Lutheran Church, which met first in a chapel within Stiegel's mansion and later on land that Stiegel deeded for a new church in 1772. Although family tradition claims that Andreas Bartruff Sr. commissioned the chest, it is also possible that his son Andreas Jr. was the first owner. The elder Bartruff was born in 1724, immigrated in 1752, married Christiana Sophia Klein (1739–1777) in 1758, and died in 1795. He was buried at Zion Lutheran Church in Manheim, where an elaborate relief-carved tombstone marks his final resting place. Andreas Bartruff Jr. was born in 1760 and died

Figure 109 Chest, made for Barbara Stauffer, Lancaster County, Pennsylvania, 1790. Walnut and sulfur inlay with white pine; iron, brass. H. 30½", W. 52½", D. 24½". (Courtesy, Salvatore A. Rizzuto; photo, Gavin Ashworth.) The feet are replaced.

Figure 110 Detail of the inlay on the chest illustrated in fig. 109. (Photo, Gavin Ashworth.)

in 1826. He was a house carpenter by trade, and thus it is possible that he made the sulfur-inlaid chest for either himself or his father.[50]

Another probable Lancaster County object is a chest with quarter columns and the sulfur-inlaid inscription "Barra [Barbara] Staufer" flanking a six-point star positioned above the date 1790 (figs. 109, 110). Multiple women named Barbara Staufer/Stauffer lived in Lancaster County in the late 1700s. One possible candidate is the daughter of Jacob and Anna Stauffer of Rapho Township, who is named in her father's will of 1798. Another possibility is Barbara Stauffer, daughter of John Stauffer (d. 1799) and his wife Barbara (d. 1809) of Warwick Township; she married Christian Knoll in or before 1798.[51]

Lebanon-Lancaster County Border Region

The current borders of Lancaster County were not established until 1813 with the formation of Lebanon County. Prior to 1785, what is now Lebanon County was part of Dauphin County, and before 1785 what is now

Dauphin County was part of Lancaster County. With dates ranging from 1766 to 1792, the next two groups of sulfur-inlaid furniture were thus made in a geographic region with shifting political boundaries. The area in which these objects were made is along the present-day border of northern Lancaster and southern Lebanon counties.

The Ley Schrank
One of the better documented examples of sulfur-inlaid furniture is the massive schrank made in 1771 for Michael Ley (1739–1824) and his wife Eva Magdalena Lauer (1743–1815), who lived on a property known as Tulpe-

Figure 111 Schrank, made for Michael and Eva Magdalena Ley, probably made by Christoph Uhler, Lebanon, Lancaster (now Lebanon) County, Pennsylvania, 1771. Walnut and sulfur inlay with tulip poplar and white pine; brass. H. 99¼", W. 91", D. 26". (Courtesy, Rocky Hill Collection; photo, Winterthur Museum, Laszlo Bodo.)

hocken Manor, located just west of Myerstown in what is now Jackson Township, Lebanon County. Highly architectural in detail, the tall and shallow proportions of the schrank give it the appearance of a freestanding paneled wall (fig. 111). At the bottom of the cornice is a distinctive border made of alternating squares and triangles. The central panel of the frieze is inlaid in sulfur with the inscription "ML / & / EML / 1771," surrounded by tulips and stars (fig. 112). A nearly identical schrank, also dated 1771, bears no initials but has a history of being found in Lebanon County (figs. 113, 114). It is possible that this schrank could also have been made for the Leys.[52]

Myerstown was a small settlement, totaling only eighty-four inhabitants in 1779. Fifteen years later, when Theophile Cazenove traveled through the town, he arrived just as a church service ended and observed, "It seemed to me I saw people coming out of church in Westphalia, so much have these

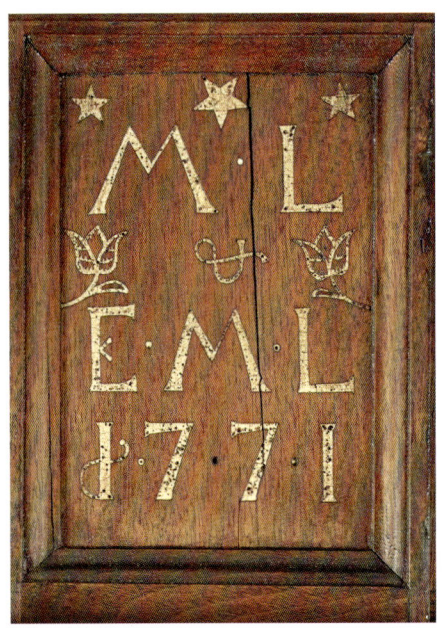

Figure 112 Detail of the inlay on the schrank illustrated in fig. 111.

144 LISA MINARDI

farmers kept their ancestors' costume." Situated along the Tulpehocken Creek and on a major east-west thoroughfare to Philadelphia, Tulpehocken Manor was a tract of 1,000 acres first settled by Michael Ley's father, the immigrant Christopher Ley (or Loy). Michael acquired the property in 1760; nine years later, he built a large, five-bay stone house there (fig. 115).

Figure 113   Schrank, probably made by Christoph Uhler (1741–1804), Lebanon, Lancaster (now Lebanon) County, Pennsylvania, 1771. Walnut and sulfur inlay with pine and tulip poplar; iron, brass. H. 91½", W. 86½", D. 26". (Private collection; photo, Gavin Ashworth.)

Figure 114   Detail of the inlay on the schrank illustrated in fig. 113. (Photo, Gavin Ashworth.)

Figure 115   Tulpehocken Manor, built for Michael and Eva Magdalena Ley, Lebanon County, Pennsylvania, 1769, remodeled 1883, photo ca. 1885. (From Rev. P.C. Croll, *Ancient and Historic Landmarks in the Lebanon Valley* [Philadelphia: Lutheran Publication Society, 1895].)

Figure 116 Door pediment from Tulpehocken Manor, signed by Christoph Uhler, Lebanon, Lancaster (now Lebanon) County, 1769. White pine; paint. H. 21¾", W. 70¼", D. 3¾". (Courtesy, James C. Keener; photo, Winterthur Museum, Laszlo Bodo.)

Figure 117 Corner cupboard from Tulpehocken Manor, probably made by Christoph Uhler, Lebanon, Lancaster (now Lebanon) County, ca. 1769. Pine and tulip poplar; paint; glass. H. 101", W. 57", D. 40". (Courtesy, Greg K. Kramer and Co.)

Figure 118 Fireplace surround from Tulpehocken Manor, probably made by Christoph Uhler, Lebanon, Lancaster (now Lebanon) County, ca. 1769. (Courtesy, Lynda and Richard Levengood; photo, Lisa Minardi.)

Figure 119 Tall clock, probably made for Henry Eshleman, movement signed by John Heinselman, Manheim, Lancaster County, Pennsylvania, 1795. Walnut and sulfur inlay with tulip poplar. H. 86", W. 18¼", D. 10¼". (Courtesy, Rock Ford Plantation, bequest of John J. Snyder Jr.; photo, Gavin Ashworth.)

Directly above the front door was a triangular pediment with a dentil cornice and relief-carved floral design flanked by the German inscription (translation): "God alone the Glory / Michael Ley and Eva Magdalena Ley / Christoph Uhler 1769 of Lebanon" (fig. 116). The interior woodwork of the house, no longer in situ, included a fireplace surround with a triangular overmantel resembling the door pediment and a built-in corner cupboard with cornice of alternating square and triangular blocks like that on the schrank (figs. 117, 118).[53]

The inscription at the bottom of the door pediment—Christoph Uhler of Lebanon—reveals the identity of the master craftsman who built the house and in all likelihood also the interior woodwork and pair of schranks. Born on February 2, 1741, Christoph was the son of Anastasius Uhler, who emigrated from Germany in 1732, settled in Lebanon, and married Dorothea Jerg in 1737. In 1766 Christoph married Margaretha Barbara Speicher/Spycker, who was born in 1749 to John and Regina Speicher and baptized at Christ Lutheran Church near Stouchsburg, Berks County. They had seven children. After her death in 1794, Christoph married the widow Judith Stine (also in 1794), with whom he had five more children. A lifelong resident of Lebanon, Christoph Uhler is first listed in the tax records in 1769 as a "chine" and again in 1771 (the same date as on the two schranks) as a "chiner," a phonetic spelling of the German pronunciation of the word joiner. He also served as a tax assessor and county commissioner in 1783. A lifelong member of Salem Lutheran Church, Uhler served as an elder, treasurer, and chairman of the building committee when the congregation embarked on the construction of a new church in 1796, with instructions that it "must be larger than any other building in Lebanon, and of the most substantial material and workmanship possible." He was well-suited to oversee this project, having supervised the construction of the church's parsonage in 1783 and a new German Reformed church from 1792 to 1796. At the time of his death in 1804, Christoph was an affluent and highly respected citizen. He identified himself as a joiner in his will, and his inventory included a "lott of carpenter tools" worth £4.10.0 in addition to 15,000 feet of pine boards, 500 feet of clapboards, and 6,000 shingles. Uhler also owned two sawmills and a gristmill. He was one of the largest property holders in Lebanon, assessed in 1798 for owning six tenant houses in addition to his own two-story stone house, which also included a stone kitchen, a log barn, and a stone joiner's shop measuring twenty by twenty-nine feet—all on more than 200 acres.[54]

Star Inlay Group
At least six clock cases, two schranks, a chest, a cradle, and a table have been identified that together form another distinctive group of sulfur-inlaid furniture. Each piece includes one or more six-point stars, as well as dates and initials or names, inlaid in sulfur. The clock cases are inlaid at the top of the pendulum doors and include an arched or shield-shape border with a small star or flower at the top or bottom (figs. 119, 120). Most of the clocks and at least one of the schranks have cornice moldings consisting of alternating

Figure 120 Detail of the inlay on the clock illustrated in fig. 119. (Photo, Gavin Ashworth.)

Figure 121 Detail of the cornice on the clock illustrated in fig. 119. (Photo, Gavin Ashworth.)

Figure 122 Detail of the groove for the hood on the clock illustrated in fig. 119. (Photo, Gavin Ashworth.)

squares and triangles, like that on the Ley schrank, but with an ogee rather than a flat profile (fig. 121). A distinctive feature of the clock cases is that the hood sits in a recessed groove rather than sliding on and off the case (fig. 122). The clocks have often been associated with the Lancaster–Lebanon border, but identifying a more precise locale is made difficult by the use of initials rather than full names on the cases. The linkage of the clocks to the two schranks (both of which have full names inlaid on the frieze) and the chest thus provides an opportunity to confirm this point of origin.

The earliest known clock case is dated 1766 and bears the initials "H h" for the unknown original owner (fig. 123, 124). It has a thirty-hour movement signed by Christian Forrer of Lampeter, Lancaster County. The same craftsman made at least one other clock case in 1766, but only the pendulum door survives. It is inlaid in sulfur with the date and initials "J S," said to be for Joseph Sturgis, a Moravian potter. He is listed in the Lebanon tax records of 1772, 1779, 1780, and 1781; in the latter two years his occupation is given as potter. Born in Philadelphia in 1738, Joseph Sturgis married Margaret Stoehr in 1766 and settled in Lebanon, where he worked as a potter

Figure 123 Tall clock, made for "H h," movement signed by Christian Forrer, Lampeter, Lancaster County, Pennsylvania, 1766. Walnut and sulfur inlay. H. 89¾", W. 21," D. 11¼". (Courtesy, Ed and Mary Ann Dixon; photo, Gavin Ashworth.)

Figure 124 Detail of the inlay on the clock illustrated in fig. 123. (Photo, Gavin Ashworth.)

until moving to Lititz in 1782. From 1803 to 1811 he lived in York, then returned to Lititz where he died in 1817. Given the location of Joseph Sturgis in Lebanon, a search of the Lebanon tax records for individuals with the initials "H H" to match those on the other clock dated 1766 reveals a Henry Heilman as a possible candidate.[55]

The next clock case is dated 1784 and bears the initials "A W" within a shield-shape surround, surmounted by a tulip and with a six-point star below. It has a thirty-hour square dial movement signed by George Hoff of Lancaster. The original owner was probably Abraham Witmer (1753–1836) of Rapho Township, Lancaster County, where he is listed in the 1780 tax records. His father, Ulrich Witmer (1702–1769), and grandfather Michael Witmer (1668–1763) immigrated to Pennsylvania in 1733 and settled in Rapho Township. A nearly identical clock, also containing a George Hoff movement, was made the following year. It is inlaid with the initials "M H," which are thought to stand for Michael Horst (1751–1830) of Rapho Township, Lancaster County (fig. 125). A Mennonite deacon and a miller by trade, Horst built a stone house in 1780 that still stands. The inventory of his estate, taken in 1830, includes "1 House Clock & Case" valued at $12. The

Figure 125 Tall clock, probably made for Michael Horst, movement signed by George Hoff, Lancaster, Lancaster County, Pennsylvania, 1785. Walnut and sulfur inlay with white pine. H. 84¾", W. 22," D. 12". (Courtesy, Clarke Hess; photo, Gavin Ashworth.) The base has been shortened.

original base section of the clock was replaced with the present, shorter section, to which the original base molding was then reapplied.[56]

The two latest clock cases are both dated 1795. One has the initials "A M" and an unsigned painted sheet iron dial (figs. 126, 127); the other bears the initials "HEM" and houses a movement signed by clockmaker John Heinselman (1766–1804) of Manheim, Lancaster County. A Lutheran, Heinsel-

Figure 126 Tall clock, made for "A M," probably Lancaster County, Pennsylvania, 1795. Walnut and sulfur inlay with tulip poplar; brass. H. 87", W. 20½," D. 10¾". (Courtesy, Carl and Yvonne De Paulis; photo, Gavin Ashworth.)

Figure 127 Detail of the inlay on the tall clock illustrated in fig. 126. (Photo, Gavin Ashworth.)

Figure 128 Chest, probably made for Jacob Ebersole, probably Lancaster County, Pennsylvania, 1785. Walnut and sulfur inlay; iron, brass. H. 28", W. 52", D. 25". (Courtesy, Leslie Miller and Richard Worley; photo, Gavin Ashworth.)

man appears in the tax records of Rapho Township from 1792 through 1803. The "HEM" initials probably stand for Henry Eshleman, a wheelwright who lived on the Chiques Creek in Rapho Township, Lancaster County (see figs. 119–122). He died intestate in 1796.[57]

Based on the close relationship of the sulfur inlay and the cornice moldings, the same cabinetmaker also built a chest, a table, and two schranks. The chest is dated 1785 and bears the name "Jacob Ebs" together with six-point stars and small six-petal rosettes on the façade (fig. 128). The manner in which the numerals of the date are rendered is virtually identical to the numerals on the MH / 1785 clock case, including the small, curved serif at the foot of the "1" and the short, angled top of the "5" (see fig. 125). The inlaid surname "Ebs" is probably an abbreviation of Ebersole. A Jacob Ebersole is listed in the 1790 and 1800 U.S. censuses as a resident of Mount Joy Township, Lancaster County, which borders on the west side of Rapho Township. He may have been the son or grandson of Jost/Joseph Ebersol (1710–ca. 1792), who emigrated from Germany in 1739 and settled in Rapho Township. The table, of which only the drawer has sulfur inlay, is dated 1782 and bears the initials "PA" and "AA" (likely for a married couple) flanking two six-point stars (fig. 129). Tiny six-petal rosettes are also inlaid in the corners of the drawer.[58]

Figure 129 Drawer from a table, made for "PA AA," probably Lancaster County, Pennsylvania, 1782. Walnut and sulfur inlay. Dimensions unrecorded. (Private collection; photo, Gavin Ashworth.)

Figure 130 Schrank, made for Christian and Elisabeth Schneider, probably Lancaster County, Pennsylvania, 1780. Walnut and sulfur inlay; iron. H. 80½", W. 74", D. 24¼". (Private collection; photo, Joseph Schneider Haus.)

Figure 131 Frieze of a schrank, made for John and Mary Mennig/Minnich, probably Lancaster County, Pennsylvania, 1789. Walnut and sulfur inlay. H. 8¾", W. 68¾", D. 1". (Courtesy, David A. Schorsch; photo, Gavin Ashworth.)

The earlier of the two schranks was made in 1780 for Christian Schneider (1725–1795) and his second wife, Elisabeth (fig. 130). A wealthy Mennonite farmer and miller, Christian Schneider lived in what is now Londonderry Township, Dauphin County, near the western Lancaster County border. He immigrated to Pennsylvania in 1736 as a young boy with his parents Johannes and Susanna (Bauman) Schneider. His first wife was Barbara Reist, sister of Abraham Reist who owned a sulfur-inlaid schrank dated 1775 (see fig. 38). After Barbara's death, Christian married a woman named Elisabeth prior to 1780, the date on the schrank. The cornice of the schrank has a border of alternating rectangles and triangles with ogee profiles identical to those found on all but the earliest of the clock cases. The six-point stars and astragal-ends of the inlaid frieze are virtually the same as the inlay on the top of the clock doors.[59]

Of the second schrank, made in 1789, only the sulfur-inlaid frieze survives, which bears the couple's names flanked by six-point stars and the date in the

152   LISA MINARDI

center: "IOHN MENNIG 1789 MERY MENNIG" (fig. 131). Numerous men named John Mennig/Minnich/Muench lived in southeastern Pennsylvania in the late 1700s, including in Lancaster, Lebanon, and Dauphin counties, making it difficult to determine which one was the original owner of the schrank. A probable candidate is Johannes Minnich/John Minnig (1735–1813) of Rapho Township, Lancaster County, who is listed in the 1770 tax list as a carpenter. His wife's name was Anna Maria, which would fit the name "Mery" or Mary inlaid on the frieze. This couple also lived near Henry Eshleman, for whom a sulfur-inlaid clock case dated 1795 was probably made (see fig. 119). John Minnich died in 1813, naming children Adam and Jacob in his will.[60]

The final piece of the group, also dated 1789, is a cradle with the date inlaid in sulfur on the footboard and the initials "EV MI" on the headboard, probably for an Eva Miller or similar surname (figs. 132–134). Although cradles were not a major output for most cabinetmakers—Abraham Overholt of Bucks County, for example, made only two cradles at a cost of fifteen

Figure 132 Cradle, made for "EV MI," probably Lancaster County, Pennsylvania, 1789. Walnut and sulfur inlay. H. 22¾", W. 28⅛", D. 38⅜". (Courtesy, Winterthur Museum, promised gift of David A. Schorsch and Eileen M. Smiles; photo, James Schneck.)

Figure 133 Detail of the inlay on headboard of the cradle illustrated in fig. 132.

Figure 134 Detail of the inlay on the footboard of the cradle illustrated in fig. 132.

shillings each between 1790 and 1833—they did reflect local preferences of ornament and construction. The shape of the numerals and initials on this cradle relate very closely to the frieze of the 1789 schrank made for John and Mary Mennig. The cradle also has heart-shape cutouts similar to those found in the backs of Pennsylvania German plank seat chairs (*Brettstühle*) and the horizontal projections from either side of the headboard—known as pillow panels—which are diminutive versions of those found on full-size Pennsylvania German bedsteads.[61]

Tulpehocken Valley Chests

Derived from an Indian word meaning "land of turtles," the Tulpehocken Valley is a fertile region that extends across what is now eastern Lebanon and western Berks counties. Much of the valley was originally part of Heidelberg Township, Lancaster County. The Tulpehocken Creek begins just west of Myerstown and flows east approximately twenty-six miles to join the Schuylkill River outside of Reading. The largest settlement in the valley was Schaefferstown, laid out in 1758 by Alexander Schaeffer (1712–1786) and initially known as Heidelberg. Approximately 95 percent of the original Tulpehocken settlers were of German heritage. This was reflected in the region's early architecture, from small log dwellings to the massive stone house built in 1752 by George and Maria Catharina Miller, later taken over by their son Michael (fig. 135). Many contemporary observers remarked on the Germanic character of the region. In 1783, traveler Johann David Schoepf wrote, "We crossed Tulpehacken [sic] Creek, and passed through a part of the Tulpehacken valley, an especially fine and fertile landscape . . . the inhabitants are well-to-do and almost all of them Germans." The region is also noted for having produced many distinctive examples of Pennsylvania German material culture, including a large group of painted chests associated with the so-called "Embroidery Artist," possibly made by Samuel Ache of Schaefferstown, Lebanon County, and decorated manuscripts or fraktur.[62]

Figure 135 House of George and Maria Catharina Miller, Millbach, Lebanon County, Pennsylvania, 1752. (Courtesy, Millbach Foundation; photo, Winterthur Museum, Laszlo Bodo.)

Figure 136 Chest, probably made for Eva Koppenhefer, Lebanon County, Pennsylvania, 1785. Walnut and sulfur inlay with white pine and tulip poplar; iron, brass. H. 28½", W. 54⅞", D. 24⅜". (Courtesy, Philip H. Bradley Co.; photo, Gavin Ashworth.)

Figure 137 Detail of the inlay on the chest illustrated in fig. 136. (Photo, Gavin Ashworth.)

Figure 138 Christ Lutheran Church, near Stouchsburg, Marion Township, Berks County, Pennsylvania, built in 1786. (Courtesy, Mr. and Mrs. Michael Emery.)

A group of three sulfur-inlaid chests can now be identified as products of the Tulpehocken Valley. The earliest example is dated 1785 and inscribed for "Eefa [Eva] Kobehn" or Koppenhefer, a common local surname (figs. 136, 137). The family patriarch, Johann Thomas Koppenhefer (ca. 1710–1762), emigrated from Germany in 1728. Three of his granddaughters were named Eva and are equally probable candidates to be the original owner of the chest: Eva, born in 1763 to Simon and Maria Elisabeth Koppenhefer; Eva, born in 1763 to Henrich and Christina Koppenhefer; and Eva Margaret, born in 1768 to Henrich and Anna Catharina Koppenhefer. All three Evas were baptized at Christ Lutheran Church, located near the village of Stouchsburg along the western border of Berks County (fig. 138). Founded in 1743, Christ Lutheran was one of the most affluent congregations in colonial Pennsylvania and the center of a large parish that extended into Lebanon and Lancaster counties. Thomas Koppenhefer and his sons were significant supporters of Christ Lutheran Church, as was Michael Ley, owner of the impressive sulfur-inlaid schrank made in 1771 (see fig. 111). In 1752 Thomas donated £2 to the church for the purchase of an organ, which cost nearly £130 and was made by Johann Gottlob Clemm, a Moravian, of

Figure 139   Chest, made for John Illig, Lebanon County, Pennsylvania, 1797. Walnut and sulfur inlay. H. 25", W. 52½", D. 23". (Private collection; photo, Conestoga Auction Co.)

Philadelphia. When the congregation was raising funds from 1771 to 1773 for building a new parsonage, Michael Ley and the Koppenhefers were among the highest contributors, with donations ranging from £5 to £6.[63]

Siblings Margaret and John Illig owned the other two chests. Margaret's, dated 1792, is inlaid in sulfur with her name and the date in an undulating horizontal line similar to that on Eva Koppenhefer's chest. Its original feet were replaced with turned, empire-style feet at a later date. The chest owned by John Illig is dated 1797 and includes small geometric motifs as dividers between the name and date (fig. 139). The Illigs lived near Millbach in Heidelberg Township, Lancaster County (now Mill Creek Township, Lebanon County). Margaret Illig was born on January 31, 1774; married Christopher Rieth (1783–1865) on July 3, 1802, at Christ Lutheran Church; and died on October 24, 1842. John Illig was born on August 22, 1776; married Catharine Stahly (1773–1848); died on October 2, 1824; and was buried at Christ Lutheran Church. Their parents were Leonard Illig (1732–1797) and Dorothea Bassler (1746–1816). The family patriarch, Andreas Illig (d. 1761), emigrated from Germany in 1727 and settled in the Millbach area of what is now Lebanon County. In 1744 Andreas and his wife Philippina had their son Georg Michael Illig baptized at Christ Lutheran Church. Seven of Leonard and Dorothea Illig's children were also baptized there, including Margaret, John, and five siblings. Both Andreas and Leonard Illig were financial supporters of the church, donating to efforts such as building a new parsonage and building a wall around the cemetery. Although the Illigs were staunch Lutherans, their German Reformed neighbor, Michael Miller of Millbach (see fig. 135), served as co-executor of Andreas Illig's estate. In 1798, Leonard Illig owned a two-story log house measuring thirty by twenty-eight feet on land adjoining that of Michael Miller, and he also owned a smaller log house in Newmanstown, two large stone barns, and 537 acres of land. As further evidence of the Illig's German heritage, several plates from a five-plate stove dated 1760 and inscribed with the Tenth Commandment in German were removed in 1909 from "Mr. John Illig's old house, built in 1732, at Millbach, Lebanon County."⁶⁴

The close proximity of the Koppenhefer and Illig families to one another provides an opportunity to consider which local woodworker might have been responsible for building these chests. A strong candidate is the joiner Samuel Betz (1766–1828) of Newmanstown, Lebanon County. On April 21, 1791, he married Esther "Hester" Miller (1769–1829) at Christ Lutheran Church, where most if not all of their eleven children were subsequently baptized. In the 1798 federal Direct Tax list, Samuel Betz is noted as a resident of Newmanstown, where he owned a two-story house built of hewn logs, measuring twenty-four by eighteen feet; a joiner's shop of hewn logs (eighteen by twelve feet); and a stable of round logs (eighteen by twelve feet. In his will of 1828, Samuel identified himself as a carpenter and bequeathed to Hester "my large brass kettle, my best bed and bedstead, and clock" together with one-third of his personal estate. He died in May of 1828 and was buried at the Millbach Reformed Church, as was Hester after her death the following year.⁶⁵

Dauphin County

Established in 1785 when it was subdivided from Lancaster County, Dauphin County is located along the east bank of the Susquehanna River. This area was known in the 1700s as "Paxtang" after an Indian word meaning "place where water stands" and was first settled in 1719 by John Harris Sr. In 1733 he secured a land grant of 800 acres and a license to operate a ferry across the Susquehanna. The county seat, Harrisburg, was laid out in 1785 by John Harris Jr., and in 1812 it succeeded Lancaster as the state capital. Although Dauphin County had a sizeable Scots-Irish population in the early 1700s, German-speaking people began to move there by the mid-1700s. A log house in Middletown, built in 1764, had a door lintel carved with a German language inscription (translation): "I go out or in, so death stands and waits for me" (fig. 140). An elaborate birth and baptismal cer-

Figure 140 Detail of a door lintel, probably Middletown, Dauphin County, Pennsylvania, 1764. Pine. H. 9", W. 40½", D. 5¼". (Courtesy, Pennsylvania Historical and Museum Commission, State Museum of Pennsylvania.)

Figure 141 Birth and baptismal certificate, made for Johannes Poorman, Paxton Township, Dauphin County, Pennsylvania, ca. 1785. Watercolor and ink on laid paper. 12½" x 15½". (Courtesy, Susan and Stephen Babinsky; photo, Winterthur Museum, James Schneck.)

Figure 142 Chest, made for Magdalena Fischborn, Dauphin County, Pennsylvania, 1781. Walnut, sulfur inlay, and mixed-wood inlay with pine; iron. H. 27½", W. 52¾", D. 24¼". (Courtesy, Carl and Yvonne De Paulis; photo, Gavin Ashworth.)

Figure 143 Detail of the inlaid star on the chest illustrated in fig. 142. (Photo, Gavin Ashworth.)

tificate with watercolor and pinpricked decoration—made for Johannes Poorman, born December 9, 1769, in "Beckstein" Township, "Daven" County—also speaks to the region's early Germanic heritage (fig. 141). Heretofore little Pennsylvania German furniture has been associated with Dauphin County, but two groups of sulfur-inlaid furniture can now be linked to this region.[66]

The first and larger group of Dauphin County sulfur-inlaid furniture includes at least ten chests decorated with sulfur-inlaid names or initials and dates ranging from 1769 to 1793. At the center of the façade, most of the chests have an inlaid compass star made of alternating light and dark wood inlay—probably maple and red cedar in at least some instances (fig. 142). On the earlier chests this inlaid star has six points, but beginning in 1781 nearly

158 LISA MINARDI

all of the chests have twelve point stars (fig. 143). Most of the chests in this group are constructed with a distinctive sloped till compartment, in which the front board of the till is set at an angle rather than vertically (fig. 144). The wrought iron strap hinges are also typically of a distinctive form with a pear-shape terminal. The earlier chests have ball feet, while the later examples have bracket feet with unusually large glue blocks (figs. 145, 146).

Figure 144   Detail of the till compartment of the chest illustrated in fig. 142. (Photo, Gavin Ashworth.)

Figure 145   Detail of the bracket foot of the chest illustrated in fig. 142. (Photo, Gavin Ashworth.)

Figure 146   Detail of the glue block of the chest illustrated in fig. 142. (Photo, Gavin Ashworth.)

Figure 147 Façade of a chest, made for Ludwig Brandt, Dauphin County, Pennsylvania, 1769. Walnut with sulfur inlay; iron. H. 18⅜", W. 51¾", D. 1". (Courtesy, Edward and Linda Rosenberry; photo, Winterthur Museum, James Schneck.)

The earliest known example was made in 1769 for Ludwig Brandt; only the façade, sides, and back board survive (fig. 147). Although the till compartment is no longer present, the angled mortises in the front and back boards indicate that it had a sloped front board. The next chest was made in 1775 for Elisabetha Brandt. Built over three drawers, it retains its original ball feet (fig. 148). The sloped front board of its till compartment is removable, allowing access to two hidden drawers (figs. 149, 150). Ludwig and Elisabeth were siblings. Their father, Martin Brandt (1722–1809), emigrated from Germany in 1742 and settled near Hummelstown in what is now Derry Township, Dauphin County. In his will of 1809, he bequeathed to

Figure 148 Chest, made for Elisabetha Brandt, Dauphin County, Pennsylvania, 1775. Walnut with sulfur and wood inlay and white pine and tulip poplar; iron. H. 30½", W. 58¾", D. 25¾". (Courtesy, Renfrew Museum; photo, Gavin Ashworth.)

Figure 149 Detail of the till compartment of the chest illustrated in fig. 148. (Photo, Gavin Ashworth.)

Figure 150 Detail of the hidden drawers of the chest illustrated in fig. 148. (Photo, Gavin Ashworth.)

Ludwig a "certain tract of land which I bought of my son Adam near new Lancaster" (New Lancaster is located in Perry County, Ohio). Elisabeth and her two sisters each received a bond of £150. The will was witnessed by Frederick Hummel Jr. and George Gish, who also appraised the estate and enumerated items such as a tall clock, six delft dishes, a lot of Queensware, and twenty-five books. Martin's tombstone is inscribed with the date of his death in both German and English—an extremely rare occurrence. His widow, Esther Brandt, died in 1822, and John Minnich (possibly the owner of a sulfur-inlaid schrank dated 1789; see fig. 131) was one of the two witnesses to her will. Ludwig was born on October 1, 1747. By 1777 he resided in Allen Township, Cumberland County, where he served in a battalion during the Revolutionary War. He later moved to Perry County, Ohio, where he died about 1828. Elisabeth Brandt was born on October 14, 1757, and is named in her father's will of 1809; it remains unknown whether or not she ever married.[67]

The next chest was made in 1776 for Elisabeth Landis. It is nearly identical in appearance to the Elisabeth Brandt chest but lacks the wood inlaid star; its wrought iron strap hinges are identical to those in the Ludwig Brandt chest. Pasted under the lid are remnants of a birth and baptismal certificate printed in the 1780s at the Ephrata Cloister in Lancaster County.

Figure 151 Chest, made for Elisabeth Brua, Dauphin County, Pennsylvania, 1776. Walnut, sulfur inlay, and wood inlay with tulip poplar; iron. H. 26", W. 49½", D. 24". (Courtesy, Pook & Pook.)

Elisabeth Landis was the daughter of Felix Landis III (1728–1805) of Derry Township and his wife Elisabeth. She was born in about 1762 and married Abraham Welter. The family patriarch, Felix Landis I, emigrated in 1717 from the Alsatian region of what is now eastern France and settled in Lampeter Township, Lancaster County, where he died in 1739. Felix Jr. (1708–1770) emigrated from Alsace with his father, served as a ranger for British troops, and owned extensive land in Lampeter, Lebanon, Hanover, and Derry townships (the latter along the Swatara Creek).[68]

Another chest, also dated 1776, is inscribed for Elisabeth Brua (fig. 151). The Brua/Bruah/Brewer family is descended from Johann Theobald/Dewalt Brua (1698–ca. 1756), who immigrated to Pennsylvania in 1741 and settled

Figure 152 Chest, made for Henrich Miller, Dauphin County, Pennsylvania, 1781. Sycamore, sulfur inlay, and mixed-wood inlay with tulip poplar; iron, brass. H. 27¾", W. 54¼", D. 24". (Courtesy, Rocky Hill Collection; photo, Gavin Ashworth.)

in Strasburg Township, Lancaster County. Several of Theobald's granddaughters were named Elisabeth, but only one fits chronologically with the 1776 date on the chest. She was born to Johann Peter Brua (1729–1808) and his wife Anna Maria (1731–1804) on March 17, 1766, in Tulpehocken Township, Berks County, and died unmarried on September 24, 1830. The Bruas had extensive connections to several other families who owned sulfur-inlaid furniture. One of Theobald Brua Sr.'s sons, Jacob Brua (1722–1800), married Hannah Ferree (b. 1733), a first cousin of Peter Ferree who owned the sulfur-inlaid clock dated 1765 (see fig. 61). The Tulpehocken branch of the Brua family had close ties with both Michael Ley and Thomas Koppenhefer (see figs. 111, 136), who also commissioned sulfur-inlaid furniture for themselves or their children. In 1754, both Ley and Koppenhefer had children who attended the same confirmation class as Theobald Brua Jr.'s son Gustavus at Christ Lutheran Church near Stouchsburg, Berks County. Most of Peter Brua's children were baptized at Christ Lutheran Church and he, his wife, and two of their children are buried there. Although it is unknown how

Figure 153 Interior of the chest illustrated in fig. 152. (Photo, Gavin Ashworth.) The maker used a sliding batten to stabilize the three-board lid and installed a slanted till compartment.

Elisabeth Brua of Berks County came to own a chest thought to have been made in Dauphin County, an intriguing connection is that her brother, Peter Brua Jr. (1771–1842), was a carpenter who moved to Harrisburg in about 1792. There Peter and his wife, Catharina Rupley, joined Zion Lutheran Church, where seven of their children were baptized between 1797 and 1814.[69]

A chest made in 1781 for Heinrich Miller is unique among known examples of Pennsylvania German sulfur-inlaid furniture for its use of sycamore as the primary wood (fig. 152). The narrow dimensions of the quarter-sawn sycamore boards required the cabinetmaker to use three pieces for the top, which he joined together with six butterfly dovetails on the interior. The lid also has sliding dovetailed battens, made of walnut, to prevent it from warping (fig. 153). In keeping with this chest's over-the-top nature, both the façade and ends have additional inlaid embellishments (figs. 154–156). Identifying the exact Heinrich Miller for whom this chest was made is complicated by the fact that there were multiple men of that name present in

Figure 154 Side of the chest illustrated in fig. 152. (Photo, Gavin Ashworth.)

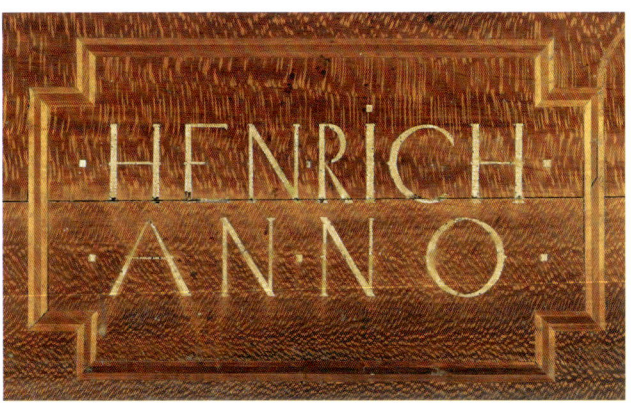

Figure 155 Detail of the inlay on the façade of the chest illustrated in fig. 152. (Photo, Gavin Ashworth.)

Figure 156 Detail of the inlay on the façade of the chest illustrated in fig. 152. (Photo, Gavin Ashworth.)

163   SULFUR INLAY IN PENNSYLVANIA

Dauphin and Lebanon counties at the same time. One possible candidate is the Henry Miller Jr. who was baptized in 1767 at St. Jacob's (Kimmerling's) Reformed Church in Lebanon County and was the son of Henry Miller Sr. and Anna Maria Kimmerling. Another is a Heinrich Miller, who along with his wife Magdalena was a sponsor at a 1767 baptism at the German Lutheran Church in Hummelstown; he is likely the same Heinrich Miller who died on June 10, 1802, and was buried in the Lutheran cemetery. A third possibility is a Heinrich Miller who signed the petition to establish Dauphin County in 1785.[70]

The next two chests were made in 1781 and 1783, respectively, for siblings Magdalena and Ludwig Fischborn/Fishburn (figs. 157, 158; see also fig. 142). Although nearly identical in overall appearance as well as size, the chests

Figure 157 Chest, made for Lutwig Fischborn, Dauphin County, Pennsylvania, 1783. Walnut, sulfur inlay, and mixed-wood inlay with tulip poplar; brass, iron. H. 27½", W. 51½", D. 23¾". (Courtesy, Carl and Yvonne De Paulis; photo, Gavin Ashworth.)

Figure 158 Detail of the inlay on the chest illustrated in fig. 157. (Photo, Gavin Ashworth.)

have some minor differences. Most notably, Magdalena's chest is constructed with exposed dovetails, whereas Ludwig's is built with half-blind dovetails. Their father, Johann Philip Fischborn (1722–1795), was born in Hesse-Darmstadt, Germany, immigrated to Pennsylvania in 1749, and settled in Londonderry Township, now part of southern Dauphin County. Philip identified himself as a yeoman in his will and owned extensive livestock and farm equipment at the time of his death, but also a clock valued at £9 and a ten-plate stove worth £4.10. Although Philip Fischborn was Lutheran, not all of his children remained in that denomination: his son, Philip Jr. (1754–1851), is buried at the Fishburn United Methodist Cemetery in Hershey. Magdalena Fischborn was born in 1765, married John Ricker, and died in 1836. Ludwig Fischborn was born in 1756, married Catharine Grim in 1789, and died in 1846. He resided in Derry Township, Dauphin County, where he owned 123 acres at the time of his death. Magdalena, Ludwig, and their spouses are buried in the cemetery of Zion Lutheran Church in Hummelstown.[71]

The latest sulfur-inlaid chest of this group bearing a complete name was made in 1792 for Maria Klinger (figs. 159–161). The Klinger family is often

Figure 159   Chest, made for Maria Klinger, Dauphin County, Pennsylvania, 1792. Walnut, sulfur inlay, and mixed-wood inlay with tulip poplar and white pine; brass, iron. H. 27", W. 51½", D. 24". (Courtesy, Rock Ford Plantation, bequest of John J. Snyder Jr.; photo, Gavin Ashworth.)

Figure 160   Detail of the inlay on the chest illustrated in fig. 159. (Photo, Gavin Ashworth.)

Figure 161   Detail of the inlay on the chest illustrated in fig. 159. (Photo, Gavin Ashworth.)

associated with northern Dauphin County, in the vicinity of Klingerstown and Erdman, but there was a George Klinger listed in the 1783 tax list for Lebanon Township. Numerous Klingers were also baptized at Christ Lutheran Church near Stouchsburg, Berks County. Four related chests are also known with only initials and dates. The earliest example is dated 1788 and bears the initials "CH KM" flanking a six-point star (figs. 162, 163).

Figure 162 Chest, made for "CH KM," probably Dauphin County, Pennsylvania, 1788. Walnut and mixed-wood inlay with tulip poplar; brass, iron. H. 26", W. 54", D. 23". (Courtesy, Clarke Hess; photo, Gavin Ashworth.)

Figure 163 Detail of the star inlay on the chest illustrated in fig. 162. (Photo, Gavin Ashworth.)

Figure 164 Chest, made for "ML," probably Dauphin County, Pennsylvania, 1789. Walnut, sulfur inlay, and mixed-wood inlay with tulip poplar; brass, iron. H. 27 1/8", W. 50", D. 23 3/4". (Courtesy, Mr. and Mrs. Stephen D. Hench; photo, Gavin Ashworth.)

Although it is not possible to identify the original owner, the initials likely stand for a name such as Christian or Christopher Karmene, Kitzmiller, Kemmerer, or Kimmerling. The other three chests have a sulfur-inlaid horizontal plaque with ovolo ends that frames the date and initials. The earliest example was made in 1789 and bears the initials "ML" along with a twelve-point compass star (fig. 164). Another chest was made in 1790 bearing the initials "I S" (fig. 165). The last of the three chests, dated 1793, has the initials "S A C" inlaid in sulfur but no compass star (fig. 166). The latest

known chest associated with this group is dated 1798 and has a twelve-point compass star inlaid on the façade. Both the date and the owner's name, Magdalena Baum, are painted in a yellowish-white color rather than inlaid in sulfur (figs. 167, 168). She may be the daughter of Adam and Veronica (Gingerich) Baum, who were married in 1752 and lived near Hummelstown in what is now Derry Township, Dauphin County.[72]

Figure 165 Chest, made for "IS," Dauphin County, Pennsylvania, 1790. Walnut and sulfur inlay with tulip poplar; brass, iron. H. 27½", W. 49½", D. 23". (Courtesy, Winterthur Museum, bequest of John J. Snyder Jr.; photo, Gavin Ashworth.)

Figure 166 Chest, made for "S A C," probably Dauphin County, Pennsylvania, 1793. Walnut and sulfur inlay with tulip poplar; brass, iron. H. 29⅝", W. 50½", D. 23¾". (Courtesy, Pennsylvania Historical and Museum Commission, Landis Valley Village and Farm Museum, bequest of John J. Snyder Jr.; photo, Gavin Ashworth.)

Figure 167 Chest, made for Magdalena Baum, probably Dauphin County, Pennsylvania, 1798. Walnut and mixed-wood inlay with white pine and tulip poplar; brass, iron; paint. H. 27", W. 55½", D. 23". (Courtesy, Historical Society of Dauphin County, Harrisburg, Pa.; photo, David Pickel.)

Figure 168 Detail of the inlay and paint on the chest illustrated in fig. 167.

167   SULFUR INLAY IN PENNSYLVANIA

Alleman Chests

Two more Dauphin County sulfur-inlaid chests are known, which were made for Margaret Alleman and her first cousin, Martin Alleman. Margaret's chest is dated 1786 and includes numerous sulfur-inlaid dots interspersed with the letters and numerals of the inscription (fig. 169). The original owner can be identified as Margaret Alleman (1775–1838), daughter of Conrad Alleman (1738–1792) and Margaret (Eshenauer) Alleman who lived near Middletown in Lower Paxton (now Lower Swatara) Township,

Figure 169 Chest, made for Margaret Alleman, Dauphin County, Pennsylvania, 1786. Walnut and sulfur inlay; iron. H. 22", W. 48", D. 24". (Photo, Pook & Pook.)

Dauphin County. She married Andrew Schott of Derry Township in 1802; they later moved to the town of Waterloo in Seneca County, New York. A closely related chest with the sulfur-inlaid name of "Chatharina Fuscherin" and the date 1786 is also known. She may have been a relative of Margaret Alleman by marriage, since Margaret's sister Anna Maria Alleman married a John Fisher. The other chest was made in 1792 for Martin Alleman (1768–1840), son of Christopher and Elisabeth (Shaffner) Alleman of Swatara Township, Dauphin County (figs. 170, 171). Probably made by a different craftsman than the Margaret Alleman chest, it was originally built over

Figure 170 Chest, made for Martin Alleman, Dauphin County, Pennsylvania, 1792. Walnut and sulfur inlay with white pine, tulip poplar; iron. H. 20½", W. 52", D. 24¼". (Courtesy, Clarke Hess; photo, Gavin Ashworth.) The chest was originally over drawers and has been reduced in height.

Figure 171 Detail of the inlay on the chest illustrated in fig. 170. (Photo, Gavin Ashworth.)

drawers and has been reduced in height. Christopher and Conrad Alleman were brothers, both descended from German immigrant John Christian Alleman (d. 1790). Of Lutheran heritage, many members of the Alleman family were baptized or married at Zion Lutheran Church in Harrisburg, including Martin Alleman and his wife Rosina Pancake, who had three children baptized there between 1795 and 1801.[73]

York County

Located on the west side of the Susquehanna River, York County was formally established in 1749 when it was subdivided from Lancaster County. The town of York, which became the county seat, was founded in 1741 and within thirty years developed into a thriving market town with a population of nearly 2,500 (fig. 172). During the British occupation of Philadelphia in 1777–1778, York hosted the Continental Congress for nine months. More than half of the town's taxpayers in 1779 were artisans, who represented some forty distinct trades. According to German traveler Johann David Schoepf, who visited York in 1783, the inhabitants were "very largely Germans." One of the most talented craftsmen in York was John Fisher (1736–1808), a clockmaker, engraver, sign painter, carver, and musical instrument builder. Born in Germany, Fisher immigrated to Pennsylvania

Figure 172 William Wagner, view of York, York County, Pennsylvania, 1830. (Courtesy, York County Heritage Trust, York, Pa.)

Figure 173 Tall clock, made for "A G and AMG," movement signed by John Fisher, York, York County, Pennsylvania, 1773. Walnut and sulfur inlay. H. 99", W. 17½", D. 11½". (Private collection; photo, Winterthur Library, Decorative Arts Photographic Collection.)

Figure 174 Detail of the clock illustrated in fig. 173.)

in 1749 and settled in York by 1756. One of his movements is housed in a walnut clock case that has the sulfur-inlaid initials "AG" flanking a scrolled bracket at the center of the hood and the date "1773" inlaid in the corners of the bonnet door. The initials "AMG" are inlaid on the waist, above a stylized shell motif inlaid at the top of the pendulum door (figs. 173, 174). This is the earliest known dated example of sulfur-inlaid furniture that can be associated with York County. Although the identity of the original owners is unknown, the use of two sets of initials suggests that the clock was owned by a married couple, most likely an Adam and Anna Maria whose surname began with a G. It is possible that John Fisher may have assisted in the selection of the case, since a 1789 contract between Fisher and a customer stipulated that Fisher was to procure a case "of fine cured walnut or cherry . . . [and] assures the buyer of the latest style and design that is to be had at the hands and mind of himself and the most skillful and renowned joiner it is his responsibility to hire."[74]

Conewago Area Sulfur Inlay

The Conewago settlement of southern York County straddled the Pennsylvania–Maryland line, a hotly disputed border until the completion of the Mason-Dixon Line in 1768. First settled in the late 1720s by Roman Catholics and German Protestants, much of the Conewago settlement was on a tract of 10,000 acres known as Digges Choice—named after John Digges, a Catholic settler from Maryland who was granted the land in 1727 by Charles Calvert, fourth Lord Baltimore of Maryland. Today the Digges Choice tract comprises the borough of Hanover, Penn and Heidelberg townships in York County and Conewago, Germany, and Union townships in Adams County, Pennsylvania. As the Conewago settlement grew, German Lutheran and Reformed inhabitants joined together to form a union congregation. By 1762 they had erected a church, St. Mary's, near the Silver Run in what is now Carroll County, Maryland (the area was part of Frederick County, Maryland, until 1837). Two pieces of sulfur-inlaid furniture and several dozen gravestones with sulfur-inlaid decoration are associated with the Conewago region.[75]

A slant-front desk made in 1790 for George Gelwicks (1739–1817) is the second earliest dated example of York County sulfur-inlaid furniture (figs. 175, 176). George was the son of Friedrich Heinrich Gelwicks (1712–1783), who emigrated from Germany by 1733, when he married Maria Dorothea Euler/Eiler at Providence (now Trappe), Montgomery County, Pennsylvania. The couple's first child was baptized at Trappe in 1734 and their next three at the Muddy Creek Church in northern Lancaster County between 1736 and 1739, including son George Carl Gelwicks, who was born on September 16, 1739. By the mid-1700s the Gelwicks family had moved to Manheim Township, York County, where Friedrich worked as a farmer, shoemaker, and distiller. He was a founding member and probably the schoolmaster of the "Lutheran Church on the Conewago" (later known as St. Matthew's) in Hanover. In 1756, Friedrich became treasurer of York County, the first

Figure 175 Desk, made for George Gelwicks, York County, Pennsylvania, 1790. Walnut with sulfur inlay and pine. H. 44¼", W. 41¼", D. 22". (Private collection; photo, Rob Manko.)

Figure 176 Detail of the inlay on the desk illustrated in fig. 175.

German to hold that office. His son George, the owner of the desk, married Maria Eva Forney in 1765; after her death in 1770, he married a woman named Elisabeth Maria Barbara.[76]

During the American Revolution, George Gelwicks served in the Flying Camp under Captain Peter Ickes. He may have been one of the men who presented Ickes with an engraved pewter mug after the war celebrating the American victory. Like his father, George worked as a shoemaker and innkeeper. He remained in Hanover until at least 1783 and later moved just south of the Pennsylvania border to Hagerstown, Maryland, where his son Johannes was born and baptized in 1786 (fig. 177). George Gelwicks died on April 1, 1817. His younger sister, Eva Dorothea Gelwicks (1743–1792), mar-

Figure 177 Birth and baptismal certificate for Johannes Gelwicks, decoration and infill attributed to the Pseudo-Otto Artist, printed form attributed to the Ephrata Cloister, Lancaster County, Pennsylvania, ca. 1788. Watercolor and ink on laid paper. 13" x 16". (Courtesy, Philadelphia Museum of Art, promised gift of Joan and Victor Johnson; photo, Graydon Wood.)

ried Philip Meyer/Meier (d. 1800) of Hanover. A joiner by trade, Meyer is a likely candidate to have made the desk owned by his brother-in-law George Gelwicks. From 1771 to 1772 Meier provided joinery work for the Emanuel Reformed Church in Hanover, of which he was a member. In 1783 Meyer also served as co-executor of his father-in-law Friedrich Heinrich Gelwick's estate together with Nicholas Gelwicks. Another possible maker is the joiner John Ritz, who worked on the Lutheran congregation's new church, built from 1802 to 1805.[77]

Also from the Conewago area is an undated chest of drawers made for Casper Renaker/Reinecker of Hanover, York County (figs. 178, 179). Born in Germany on July 30, 1733, to Adam and Elisabeth Reinecker, Casper immigrated in 1750 and settled near the border of what is now York and Adams counties. On October 17, 1751, he married Anna Maria Carl (1738–1789) of Berwick Township, now in Adams County. Deeds list his occupation variously as yeoman, merchant, and gentleman. In his will of 1789, he described himself as an innkeeper. Casper also acquired substantial land holdings,

Figure 178 Chest of drawers, made for Casper Renaker, York County, Pennsylvania, ca. 1790. Walnut and sulfur inlay with pine and tulip poplar. H. 51½", W. 41¼", D. 22". (Courtesy, Carl and Yvonne De Paulis; photo, Gavin Ashworth.) The feet, top, and knobs are replaced.

Figure 179 Detail of the inlay on the chest of drawers illustrated in fig. 178. (Photo, Gavin Ashworth.)

including four lots in Hanover and 250 acres in nearby Manchester Township. He died on August 17, 1790, and the inventory of his estate, taken only two days later, totaled an impressive £7,158.18.7. It includes many detailed lots of ceramics and a reference to what is likely the sulfur-inlaid chest of drawers: "1 Large Walnut Droor, high feet," valued at £3.10. Although the chest of drawers is undated, given Renaker's date of death, the chest of drawers must have been made in 1790 or earlier—about the same time as the Gelwicks desk that is dated 1790. Of note is that Philip Meyer, the joiner who was the brother-in-law of George Gelwicks, was also one of the witnesses to Renaker's will. However, construction differences between the two pieces suggest that different craftsmen made them. The drawer bottoms of the Renaker chest are recessed and nailed through the drawer sides rather than being pegged up or slid into a groove, and there are also spring locks on the two smaller drawers at the top. The dovetails are wedged as is often seen in Pennsylvania German furniture. The Gelwicks desk, on the other hand, has chamfered drawer bottoms slid into grooves and the dovetails are not wedged.[78]

Gelwicks and Renaker intersected with one another in multiple ways. Both owned sulfur-inlaid furniture, and both were German Lutherans who supported the Conewago church. In 1762, Renaker purchased 120 acres of the Digges Choice tract. On this land stood the first log church used by the Lutheran congregation at Conewago, for which they did not have clear title. Friedrich Gelwicks and Casper Renaker later donated money to help the congregation acquire land for a new church and cemetery. As a tavern keeper, Renaker also did a substantial business with Friedrich Gelwicks, from whom he purchased large quantities of liquor. In 1767, Renaker bought seventy-seven gallons of "cider royal" from Gelwicks; another 104 gallons in 1768; 188 gallons in 1769; 100 gallons in 1770; and fifty more gallons plus one barrel of applejack in 1772.[79]

Gravestones

At least three churches in the Conewago area have gravestones with remnants of sulfur inlay in either the decoration, inscriptions, or both: St. Mary's Church near Silver Run, St. Luke's (Winters) Church near New Windsor, and St. Benjamin's (Pipe Creek or Krider's) Church near Westminster—all located in what is now Carroll County, Maryland, near the Pennsylvania line. Each of these churches functioned as a so-called "union" or joint Lutheran and Reformed church during the 1700s. At one time St. John's Lutheran Church in Littlestown, Adams County, Pennsylvania, was also said to have tombstones with sulfur inlay. The sulfur-inlaid gravestones—several dozen remain—are consistently made of slate, although stylistic differences indicate that they were probably made by several different craftsmen. Most of the gravestones were made for people who died during the 1790s or early 1800s. On gravestones where the sulfur inlay is no longer present, tool marks are clearly visible where the maker gouged the stone to provide a surface to which the inlay could adhere (see p. 74 figs. 9, 11 in this volume).[80]

Figure 180 Tombstone for Michael Gibler, St. Mary's Church, Carroll County, Maryland, 1791. (Photo, Lisa Minardi.)

Figure 181 Tombstone for Anna Elisabeth Margreth Gibler, St. Mary's Church, Carroll County, Maryland, 1791. (Photo, Lisa Minardi.)

Casper Renaker, the owner of the sulfur-inlaid chest of drawers, is directly linked to the sulfur-inlaid tombstones at St. Mary's. His younger brother, Paul Renaker (1745–1799), married Anna Margaret Gibler. In 1762, her father, Michael Gibler is listed as a member of St. Mary's, then part of Frederick County, Maryland. Between 1771 and 1795 Paul and Anna Margaret Renaker had twelve children baptized by the Lutheran pastor of St. Mary's. Casper Renaker and his wife Anna Maria served as sponsors for the baptism of Paul and Anna Margaret's first child, Catharine, born in 1771. Both Michael Gibler and his wife, Anna Elisabeth Margaret, died in 1791. A pair of nearly identical tombstones inscribed in German, with sulfur-inlaid stars at the top, marks their graves (figs. 180, 181). When Paul Renaker died only eight years later in 1799, a sulfur-inlaid tombstone was commissioned. It is inscribed in English and the letters themselves are inlaid in sulfur (fig. 182).[81]

Figure 182 Tombstone for Paul Renecker, St. Mary's Church, Carroll County, Maryland, 1799. (Photo, Lisa Minardi.)

SULFUR INLAY IN PENNSYLVANIA

Floral Group

A third group of sulfur-inlaid furniture that can now be linked to York County is characterized by floral designs made of very shallow sulfur inlay or yellowish paint along with traces of polychrome painted decoration. The earliest example, a chest, is dated 1789 and has the initials "MS WS" on the facade (fig. 183). Rather than being inlaid in sulfur, the inscription and floral designs were rendered in a yellow-colored paint. The shape of the flowers, however, is closely related to that on the other two sulfur-inlaid examples. The chest descended in the family of Beulah Bowers Coffman (1900–1997) of Shenandoah County, Virginia. She was a descendant of Jacob Emswiler (1755–1832), who moved to Shenandoah County from York County, Pennsylvania, by 1782. His father, Peter Imbsweiller/Imschwiller (d. 1772), emigrated from Germany in 1749 and settled in Windsor Township, York County. Jacob was baptized on October 5, 1755, at Christ Lutheran Church in York.[82]

Figure 183   Chest, probably York County, Pennsylvania, 1789. Yellow pine; paint; iron. H. 22½", W. 49", D. 21½". (Courtesy, Museum of the Shenandoah Valley, Winchester, Va.; photo, Ron Blunt.) The left foot is restored. It is also possible that this chest was made in Shenandoah County, Virginia.

The next piece is a miniature chest, dated 1790 and inscribed with the name "ANAS ZEEL" (figs. 184, 185). This inscription probably refers to the Anna Zell/Sell/Sill (1777–1845) who was the granddaughter of Abraham Sell (1715–1786; interred in Littlestown in Germany Township, York [now Adams] County). Abraham's son, Adam Sell, had a daughter named Anna

176   LISA MINARDI

Figure 184 Miniature chest, probably made for Anna Sell/Zell, York County, Pennsylvania, 1790. Walnut and sulfur inlay with pine. H. 11⅜", W. 19¼", D. 11½". (Private collection; photo, Gavin Ashworth.)

Figure 185 Detail of the inlay on the chest illustrated in fig. 184. (Photo, Gavin Ashworth.)

or "Hannah" who was probably the original owner of the chest. She married Dr. John Study (1770–1853); both Hannah and John Study are buried at St. Mary's Church near Silver Run in Carroll County, Maryland. A 1762 list of members at St. Mary's includes Martin Studi, John Study's grandfather; Hans Adam Forne, father-in-law of Abraham Sell (m. Louisa Charlotte Forney); and Michael Gibler, whose sulfur-inlaid tombstone is illustrated in figure 180.[83]

Figure 186 Chest, probably made for Peter Holtzappel, York County, Pennsylvania, 1791. Walnut and sulfur inlay with pine; paint. H. 24½", W. 49", D. 20¼". (Courtesy, Clarke Hess; photo, Gavin Ashworth.) The feet and base molding are replaced.

Figure 187 Detail of the inlay on the chest illustrated in fig. 186. (Photo, Gavin Ashworth.)

The latest piece in the group is dated 1791 and inscribed "PTR HLSLE" (figs. 186, 187). It was probably made for Peter Holtzappel/Holsapple, great-grandson of German immigrant Hans Leonard Holtzappel and his wife Anna Barbara. The Holtzappels emigrated from Germany in 1731 along with their daughter, Anna Barbara; son-in-law, Johann Adam Rupert; and son Erasmus Holtzappel (1710–1793). The family settled in York County, where Erasmus married Christina Rausher in 1738 at Christ Lutheran Church in York. Erasmus and Christina lived in Manchester Township, York County, and had at least twelve children. Although none was named Peter, given the 1791 date of the chest, it was likely made for one of their grandchildren. The chest was found in the late 1900s in Tuscarawas County, Ohio, in the possession of an Amish family. Beginning in the 1770s, the Moravian missionary David Zeisberger established several missions in the Tuscarawas Valley, including Goshen in 1798. Farmers from Pennsylvania soon began moving to the region and by 1808 had established the first permanent settlement, New Philadelphia, near the Goshen mission. One of Erasmus Holtzappel's daughters, Maria Barbara (1753–ca. 1822), married Gottlieb Fackler and moved to the Goshen area of Tuscarawas County, Ohio, by 1820, probably taking the chest with her.[84]

Other Sulfur-Inlaid Furniture

There are a number of pieces of sulfur-inlaid furniture that fall into distinctive groups but cannot yet be linked to a particular county or locale. There are also singular objects which, so far as can be determined, are the only known examples of their type. The following section will provide an overview of some of these groups and singular objects.

Double Eagle Group

During the 1760s, at the same time when Lancaster County joiners were building extraordinary sulfur-inlaid tall clocks, schranks, and chests for local families, another as-yet unidentified maker in southeastern Pennsylvania crafted two distinctive pieces of furniture inlaid in sulfur and wood. The earlier example is a tall clock dated 1766 with the initials "i r" flanking a spread-wing, double-headed eagle (fig. 188). Unfortunately, because the dial of the clock appears to be unmarked, its place of origin remains obscure. The second known object is a corner cupboard dated 1768 with the initials "i b" and a double-headed eagle motif inlaid in the top (figs. 189, 190). The date and the body of the bird are inlaid in sulfur, while the

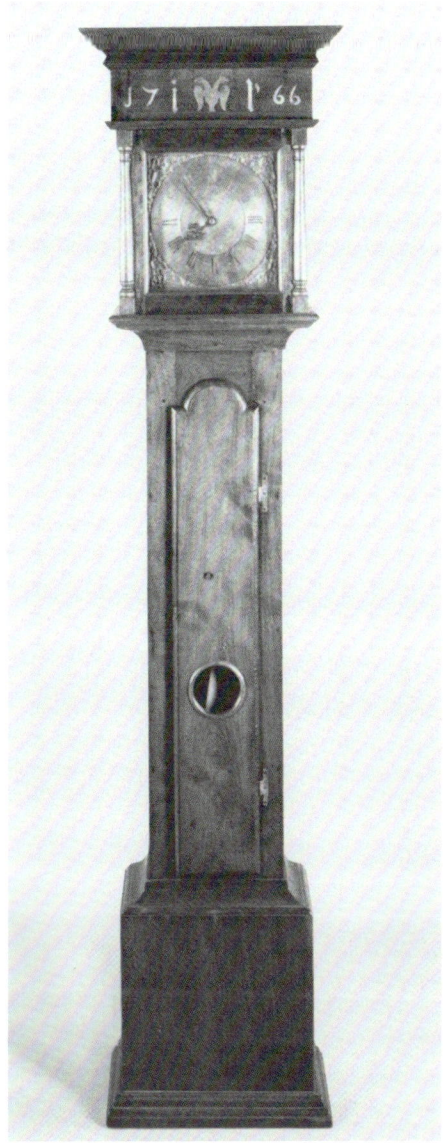

Figure 188 Tall clock, southeastern Pennsylvania, 1766. Walnut, sulfur inlay, and mixed-wood inlay; secondary woods unrecorded. H. 88", W. 19", D. 10½". (Location unknown; photo, Christie's.)

Figure 189 Corner cupboard, southeastern Pennsylvania, 1768. Walnut, sulfur inlay, and mixed-wood inlay with tulip poplar and pine; iron, brass. H. 85½", W. 47", D. 22½". (Courtesy, Renfrew Museum; photo, Gavin Ashworth.) The upper door is missing.

179 SULFUR INLAY IN PENNSYLVANIA

Figure 190 Detail of the inlay on the cupboard illustrated in fig. 189. (Photo, Gavin Ashworth.)

Figure 191 Detail of the inlay on the cupboard illustrated in fig. 189. (Photo, Gavin Ashworth.)

initials as well as the legs and heads of the bird are inlaid in wood (fig. 191). The corner cupboard has heavily pegged construction and wedged dovetails, indicating that its maker was trained in Germanic woodworking techniques. Although other cabinetmakers also used sulfur and wood inlay on the same objects, the combination of both materials here in the eagles is highly distinctive, as is the double-headed eagle shape itself, which does not appear on any other Pennsylvania German sulfur-inlaid furniture and only rarely in Pennsylvania German art of any kind.[85]

Hearts and Flowers Group

Another distinctive group includes a pair of sulfur-inlaid chests, each with a central heart motif containing a spray of flowers flanked by the owners' names and dates, set within horizontal tablets. The earlier of the two chests is dated 1785 and inscribed for Veronica Miller (figs. 192–194). Multiple Veronica Millers lived in Pennsylvania at that time. One, who was born in 1753 to Nicholas Miller (1730–1784) and his wife Barbara of Bern Township, Berks County, married Jacob Kauffman (b. 1751), and they later moved to Somerset County, Pennsylvania. Another was born in 1763 and died 1799; she is buried in the Fackler graveyard in Lower Paxton Township, Dauphin County. A third Veronica Miller, wife of Daniel Kinports (Kihports/Keeports) is named as a daughter in the 1803 will of Christian Miller of Lampeter Township, Lancaster County.[86]

Figure 192 Chest, made for Veronica Miller, southeastern Pennsylvania, 1785. Walnut and sulfur inlay with tulip poplar; iron, brass. H. 20", W. 52", D. 23¾". (Courtesy, Clarke Hess; photo, Gavin Ashworth.) The feet and base molding are replaced; the chest used to be over two drawers.

Figure 193 Detail of the inlay on the chest illustrated in fig. 192. (Photo, Gavin Ashworth.)

Figure 194 Detail of the inlay on the chest illustrated in fig. 192. (Photo, Gavin Ashworth.)

The later of the two chests is dated 1792 and inscribed for "Fridrich Schweizer." It was first published in Monroe Fabian's article on sulfur inlay and attributed to Lancaster County. According to Fabian, the chest was probably made in Lancaster County but accompanied Schweizer when he moved to what is now Jackson Township, Snyder County, where he died and was buried. However, no source was provided for this information and no record of a Frederick Schweizer has been found in Snyder County (which was established in 1855 out of Union County). New research has uncovered several other possible candidates as the original owner of this chest. The first is Johann Friederich Schweizer (1763–1839) of Brecknock Township, Berks County, son of Peter and Elizabeth (Heffelfinger) Schweizer. He married Anna Barbara Burkhart (b. 1770) and is buried at the Old Allegheny Union Cemetery in Brecknock Township. The second is Friederich Schweizer, who with his wife, Magdalena, had two children baptized (in 1792 and 1794, respectively) at Tabor First Reformed Church in Lebanon, Lebanon County.[87]

Slide-lid Boxes

Another distinctive but as-yet unidentified group of sulfur-inlaid objects comprises three slide-lid boxes, each inlaid with initials that include a surname beginning with the letter D and dates of either 1796 or 1797

Figure 195   Slide-lid box, made for "H D," probably Lancaster County, Pennsylvania, 1796. Walnut and sulfur inlay. H. 3¼", W. 6⅝", D. 12". (Private collection; photo, Gavin Ashworth.)

Figure 196   Slide-lid box, made for "C D", probably Lancaster County, Pennsylvania, 1796. Walnut and sulfur inlay. H. 4⅜", W. 8", D. 13⅜". (Private collection; photo, Gavin Ashworth.)

Figure 197   Slide-lid box, made for "M D," probably Lancaster County, Pennsylvania, 1797. Walnut and sulfur inlay. H. 4⅜", W. 8", D. 13⅜". (Courtesy, Mr. and Mrs. Stephen D. Hench; photo, Gavin Ashworth.)

(figs. 195–200). No two are exactly identical, although the boxes are clearly the work of the same unknown maker. Two have border treatments with ovolo ends; one has a more complex border resembling the outline of a Germanic raised panel. The two boxes dated 1796 both have a small quatrefoil device inlaid between the initials; the 1797 box has a six-point compass star. The HD / 1796 box is inscribed in pencil on the underside of the lid with the name "Mrs. Wolfinger" and once had an internal partition that divided the box into two compartments.

Figure 198 Detail of the inlay on the lid of the box illustrated in fig 195. (Photo, Gavin Ashworth.)

Figure 199 Detail of the inlay on the lid of the box illustrated in fig 196. (Photo, Gavin Ashworth.)

Figure 200 Detail of the inlay on the lid of the box illustrated in fig 197. (Photo, Gavin Ashworth.)

Figure 201   Chest, made for "HA BE," possibly Lancaster County, Pennsylvania, 1768. Walnut and sulfur inlay with walnut and oak; brass, iron. H. 27⅝", W. 48¾", D. 22¼". (Private collection; photo, Gavin Ashworth.) The feet are replaced.

Figure 202   Detail of the inlay on the chest illustrated in fig. 201. (Photo, Gavin Ashworth.)

Figure 203   Kitchen cupboard, possibly made for Adam and Anna Brandt, Lebanon County, Pennsylvania, 1770. Walnut and sulfur inlay with pine and tulip poplar; brass, iron. H. 89½", W. 76½", D. 20¾". (Courtesy, Rocky Hill Collection; photo, Gavin Ashworth.) The pie shelf section and brasses are restored.

Singular Objects

A walnut chest over drawers, dated 1768 and with the initials "HA BE," is one of the earlier known examples of sulfur-inlaid furniture (figs. 201, 202), yet it does not appear to fit into any of the identifiable groups of sulfur-inlaid furniture made during the 1760s. Another object, the only known kitchen cupboard with sulfur-inlaid decoration, has tulips with vines flanking the initials "AD B" and "AN B" (fig. 203). A central rose motif and the date 1770 are also set within a series of three plaques (figs. 204–206). No other objects with sulfur inlay are known that appear to have been made by the same hand. Given the conventions of abbreviating names with initials on Pennsylvania German furniture, this piece was likely made for an Adam and Anna B. Numerous couples can be found whose names match these initials, but one intriguing possibility is Adam and Anna Brandt of Lebanon County. Adam's father, the German émigré Adam Brandt Sr., initially settled in the area of Strasburg, Lancaster County, but by 1745 had moved to Lebanon Township, now part of Lebanon County. Adam Brandt Jr. was born in about 1732 and died in 1803. Both he and his father are listed in the Lebanon Township tax records during the 1750s but Adam Jr. later moved to Bethel Township. There he served in various official capacities, including constable in 1775, overseer of roads in 1778, and overseer of the poor in 1782. His wife, Anna, predeceased him. In his will, dated April 6, 1799, Adam Brandt Jr. identified himself as a farmer and directed his executors to divide his estate equally among his three grandchildren—Christian, Anna, and Elizabeth Franck—born to his daughter, Barbara, whose husband Christian Franck had died prior to 1799. He then added a specific bequest, writing "To Barbara Brand my own Dauther I give and bequeath out of my Personel Estate unto her my Kitchen Dresser, or Closet." Whether or not this is the sulfur-inlaid kitchen cupboard is impossible to say with certainty, but given the nature of this bequest it must have been a special object—and this Adam and Anna Brandt fit the date and initials.[88]

Figure 204 Detail of the inlay on the cupboard illustrated in fig. 203. (Photo, Gavin Ashworth.)

Figure 205 Detail of the inlay on the cupboard illustrated in fig. 203. (Photo, Gavin Ashworth.)

Figure 206 Detail of the inlay on the cupboard illustrated in fig. 203. (Photo, Gavin Ashworth.)

Figure 207 Hanging cupboard, probably Lancaster County, Pennsylvania, 1772. Walnut and sulfur inlay with pine. H. 33", W. 18", D. 11⅞". (Courtesy, Philadelphia Museum of Art, 1953-125-9; photo, Gavin Ashworth.) The bottom lip of the drawer is replaced.

Figure 208 Detail of the inlay on the cupboard illustrated in fig. 207. (Photo, Gavin Ashworth.)

Figure 209 Detail of the inlay on the cupboard illustrated in fig. 207. (Photo, Gavin Ashworth.)

Figure 210 Tall clock, made for "J.K.," movement signed by George Hoff, probably Lancaster County, Pennsylvania, 1774. Walnut and sulfur inlay with tulip poplar. H. 86 3/8", W. 20", D. 10 1/8". (Courtesy, Philip H. Bradley Co.; photo, Gavin Ashworth.) The feet are replaced and the inlay is restored.

Another singular object is a hanging cupboard, dated 1772, with a heart, tulips, and ovolo-end borders framing the raised panel door and drawer below (figs. 207–209). The maker used a compass to lay out the arcs of the design, filling the compass point holes with sulfur. No provenance is known prior to the acquisition of this piece by collector Titus C. Geesey in the early 1900s. This is one of at least two hanging cupboards embellished with sulfur inlay; the other, which has a glazed door and does not appear to be from the same workshop, bears the initials "B R" inlaid in sulfur above the door. Other singular objects include a tall clock inlaid on the pendulum door with the initials "J K" and a motif that appears to be a wheel (figs. 210, 211). The clock movement was made by George Hoff of Lancaster, suggesting a probable Lancaster County origin for the case. Another tall clock has the sulfur-inlaid initials "H S" and an elongated diamond-shape motif at the center of the tympanum

Figure 211 Detail of the inlay on the clock illustrated in fig. 210. (Photo, Gavin Ashworth.)

Figure 212 Tall clock, made for "H.S.," movement signed by Jacob Gorgas, Ephrata, Lancaster County, Pennsylvania, ca. 1790. Walnut and sulfur inlay with tulip poplar. H. 95½", W. 23½", D. 12¾". (Private collection; photo, Gavin Ashworth.)

(figs. 212, 213). It has a distinctive border of pointed ovals carved into the edge of the broken scroll pediment. The white painted dial is signed by Jacob Gorgas of Ephrata, also suggesting a Lancaster County origin.[89]

Sulfur inlay was used to decorate a wide range of furniture forms and sizes, from massive schranks and tall clocks to work tables and small wooden boxes.

Figure 213 Detail of the inlay on the clock illustrated in fig. 212. (Photo, Gavin Ashworth.)

Figure 214 Table, possibly Lancaster County, Pennsylvania, ca. 1790. Walnut and sulfur inlay; brass. H. 30", W. 41", D. 29½". (Courtesy, Carl and Yvonne De Paulis; photo, Gavin Ashworth.)

Figure 215 Slide-lid box, made for "W B," probably Lancaster County, Pennsylvania, ca. 1790. Walnut and sulfur inlay with pine. H. 5", W. 11¼", D. 5 ⅞". (Courtesy, Rocky Hill Collection; photo, Gavin Ashworth.)

Figure 216 Box with drawer, made for "M E," probably Lancaster County, Pennsylvania, 1799. Walnut, sulfur inlay, and mixed-wood inlay with tulip poplar; brass. H. 9¼", W. 18", D. 8¾". (Courtesy, Rocky Hill Collection; photo, Gavin Ashworth.)

Probably due to their utilitarian function, objects such as tables are rarely decorated with sulfur inlay. A single-drawer table with sulfur-inlaid stringing and fans in the drawer corners is a rare exception (fig. 214). At least one other sulfur-inlaid table is known, a stretcher-base model with three drawers inlaid in sulfur with flowers, initials, and the date 1788 (see fig. 91). In addition to the sulfur-inlaid boxes illustrated in figures 195–197, several more boxes of varying forms are known. One is a slide-lid walnut box with the initials "W B" inlaid in sulfur on one of the long sides (fig. 215). Another walnut box, with a hinged lid and drawer, is inlaid with a combination of wood and sulfur to form the initials "M E" flanking a star and the date 1799 (fig. 216).

Conclusion

From its origins in Lancaster County during the 1760s, sulfur inlaid decoration spread rapidly throughout portions of southeastern Pennsylvania—including Dauphin, Lebanon, and York counties. Distinctly local groups of sulfur inlay can now be identified, ranging from the fleur-de-lis motifs on central Lancaster County furniture to the chests with compass star inlay from southern Dauphin County. Identifying this furniture sheds new light on our understanding of Pennsylvania German culture during the mid- to late 1700s and provides an excellent case study of the information that can be gleaned from such objects—especially when combined with solid genealogical research to document them to specific people and places. Many other locally-distinctive schools of furniture decoration existed in southeastern Pennsylvania, which scholars have only begun to explore. As Pennsylvania Germans began moving into the Shenandoah Valley, the use of sulfur inlay spread into Maryland, Virginia, and the North Carolina Piedmont. Yet despite this rapid expansion, sulfur inlay enjoyed only a brief period of popularity and largely ceased to be used after 1800. Nonetheless, more than 125 examples of sulfur-inlaid furniture have been documented to date, revealing the importance of this unique contribution to the field of American furniture by Pennsylvania German craftsmen.

ACKNOWLEDGMENTS For assistance with this article, the author thanks: Alan Andersen; Gavin Ashworth; Susan and Steve Babinsky; Barnes Foundation, Barbara Buckley and Deborah Lenert; Luke Beckerdite; Philip Bradley; Amy Brunner; Ray Brunner; Chester County Historical Society, Ellen Endslow; Christie's, John Hays, Andrew Holter, and Chelsea Corcoran; Colonial Williamsburg Foundation, Tara Gleason Chicirda and John Watson; Dietrich American Foundation, Debbie Rebuck and Chris Storb; Carl and Yvonne De Paulis; Ed and Mary Ann Dixon; William K. du Pont; Christina and Andreas Duhme; Jeff and Bev Evans; Vernon Gunnion; Steve and Marcy Hench; Henry Ford Museum, Charles Sable and Jim Orr; Don Herr; Caroline Nunan Hill; Historic Manheim Preservation Foundation, Jim Hosler; Historical Society of Dauphin County, Janet Bowen and Nicole McMullen Smith; Robert Hogg; Brenda Hornsby-Heindl; Barbara Hunzicker; Joan and Victor Johnson; James Keener; Alan Keyser; Kelly Kinzle; Greg Kramer; LancasterHistory.org, Wendell Zercher; Lancaster Mennonite Historical Society; Ed, Virginia, and Will LaFond; Landis Valley Museum, Bruce Bomberger, Mike Emery, Jim Lewars, and Jen Royer; Richard Levengood; Pat Levin; Dianne Loper; Niccolo Lorimer; Rob Manko; Maryland Historical Society; Clint and Cindy McCauley; Alan Miller; Leslie Miller and Richard Worley; Museum Angewandte Kunst (Frankfurt am Main), Ute Kunze; Museum of Early Southern Decorative Arts, Robert Leath, June Lucas, and Daniel Ackermann; Museum of the Shenandoah Valley, Nick Powers; National Museum of American History, Smithsonian Institution, Stacey Kluck; Olde Hope Antiques; Philadelphia History Museum, Kristen Froehlich; Drinan; Philadelphia Museum of Art, David Barquist and Alexandra Kirtley; Dave Pickel and Adrienne Staleck; Pook & Pook; Jamie Price; Todd Prickett; Sumpter Priddy; Renfrew Museum, Judy Elden and Dade Royer; Rock Ford Plantation, Sarah Drennen; Ed and Linda Rosenberry; David Schorsch and Eileen Smiles; Sotheby's, Erik Gronning; Clarence Spohn; State Museum of Pennsylvania, Bradley Smith; Jay Stiefel; Steve Still; Gary Sullivan; Helen Warnke; Sue Watkins; Carolyn Wenger; Ann and David Weston; Winterthur Museum, Mark Anderson, Stephanie Auffret, Laszlo Bodo, Wendy Cooper, Emily Guthrie, Josh Lane, Lea Lane, Jennifer Mass, Susan Newton, Lauri Perkins, Jim Schneck, and Jeanne Solensky; Carolyn Wenger; Christine Witherspoon and Warren Reynolds; York County Heritage Trust, Lila Fourhman-Shaull. Special thanks are due to Clarke Hess and the late John J. Snyder Jr., who kindly shared both their personal collections of sulfur-inlaid furniture and their extensive genealogical research on the owners.

1. Hattie Brunner to Henry Francis du Pont, December 4, 1929, folder: Brunner, Mrs. R.S., 1931–1940, Antiques Dealer Correspondence Files, box 12, Winterthur Archives, Winterthur Library. See also Wendy A. Cooper and Lisa Minardi, *Paint, Pattern & People: Furniture of Southeastern Pennsylvania, 1725–1850* (Winterthur, Del.: Henry Francis du Pont Winterthur Museum, 2011), p. xxi. Frances Lichten, "A Masterpiece of Pennsylvania-German Furniture," *Antiques* 77, no. 2 (February 1960): 176–78. Monroe H. Fabian, "Sulfur Inlay in Pennsylvania German Furniture," *Pennsylvania Folklife* 27, no. 1 (Fall 1977): 2–9. Clarke Hess, *Mennonite Arts*

(Atglen, Pa.: Schiffer Publishing, 2002), pp. 28, 34–37. Jennifer L. Mass and Mark J. Anderson, "Pennsylvania German Sulfur Inlaid Furniture: Characterization, Reproduction, and Aging Phenomena of the Inlays," *Measurement and Technology* (2003): 1598–1607; Mark J. Anderson, "A New Look at Sulfur and Other Composition Inlay," *Chester County Historical Society Antiques Show Catalogue* (West Chester, Pa.: Chester County Historical Society, 1995), pp. 36–39. In 2009 Winterthur fellow Brenda Hornsby-Heindl conducted a survey of sulfur-inlaid furniture and documented more than 100 pieces.

2. Luther R. Kelker, trans., *Baptismal and Marriage Records, Rev. John Waldschmidt, Cocalico, Moden Krick, Weisseichen Land and Seltenrich Gemeinde, Lancaster County, Pennsylvania, 1752–1786* (1906; reprint, Westminster, Md.: Heritage Books, 2007), pp. 35, 36, 43, 122–24. Charles H. Glatfelter, *Pastors and People: German Lutheran and Reformed Churches in the Pennsylvania Field, 1717–1793*, Publications of the Pennsylvania German Society, vol. 13 (Breinigsville, Pa.: Pennsylvania German Society, 1980), p. 318. Another possibility is John Musser (1762–1824), son of Veronica and Henry Musser (1730–1805). Henry immigrated in 1752, settled in Brecknock Township, Lancaster County, and was a farmer and tailor. John's oldest brother, Peter Musser (1761–1845), was a shoemaker. However, this John Musser would have been only nine years old in 1773, the date the miniature chest was made.

3. "Production of Sulphur in Italy," *Journal of the Royal Society of the Arts* 16, no. 803 (April 10, 1868): 389–90.

4. *The Pennsylvania Gazette*, October 23, 1746, Early American Newspapers Database. Inventory of Daniel Hiester, taken on August 3, 1796, Berks County, Berks County Register of Wills. Theodore G. Tappert and John W. Doberstein, trans. and eds., *The Journals of Henry Melchior Muhlenberg*, 3 vols. (1942–1958; reprint, Camden, Me.: Picton Press, 1980), 3:47, 67. Benno Forman also suggested that sulfur inlay was used as a time-saving substitute for ivory or bone inlay; see Benno M. Forman, "German Influences in Pennsylvania Furniture," in *Arts of the Pennsylvania Germans*, edited by Catherine E. Hutchins (Winterthur, Del.: Henry Francis du Pont Winterthur Museum, 1983), p. 162.

5. Gerald Kutney, *Sulfur: History, Technology, Applications & Industry* (Toronto: Chemtec Publishing, 2007), p. 42. A. Rupert Hall, *The Revolution in Science 1500–1750* (1954; rev. ed., New York: Routledge, 2014), pp. 241–42.

6. Cyril Stanley Smith and Martha Teach Gnudi, trans. and eds., *The Pirotechnia of Vannoccio Biringuccio: The Classic Sixteenth-Century Treatise on Metals and Metallurgy* (1942; rev. ed., New York: Dover Publications, 1990), pp. 88–90, 105–7. Charles I. Landis and Thomas Penn, "The Juliana Library Company in Lancaster," *Pennsylvania Magazine of History and Biography* 43, no. 1 (1919): 24–52. Inventory of William Henry, taken April 26, 1790, Lancaster History.org, INV 1790 F002H.

7. On the Pequea settlement, see Richard K. MacMaster, *Land, Piety, Peoplehood: The Establishment of Mennonite Communities in America, 1683–1790* (Scottdale, Pa.: Herald Press, 1985), pp. 81–85. On the creation of Lancaster County and Lancaster as a county seat, see Jerome H. Wood Jr., *Conestoga Crossroads: Lancaster, Pennsylvania, 1730–1790* (Harrisburg, Pa.: Pennsylvania Historical and Museum Commission, 1979), pp. 1–7, 47–49, 159.

8. On Beierle, see Annette Kunselman Burgert, *Eighteenth-Century Emigrants*, vol. 1, *The Northern Kraichgau*, Publications of the Pennsylvania German Society, vol. 16 (Breinigsville, Pa.: Pennsylvania German Society, 1983), pp. 57–58; Charles R. Freeble Jr., *The Adventures of Andrew Byerly: American, Frontiersman, Ranger & Courier* (St. Petersburg, Fla.: Valkyrie Publishing House, 1993), pp. 9–14, 67; C. H. Martin, "Life of Andrew Byerly," *Historical Papers and Addresses of the Lancaster County Historical Society* 33 (1929): 3–8; Debra D. Smith and Frederick S. Weiser, trans. and eds., *Trinity Lutheran Church Records, Lancaster, Pennsylvania*, 5 vols. (Apollo, Pa.: Closson Press, 1988–2011), 1:4, 42–43, 147, 318. On the Beierle clock, see also Cooper and Minardi, *Paint, Pattern & People*, pp. 31–32. On mold carving and bakers, see William Woys Weaver, "Mold Carving as Folk Art," in *The Legacy of Ferdinand A. Brader*, edited by Kathleen Wieschaus-Voss (Canton, Oh.: Center for the Study of Art in Rural America, 2014), pp. 55–57; also William Woys Weaver, "Cake Prints, Carved Molds and the Tradition of Decorative Confections: The Adomeit Mold Collection," *Antiques* 177, no. 4 (Summer 2010): 158–67. The chest with carved panels, previously owned by collector John J. Snyder Jr., is now in the collection of Rock Ford Plantation, Lancaster, Pa.

9. Ralph Beaver Strassburger and William J. Hinke, *Pennsylvania German Pioneers: A Publication of the Original Lists of Arrivals in the Port of Philadelphia from 1727 to 1808*, 3 vols. (Norristown, Pa.: Pennsylvania German Society, 1934), 1:169. On the Fordney genealogy, see Evajean

Fortney McKnight, *The Fortineux-Fortinet Family (Fortney, Fortna, Fordney, Furtney) in America* (Marceline, Mo.: Walsworth Publishing, 1989). On gunsmith Melchior Fordney, see Patrick Hornberger and John Kolar, *The Lancaster Long Rifle* (Trappe, Md.: Eastwind Publishing, 2012), pp. 80–81. On Freuler and Fordney, see also Mark Häberlein, *The Practice of Pluralism: Congregational Life and Religious Diversity on Lancaster, Pennsylvania, 1730–1820* (University Park: Pennsylvania State University Press, 2009), pp. 24–26, 43–44. *Pennsylvania German Church Records of Births, Marriages, Burials, etc. from the Pennsylvania German Society Proceedings and Addresses*, 3 vols. (Baltimore, Md.: Genealogical Publishing Co., 2001), 1:238, 243, 246, 253, 258.

10. On Lancaster carving, see John J. Snyder Jr., "Carved Chippendale Case Furniture from Lancaster, Pennsylvania," *Antiques* 107, no. 5 (May 1975): 964–75; also Cooper and Minardi, *Paint, Pattern & People*, pp. xvii, 100–5. On Slough, see Wood, *Conestoga Crossroads*, p. 163; Wolfgang Splitter, *Pastors, People, Politics: German Lutherans in Pennsylvania, 1740–1790* (Trier, Germany: Wissenschaftlicher Verlag, 1998), p. 356; Häberlein, *Practice of Pluralism*, p. 152. On stove patterns, see Luke Beckerdite, "Pattern Carving in Eighteenth-Century Philadelphia," *American Furniture*, edited by Luke Beckerdite (Hanover, NH: University Press of New England for the Chipstone Foundation, 2014), pp. 86–141.

11. The schrank with fleur-de-lis carving but no sulfur inlay came out of the Elizabethtown, Lancaster County, area and was sold at Christie's, New York, *Pennsylvania German Folk Art and Decorative Arts from the Collection of Mr. and Mrs. Richard Flanders Smith*, June 3, 1995, lot 139.

12. The unrecorded will is dated March 16, 1796, and was witnessed by Jacob Kilheffer and Jacob Kohler; it is in the collection of Clarke Hess. Will of Christian Herr, written May 26, 1810, proved October 11, 1811, Manor Township, Lancaster County, Pa.; LancasterHistory.org. Theodore W. Herr, *Genealogical Record of Reverend Hans Herr and His Direct Lineal Descendants*, 3rd ed. (Lancaster, Pa.: Lancaster Mennonite Historical Society, 1994), p. 5.

13. Will of Jonas Nolt, written April 18, 1775, proved June 6, 1775, Hempfield Township, Lancaster County, cited in F. Edward Wright, *Abstracts of Lancaster County, Pennsylvania, Wills, 1732–1785* (Westminster, Md.: Heritage Books, 2006), p. 173. On the John Kauffmanns, see F. Edward Wright, *Abstracts of Lancaster County, Pennsylvania, Wills, 1786–1820* (Westminster, Md.: Heritage Books, 2008), pp. 114, 117, 121–22, 233.

14. Wright, *Abstracts of Lancaster County, Pennsylvania, Wills, 1732–1785*, pp. 59, 61. Will of Mary Bachman, written April 20, 1792, proved May 28, 1805, Manheim Township, Lancaster County, in Wright, *Abstracts of Lancaster County, Pennsylvania, Wills, 1786–1820*, p. 18.

15. On the Emanuel and Mary Herr schrank, see also Forman, "German Influences in Pennsylvania Furniture," pp. 161–63; Cooper and Minardi, *Paint, Pattern & People*, pp. 80–81.

16. The Reist schrank was sold at Pennypacker Auction Centre, Reading, Pa., *Americana and Folk Art Auction*, October 10–11, 1977, lot 325. In the catalogue, it is described as having "sulphur and wax inlay." On the Reists, see Hess, *Mennonite Arts*, p. 37; also Henry G. Reist, *Peter Reist of Lancaster County, Pennsylvania, and Some of His Descendants* (Schenectady, NY: n.p., 1933), pp. 25–26. Will of Abraham Reist, written August 7, 1810, proved March 16, 1813, Warwick Township, Lancaster County, Wright, *Abstracts of Lancaster County, Pennsylvania, Wills, 1786–1820*, p. 197. For an image of the Elisabeth Reist chest, see Monroe H. Fabian, *The Pennsylvania-German Decorated Chest* (New York: Universe Books, 1978), p. 151, fig. 127. A sibling, Christian Reist (1779–1852), owned a chest from the same shop that has descended in the family; he moved to Reistville, Lebanon County. With thanks to Clarke Hess for this information. Two schranks with related molding details are illustrated in Vernon S. Gunnion, "The Pennsylvania-German *Schrank*," *Antiques* 123, no. 5 (May 1983): 1024.

17. On the MK chest and Bamberger-Kauffman genealogy, see Hess, *Mennonite Arts*, pp. 32–38. A newly discovered 18th-century family record of John and Anna (Bamberger) Kauffman provides accurate birth dates for their children (which differ from previous publications): Anna, born March 21, 1726, married David Mumma; Johannes, born September 12, 1728, married Anna Elisabeth Long; Elisabeth, born April 25, 1739, married Abraham Reist; and Michael, born October 26, 1745, married Veronica Berg. With thanks to Clarke Hess for this information.

18. Strassburger and Hinke, *Pennsylvania German Pioneers*, 1:204. On John Nicholas Wolf, see *The Pennsylvania-German*, vol. 10 (1909): 281. *Pennsylvania German Church Records*, 1:240, 243, 256, 262, 266, 272. For the 1758 Hempfield Township tax list, see Franklin Ellis and Samuel Evans, *History of Lancaster County, Pennsylvania, with Biographical Sketches of Many of Its Pioneers and Prominent Men* (Philadelphia: Everts and Peck, 1883), pp. 870–71; on Wolf, see ibid., p. 873.

19. Ellis and Evans, *History of Lancaster County*, pp. 870–71, 952.

20. A tall clock with pewter inlaid birds in the hood and a movement signed by George Faber of Sumneytown, Montgomery County, Pa. is illustrated in Robert E. Booth Jr. and Edward F. LaFond Jr., "It's About Time," *Philadelphia Antiques Show Catalogue* (2000), pp. 44, 54. A chest with floral inlay in wood and the pewter inlaid inscription "1773 HH" is illustrated in Fabian, *Pennsylvania-German Decorated Chest*, p. 123. On Stoner, see Stacy B. C. Wood Jr. and Stephen E. Kramer, *Clockmakers of Lancaster County and Their Clocks, 1750–1850* (New York: Van Nostrand Reinhold, 1977), p. 29; Stacy B. C. Wood Jr., *Clockmakers and Watchmakers of Lancaster County, Pennsylvania* (Lancaster, Pa.: Lancaster County Historical Society, 1995), pp. 62–63; also Stacy B. C. Wood Jr., "Rudy Stoner, 1728–1769: Early Lancaster, Pennsylvania, Clockmaker," *Journal of the Lancaster County Historical Society* 80, no. 2 (1976): 112–27. Landis and Penn, "Juliana Library Company," pp. 49–50. Inventory of Rudolph Stoner, taken July 31, 1769, LancasterHistory.org, INV 1769 F012S.

21. On Heyne, see Donald M. Herr, *Pewter in Pennsylvania German Churches*, Publications of the Pennsylvania German Society, vol. 29 (Birdsboro, Pa.: Pennsylvania German Society, 1995), p. 132. Inventory of Johann Christoph Heyne ("Christoph Heiney"), taken January 30, 1781, LancasterHistory.org INV 1781 F003H.

22. There were also a Frederick Stein/Stone Sr. and Jr. in Lancaster at the same time; one of them served as a baptismal sponsor in 1733 and had a daughter named Maria Catharina, who was baptized in 1739 at Trinity Lutheran with Ludwig and Maria Catharina Stein acting as her baptismal sponsors. Frederick Jr. "from Langenbach near Weylbrug" married Magdalena Haefterich in 1759; they had a daughter, Christina and a son, Johann Heinrich, baptized in 1763 and 1767, respectively. Frederick Sr., died in 1752 at the age of eighty-three and was buried at Trinity Lutheran; see Smith and Weiser, *Trinity Lutheran Church Records,* 1: 9, 33, 190, 227, 255, 288. On Nyberg, see Glatfelter, *Pastors and People*, p. 101. Anna Maria Hambrecht/Hambright was the daughter of Johann Adam Hambrecht and Elisabeth Barbara Heyl of Lancaster. Will of Ludwig Stone, written June 7, 1782, proved October 5, 1782, Lancaster, Lancaster County, LancasterHistory.org, microfilm. Inventory of Ludwig Stone, taken November 4, 1782, LancasterHistory.org, INV 1782 F0265.

23. Ellis and Evans, *History of Lancaster County*, pp. 13–14, 213, 370, 373–74, 383, 396–97, 428, 906; Splitter, *Pastors, People, Politics*, p. 357. On the Conestoga Massacre, see Kevin Kenny, *Peaceable Kingdom Lost: The Paxton Boys and the Destruction of William Penn's Holy Experiment* (New York: Oxford University Press, 2009), pp. 130–39, *passim*. Häberlein, *Practice of Pluralism*, p. 70; Glatfelter, *Pastors and People*, p. 101. F. Edward Wright, *Lancaster County, Pennsylvania, Church Records of the 18th Century*, vol. 3 (Westminster, Md.: Family Line Publications, 1994), pp. 100, 103. Smith and Weiser, *Trinity Lutheran Church Records,* 2:27, 157, 344. Ibid., 3:193. Wood, *Conestoga Crossroads*, pp. 60, 64, 77.

24. On Forrer, see Wood and Kramer, *Clockmakers of Lancaster County*, p. 19. The name boss is engraved "Christian Forrer / Lampeter / 1750," but the date appears to be a later addition.

25. On the Ferrees, see Willis L. Shirk Jr., "Assimilating into the American Milieu: French Huguenots in Eighteenth-Century Lancaster County," *Journal of the Lancaster County Historical Society* 95, no. 3 (1993): 76–78; Ellis and Evans, *History of Lancaster County*, p. 995. Peter Ferree's farm was off Bachmantown Road in East Lampeter Township, Lancaster County. Inventory of Peter Ferree, 1795, no. 1795, LancasterHistory.org. Vendue of Peter Ferree, 1795/1798, no. 1798, LancasterHistory.org.

26. On Hoff, see Wood and Kramer, *Clockmakers of Lancaster County*, p. 22–23. Will of Elizabeth Shwahr, written December 19, 1809, proved June 17, 1819, Hempfield Township, Lancaster County, Wright, *Abstracts of Lancaster County, Pennsylvania, Wills, 1786–1820*, p. 233. On Elizabeth (Hiestand) Schwar, see Charles Fahs Kauffman, *A Genealogy and History of the Kauffman-Coffman Families of North America* (York, Pa.: the author, 1940), p. 121.

27. The Besore provenance was detailed when the clock sold at Horst Auctioneers, Ephrata, Pa., *Important Two Day Public Auction*, October 23–24, 1998, lot 782. Tombstone of Daniel Beshar, Salem Church Cemetery, Franklin County, Pa.; photo accessed on Findagrave.com. On Besore's/Salem Reformed Church, see Glatfelter, *Pastors and People*, p. 297. Will of Daniel Besore, written September 10, 1804, proved March 1, 1811; Franklin County will book B, p. 436. On the Besore certificate, see also Lisa Minardi, *Drawn with Spirit: Pennsylvania German Fraktur from the Joan and Victor Johnson Collection* (Philadelphia: Philadelphia Museum of Art, 2015), pp. 216–17, 329.

28. The Meyli attribution was made by Ed LaFond on the basis of the movement's close

relationship with one signed by Samuel Meyli. The clock with sulfur inlay outlining the plaques was sold at Pook & Pook, Downingtown, Pa., *Two Day Auction*, October 13–14, 1995, lot 474. The Graff clock with horizontal supports is in the collection of Winterthur Museum, acc. no. 1965.2261; for images, see Cooper and Minardi, *Paint, Pattern & People*, pp. 132, 254.

29. Will of John Kilheffer, written April 26, 1797, proved May 27, 1797, Manor Township, Lancaster County, Wright, *Abstracts of Lancaster County, Pennsylvania, Wills, 1786–1820*, pp. 113–14. H. Frank Eshleman, *Historic Background and Annals of the Swiss and German Pioneer Settlers of Southeastern Pennsylvania* (Lancaster, Pa.: n.p., 1917), p. 95. Strassburger and Hinke, *Pennsylvania German Pioneers*, 1:60–61.

30. Strassburger and Hinke, *Pennsylvania German Pioneers*, 1:464. A. S. Brendle, *A Brief History of Schaefferstown* (Schaefferstown, Pa.: Historic Schaefferstown Inc., 1979), p. 72. Frederick S. Weiser, ed., *Records of Pastoral Acts at Emanuel Lutheran Church, Known in the Eighteenth Century as the Warwick Congregation, near Brickerville, Elizabeth Township, Lancaster County, Pennsylvania, 1734–1799*, Sources and Documents of the Pennsylvania Germans, vol. 8 (Breinigsville, Pa.: Pennsylvania German Society, 1983), pp. 5, 20, 125. Glenn P. Schwalm and Frederick S. Weiser, trans. and eds., *Records of Pastoral Acts at Trinity Evangelical Lutheran Church, New Holland, Lancaster County, Pennsylvania, 1730–1799*, Sources and Documents of the Pennsylvania Germans, vol. 2 (Breinigsville, Pa.: Pennsylvania German Society, 1977), pp. 10, 22, 28, 42, 53, 195. On Jundt and his clock, see Cooper and Minardi, *Paint, Pattern & People*, p. 136–38. Will of Michael Oberlin, written May 17, 1787, proved October 23, 1788, Earl Township, Lancaster County; see Wright, *Abstracts of Lancaster County, Pennsylvania, Wills, 1786–1820*, p. 169.

31. John J. Snyder Jr., "The Bachman Attributions: A Reconsideration," *Antiques* 105, no. 5 (May 1974): 1063. Wood, *Conestoga Crossroads*, p. 124. Ellis and Evans, *History of Lancaster County*, p. 370.

32. Snyder, "Carved Chippendale Case Furniture," pp. 965, 968; John J. Snyder Jr., "New Discoveries in Documented Lancaster County Chippendale Furniture," *Antiques* 125, no. 5 (May 1984): 1153. On the Withers desk, see Cooper and Minardi, *Paint, Pattern & People*, pp. 103–5. *Pennsylvania German Church Records*, 1:85, 244, 246, 253, 257, 261, 280. Administrative accounts of George Burkhard, filed September 21, 1784, LancasterHistory.org, Ad Acct 1784 F007B; Ad Acct 1791 F001B.

33. Wright, *Abstracts of Lancaster County, Pennsylvania, Wills, 1786–1820*, p. 216. *Pennsylvania German Church Records*, 1:17, 24, 34, 56, 69. William Henry Egle, ed., *Notes and Queries, Historical and Genealogical, Chiefly Relating to Interior Pennsylvania*, vol. 2 (Harrisburg, Pa.: Harrisburg Publishing Company, 1896), pp. 452–53; Eleni Silverman, *Sehner-Ellicott House*, April 25, 1984, Historic American Buildings Survey no. PA-372, Library of Congress, Washington, D.C.

34. On the Linds, see Snyder, "Carved Chippendale Case Furniture," pp. 967–68. *Pennsylvania German Church Records*, 1:242, 246, 250, 252, 255, 257, 260, 264, 266. Häberlein, *Practice of Pluralism*, pp. 125, 205. Strassburger and Hinke, *Pennsylvania German Pioneers*, 1:496. Ludwig Stein's will includes significant bequests to his wife Catharine; stepson Ludwig Heck, a silversmith; and £100 each to three of his son Frederick's children (Frederick, Ludwig, and Catharine). A fourth grandchild, Susanna (Stone) Weiss, received one shilling. Ludwig then specified that Frederick's other children "shall be utterly excluded & debarred" from his estate. After Ludwig's death, the will was contested in a caveat filed by Frederick Stone on behalf of his excluded children. The three witnesses to the will testified as to its validity, and depositions on behalf of the estate were given by William Henry, Michael Lind, Rev. Henry Muhlenberg Jr., schoolmaster John Jacob Loeser, Daniel Newman, Joseph Walter, Peter Row, and Captain Anthony Selim. Those who testified on Frederick Stone's behalf were Michael Hubley Esq., Thomas Doyle, Andrew Graff, Margaret Shell, Ludwig Shell, George Hoff, Catharine DeHuff, Henry DeHuff, Barbara Haas, Conrad Haas, Elizabeth Lenhere (Lenkere?), Frederick Stone Jr., and Susanna Weiss. After nearly two months of hearings and depositions, the court ruled against Frederick Stone and deemed the will valid. See estate administration papers of Ludwig Stone, 1782, Lancaster, Lancaster County, Pa., LancasterHistory.org.

35. Smith and Weiser, *Trinity Lutheran Church Records*, 1:4. Snyder, "Carved Chippendale Case Furniture," p. 975.

36. On the Mertz attribution, see Jonathan L. Fairbanks and Elizabeth Bidwell Bates, *American Furniture: 1620 to the Present* (New York: Richard Marek Publishers, 1987), p. 320. On the Holl attributions, see Beatrice B. Garvan and Charles F. Hummel, *The Pennsylvania Germans: A Celebration of Their Arts, 1683-1850* (Philadelphia: Philadelphia Museum of Art, 1982), p. 30; also Beatrice B. Garvan, *The Pennsylvania German Collection* (Philadelphia: Philadelphia

Museum of Art, 1982), p. 359. With thanks to Clarke Hess for additional information on the Holl genealogy. Inventory of Peter Holl, taken December 2, 1825, Warwick Township, LancasterHistory.org, INV 1825 F018H.

37. Lichten, "A Masterpiece of Pennsylvania-German Furniture," pp. 176–78.

38. Garvan and Hummel, *Pennsylvania Germans*, p. 31; Garvan, *Pennsylvania German Collection*, p. 360. On the schrank's presumed line of descent in the Huber family, see ibid. Ellis and Evans, *History of Lancaster County*, p. 980. Donna R. Irish, comp., *Pennsylvania German Marriages: Marriages and Marriage Evidence in Pennsylvania German Churches* (Baltimore, Md.: Clearfield Publishing Co., 1982), p. 216. George Huber's brother Christian has been described as a miller and/or millstone cutter, but those were two different Christian Hubers. A second Christian Huber (1758–1818) succeeded his father, John Huber (1737–1803), as miller at Oberholtzer's mill. A third Christian Huber (d. 1820) was a millstone cutter and farmer who lived just north of Neffsville. Christian Oberholtzer named his son-in-law George Huber as his executor in his will; see will of Christian Oberholtzer, written July 18, 1785, proved August 7, 1789, Hempfield Township, Lancaster County, in Wright, *Abstracts of Lancaster County, Pennsylvania, Wills 1786–1820*, p. 169.

39. The letter by Spangler is in the files of the National Museum of American History, Smithsonian Institution, acc. no. 76–14370, acc. no. 322631. It accompanied the chest when it was acquired by the Smithsonian at Pennypacker Auction Centre, *Rare American Folk Art from the Private Collection of Mr. & Mrs. Paul R. Flack*, Reading, Pa., April 12, 1976, lot 168. Daniel W. Dietrich is named in the will of his father, George S. Dietrich, Earl Township, Lancaster County; see will book G, vol. 2, p. 239; LancasterHistory.org. George S. Dietrich's first wife was Rachel Bowers (1809–1829). Some sources identify Elizabeth Stager's parents as John and Sarah (Levengood) Stager but this has yet to be proven.

40. Will of Jacob Kauffman, written March 3, 1807, proved July 31, 1812, Manor Township, Lancaster County, Pa.; in Wright, *Abstracts of Lancaster County, Pennsylvania, Wills, 1786–1820*, p. 121. Kauffman, *Kauffman-Coffman Families*, p. 121.

41. Barbara Lang/Long is named as the wife of Charles Rudy in her father's will; see will of John Long, written February 16, 1814, proved May 24, 1817, Manheim Township, in Wright, *Abstracts of Lancaster County, Pennsylvania, Wills 1786–1820*, p. 136. A third granddaughter named Barbara Lang lived from 1768–1849; she was the daughter of Joseph Lang but her parents moved to Maryland before 1774, so she is not a viable candidate as the original owner of the chest. On the Lang chest, see also Garvan, *Pennsylvania German Collection*, p. 362. On Peter Summy, see *Biographical Annals of Lancaster County, Pennsylvania* (Chicago: J. H. Beers, 1903), p. 657.

42. Ellis and Evans, *History of Lancaster County*, p. 980. Kauffman, *Kauffman-Coffman Family*, pp. 332, 364–65.

43. *Pennsylvania German Church Records*, 1:246. Strassburger and Hinke, *Pennsylvania German Pioneers*, 1:355. Ellis and Evans, *History of Lancaster County*, 981. Gary T. Hawbaker and Clyde L. Groff, *Lancaster County, Pennsylvania, before the Federal Census: An Index to the 1780 Tax Records*, 5 vols. (Hershey, Pa.: Gary T. Hawbaker, 1981–1989), 1:37.

44. The 1784/HN chest was advertised by Scott Tyson in *Antique Collecting* (December 1978): 45.

45. On the 1790/IO SC clock, see also Cooper and Minardi, *Paint, Pattern & People*, p. 84.

46. Another straightedge with the sulfur–inlaid inscription "18 LH 05" is also known, but the inlay is of recent manufacture. On the 1800 straightedge, see also Cooper and Minardi, *Paint, Pattern & People*, p. 85. Kelker, *Baptismal and Marriage Records, Rev. John Waldschmidt*, p. 36. The Cadarina Moser chest was offered for sale by L. J. Gilbert's, Lebanon, Pa., *Eighth Annual Spring Sale*, May 23–26, 1927.

47. On the Bamberger-Kauffman family, see Hess, *Mennonite Arts*, pp. 32–37.

48. Don Yoder, ed., "From Paoli to Frederick in 1854: An Anonymous Travel Account," *Pennsylvania Folklife* 17, no. 3 (Spring 1968): 17. On the Mumma schrank, see also Hess, *Mennonite Arts*, p. 36.

49. The 1770 / AS cradle was found in the attic of a house in Lebanon, Pennsylvania; with thanks to Clarke Hess for this information. Tappert and Doberstein, *The Journals of Henry Melchior Muhlenberg*, 3:519.

50. Strassburger and Hinke, *Pennsylvania German Pioneers*, 1:484. *Records of Rev. John Casper Stoever, Baptismal and Marriage, 1730–1779* (Harrisburg, Pa.: Harrisburg Publishing Co., 1896), p. 67. Glatfelter, *Pastors and People*, pp. 319–20.

51. Wright, *Abstracts of Lancaster County, Pennsylvania, Wills, 1786–1820*, pp. 213, 224.

52. On the Leys and the schrank, see also Cooper and Minardi, *Paint, Pattern & People*, pp. 181–83. According to notations made by former owners and pasted inside the doors of the schrank, it remained in the house until 1834, when the property was bought by Conrad Loose, who gave it to his son Isaac, a resident of Bethlehem, Pa. Isaac's granddaughter bought the schrank at his estate sale for 75 cents; she died in 1970 and the schrank was again sold but then returned to the house until being sold again in the 1990s; see also Mike Schropp, "Lebanon County Antiques: A History of the County as Seen through Its Artifacts," *Lebanon Daily News*, Apr. 1, 1970. On the Ley house, see also P. C. Croll, *Ancient and Historic Landmarks in the Lebanon Valley* (Philadelphia: Lutheran Publication Society, 1895), pp. 173–76.

53. On Myerstown, see Diane E. Wenger, *A Country Storekeeper in Pennsylvania: Creating Economic Networks in Early America, 1790–1807* (University Park: Pennsylvania State University Press, 2008), p. 18. Rayner Wickersham Kelsey, ed., *Cazenove Journal 1794: A Record of the Journey of Theophile Cazenove through New Jersey and Pennsylvania (Translated from the French)* (Haverford, Pa.: Pennsylvania History Press, 1922), p. 45.

54. Frederick S. Weiser, *Records of Pastoral Acts at Christ Lutheran Church, Stouchsburg, Berks County, Pennsylvania*, 2 vols., Sources and Documents of the Pennsylvania Germans, vols. 12–13 (Birdsboro, Pa.: Pennsylvania German Society, 1989–1990), 1:6. Theodore E. Schmauk, *Old Salem in Lebanon: A History of the Congregation and Town* (Lebanon, Pa.: 1898), pp. 118–19, 125–28, 134–39; see also Lila L. Lebo, *Reflections about Salem Lutheran Church, Lebanon, Pennsylvania* (Lebanon, Pa.: Salem Evangelical Lutheran Church, 2009), pp. 2, 78; and Glatfelter, *Pastors and People*, p. 334. Strassburger and Hinke, *Pennsylvania German Pioneers*, 1:60. See also Uhler Genealogy, Salem Lutheran Church Archives, Lebanon, Pa. With thanks to Lila Lebo for this information. Christoph Uhler will and inventory, 1804, U-1, 13,569, Dauphin County Courthouse. Federal Direct Tax of 1798, Lebanon Township, Dauphin County, in Gladys Bucher Sowers, *Lebanon County, Pennsylvania: United States Direct Tax of 1798 for Bethel Township, East Hanover Township, Heidelberg Township, Lebanon Township, and Londonderry Township* (Bowie, Md.: Heritage Books, 2004), p. 135. Gladys Bucher Sowers, *Colonial Taxes, Lebanon Township, Lancaster County, Pennsylvania, 1750–1783* (Morgantown, Pa.: Masthoff Press, 2004), pp. 54, 76, 275, 309.

55. The Hh/1766 clock was sold at Christie's East, New York, *Property from the Violette de Mazia Collection*, April 26, 1989, lot 305. On Sturgis, see Sowers, *Colonial Taxes, Lebanon Township*, pp. 83, 87, 97, 110, 143, 154, 169, 199, 214, 231, 250, 280; also Abraham Reincke, *A Register of Members of the Moravian Church, and of Persons Attached to Said Church, in This Country and Abroad, Between 1727 and 1754* (Nazareth, Pa.: n.p., 1873), p. 258.

56. Strassburger and Hinke, *Pennsylvania German Pioneers*, 1:116. Wright, *Abstracts of Lancaster County, Pennsylvania, Wills, 1732–1785*, p. 242. On Abraham Witmer, see *Biographical Annals of Lancaster County*, pp. 1463–64; Hawbaker and Groff, *Lancaster County, Pennsylvania, before the Federal Census: Index to the 1780 Tax Records*, 2:83. On Michael Horst, see *Biographical Annals of Lancaster County*, 517.

57. On Heinselman, see Wood, *Clockmakers and Watchmakers of Lancaster County*, 43.

58. Strassburger and Hinke, *Pennsylvania German Pioneers*, 1:263.

59. On Schneider, see Hess, *Mennonite Arts*, 28.

60. On John Menig/Minnich, see Hawbaker and Groff, *Lancaster County, Pennsylvania, before the Federal Census: Index to the 1770 Tax Records*, 5: 127; Will of John Minnig, written March 4, 1794, proved June 10, 1813, Rapho Township, Lancaster County, in Wright, *Abstracts of Lancaster County, Pennsylvania, Wills 1786–1820*, p. 156. In 1785 a John Minnich signed a petition for the creation of Dauphin County; see Luther Reily Kelker, *History of Dauphin County, Pennsylvania*, vol. 1 (New York: Lewis Publishing Co., 1907), p. 69.

61. For images of a *Brettstuhl* with pierced heart and a bed with pillow panels, see Cooper and Minardi, *Paint, Pattern & People*, pp. 7, 44, 154. Alan G. Keyser, Larry M. Neff, and Frederick S. Weiser, trans. and eds., *The Accounts of Two Pennsylvania German Furniture Makers: Abraham Overholt, Bucks County, 1790–1833, and Peter Ranck, Lebanon County, 1794–1817*, Sources and Documents of the Pennsylvania Germans, vol. 3 (Breinigsville, Pa.: Pennsylvania German Society, 1978), pp. 11–12.

62. Johann David Schoepf, *Travels in the Confederation [1783–1784]*, trans. and ed. by Alfred J. Morrison, 2 vols. (Philadelphia: William J. Campbell, 1911), 1:203. On painted furniture and fraktur from the Tulpehocken Valley, see Lisa Minardi, "From Millbach to Mahantongo: Fraktur and Furniture of the Pennsylvania Germans," *American Furniture*, edited by Luke Beckerdite (Hanover, NH: University Press of New England for the Chipstone Foundation, 2011), pp. 2–77.

63. Strassburger and Hinke, *Pennsylvania German Pioneers*, 1:21. Frederick S. Weiser, trans., *The Account Book of Christ Lutheran Church, Stouchsburg, Berks County, Pennsylvania, 1747–1809* (Camden, Me.: Picton Press, 1997), pp. 2, 4, 7, 9–10, 12–15, 18, 19, 22, 24, 37, 55.

64. On the inside of the Margaret Illig chest is a pencil inscription: "Remodelt 1857 by Benjamin Hook." For an image, see Fabian, *Pennsylvania-German Decorated Chest*, p. 162, fig. 152. On the Illigs, see *Biographical Annals of Lebanon County, Pennsylvania* (Chicago: J. H. Beers, 1904), pp. 33–34. Christopher Rieth was the son of Valentin and Eva Rieth; see "Rieth [Reed] Genealogy," *The Pennsylvania-German* 5, no. 2 (April 1904): 91. Weiser, *Records of Pastoral Acts at Christ Lutheran Church*, 1:1, 34, 36, 43, 51–52, 55, 66; 2:75. Weiser, *Account Book of Christ Lutheran Church*, pp. 4, 13, 24. Will of Andreas Illig, written March 13, 1758, proved 1761, Heidelberg Township, Lancaster County; see Wright, *Abstracts of Lancaster County, Pennsylvania, Wills, 1732–1785*, p. 58. Sowers, *Lebanon County, Pennsylvania, United States Direct Tax of 1798*, p. 65. For an image of an inlaid clock that descended in the Illig family, see Minardi, "From Millbach to Mahantongo," p. 25. On the Illig stove plates, see Henry C. Mercer, *The Bible in Iron: Pictured Stoves and Stoveplates of the Pennsylvania Germans*, Rev. ed. (Doylestown, Pa.: Bucks County Historical Society, 1961), p. 182.

65. Weiser, *Christ Lutheran Church*, 1:85, 90, 95, 119; 2:65. Sowers, *Lebanon County, Pennsylvania, U.S. Direct Tax of 1798*, p. 56. Will of Samuel Betz, written May 17, 1828, proved May 26, 1828, Heidelberg Township, Lebanon County, will book B, pp. 1–4.

66. The door lintel is in the collection of the State Museum of Pennsylvania, acc. no. 35.9. It came from a house owned by Dr. Charles Baum at 128 Main Street in Middletown, Dauphin County, Pa.

67. Strassburger and Hinke, *Pennsylvania German Pioneers*, 1:323. Will of Martin Brandt, written July 15, 1809, proved September 12, 1809, Derry Township, Dauphin County, will book C, pp. 132–34; FamilySearch.org. Inventory of Martin Brandt, taken October 23, 1809, Dauphin County Courthouse, Register of Wills, reel B. Will of Ludwig Brandt, written July 26, 1822, proved September 12, 1829, Reading Township, Perry County, OH, will book 2, p. 32; FamilySearch.org.

68. The Elisabeth Landis chest was advertised by Arthur J. Sussel in *Antiques* 56, no. 3 (September 1949): 154. William H. Egle, *History of the County of Lebanon in the Commonwealth of Pennsylvania* (Philadelphia: Everts and Peck, 1883), p. 217.

69. Strassburger and Hinke, *Pennsylvania German Pioneers*, 1:300–303. Jacob Brua also had a daughter named Elisabeth (1749–1790), but she was married in 1771 to Henry Kinser and thus in 1776 her surname was no longer Brua. Lynn Austin Brua, *The Brua Family and Bruaw, Bruah, Brewer* (United Kingdom: the author, 1996), pp. 11–15. Will of Peter Brua, written May 14, 1804, proved October 31, 1808, Tulpehocken Township, Berks County; Berks County will book 5, pp. 91–93; FamilySearch.org. Weiser, *Records of Pastoral Acts at Christ Lutheran Church*, 1:28, 31, 36, 39; 2:142. Frederick S. Weiser, *Records of Pastoral Acts at Zion Lutheran Church, Harrisburg, Pennsylvania, 1795–1827*, Sources and Documents of the Pennsylvania Germans, vol. 11 (Birdsboro, Pa.: Pennsylvania German Society, 1987), pp. 3, 10, 13, 16, 33, 41,50. William H. Egle, *History of the County of Dauphin in the Commonwealth of Pennsylvania* (Philadelphia: Everts and Peck, 1883), pp. 469–70.

70. At least one other piece of furniture made of sycamore is known, a hanging cupboard made about 1775 for Isaac and Susanna (Kauffman) Long of Manheim Township, Lancaster County. For an illustration, see Hess, *Mennonite Arts*, p. 37. Kelker, *History of Dauphin County*, pp. 66, 694. F. Edward Wright, *Early Church Records of Lebanon County, Pennsylvania* (Lewes, Del.: Colonial Roots, 2003), p. 75.

71. Willis Miller Kemper, ed., *Genealogy of the Fischback Family in America* (New York: Thomas Madison Taylor, 1914), p. 70. Will of Philip Fischburn, dated January 23, 1790, proved February 28, 1795, Dauphin County Courthouse, Register of Wills, will reel F-1. Inventory of Philip Fischburn, taken March 23, 1795, Dauphin County Courthouse, Register of Wills, inventories reel F-1. Will of Ludwig Fischburn, dated May 9, 1845, proved April 9, 1846, Dauphin County Courthouse, Register of Wills, will reel F-8.

72. Max E. Klinger, *The Descendants of Johann Peter Klinger and Catharina Steinbruch* (Mechanicsburg, Pa.: Sunbury Press, 2005), p. 4. Sowers, *Colonial Taxes, Lebanon Township*, p. 292. On Baum, see Kelker, *History of Dauphin County*, pp. 383–84; Egle, *Notes and Queries*, pp. 24–25, 88. Adam Baum of Derry married Veronica Gingerich on July 5, 1752; see *Records of Rev. John Casper Stoever*, p. 63.

73. Henry Snyder Alleman, *A Genealogy of the Allemans in the United States Who Are the*

Offspring of John Christian Alleman and John Frederick Christian Alleman (Harrisburg, Pa.: Mount Pleasant Press, 1954), p. 18. Another Margaret Alleman married Frederick Conrad at Zion Lutheran Church in 1799, but she was born in about 1780 and is thus too young to be the probable owner of the chest; see Weiser, *Records of Pastoral Acts at Zion Lutheran Church, Harrisburg*, pp. 1, 9, 14, 73.

74. On York, see Carl Bridenbaugh, *The Colonial Craftsman* (New York: New York University, 1950), p. 56. Schoepf, *Travels in the Confederation*, 2:20. A copy of the contract is in the John Fisher file, no. 16800, York County Heritage Trust. On Fisher, see also Cooper and Minardi, *Paint, Pattern & People*, pp. 174–8.

75. Jan Bankert, *Digges Choice, 1724–1800* (Camden, Me.: Picton Press, 1996).

76. William J. Hinke and Frederick S. Weiser, *Records of Pastoral Acts at the Lutheran and Reformed Congregations of the Muddy Creek Church, East Cocalico Township, Lancaster County, Pennsylvania, 1730–1790*, Sources and Documents of the Pennsylvania Germans, vol. 5 (Breinigsville, Pa.: Pennsylvania German Society, 1981), p. 35. Frederick S. Weiser, "*The Lutheran Church on the Conewago at Hanovertown:*" *A History of Saint Matthew Evangelical Lutheran Church, Hanover, Pennsylvania, 1735–1810* (Hanover, Pa.: St. Matthew Evangelical Lutheran Church, 1993), pp. 9, 17, 42. Larry M. Neff and Frederick S. Weiser, trans. and ed., *Friedrich Heinrich Gelwicks, Shoemaker and Distiller: Accounts, 1760–1783*. Sources and Documents of the Pennsylvania Germans, vol. 4 (Breinigsville, Pa.: Pennsylvania German Society, 1979), pp. vii–xiii, 122. Frederick S. Weiser, trans., *Records of St. Matthew's Evangelical Lutheran Church of Hanover, Pennsylvania, 1741–1831* (Camden, Me.: Picton Press, 1994), pp. 20, 59, 169. On the Gelwicks fraktur, see also Minardi, *Drawn with Spirit*, pp. 60, 283.

77. The pewter mug is in the collection of Winterthur Museum, acc. no. 1967.1369; for an image, see Lisa Minardi, *A Colorful Folk: Pennsylvania Germans & the Art of Everyday Life* (Winterthur, Del.: Henry Francis du Pont Winterthur Museum, 2015) p. 55. Will of Frederick Gelwicks, written March 20, 1783, proved April 15, 1783, York County will book vol. f, pp. 115–7. Gelwicks file, York County Heritage Trust, York, Pa. George R. Prowell, *History of York County, Pennsylvania*, vol. 1 (Chicago: J.H. Beers, 1907), pp. 146, 279, 574.

78. Reinacker and Carl Genealogical Files, York County Heritage Trust. Letter from John J. Snyder Jr. to Chris Machmer, January 23, 1990, private collection. Will of Casper Renaker/Reinecker, written November 13, 1789, proved August 30, 1790, York County will book, vol. H, pp. 159–62.

79. Weiser, "*The Lutheran Church on the Conewago at Hanovertown,*" pp. 14, 18. Neff and Weiser, *Friedrich Heinrich Gelwicks*, pp. 62–63.

80. Glatfelter, *Pastors and People*, pp. 181–2, 184–5, 227. St. John's was reported to have sulfur-inlaid tombstones by Frederick S. Weiser, but none was observed there by Brenda Hornsby-Heindl on a visit in 2009.

81. Frederick S. Weiser, trans. and ed., *Maryland German Church Records*, vol. 7, *St. Mary's Church* (Westminster, Md.: Historical Society of Carroll County, 1987), pp. v, 7–11, 13–14, 100. St. Mary's was also noted for the tinned sheet iron flowers that adorned the sounding board of the pulpit, see Frederick S. Weiser, "Die Blumme of Saint Mary's," *Der Reggeboge: Journal of the Pennsylvania German Society* 9, no. 1 (March 1975): 15–21.

82. Strassburger and Hinke, *Pennsylvania German Pioneers*, 1:419. Will of Peter Imswiller, written October 26, 1769, proved November 21, 1772, Windsor Township, York County, in F. Edward Wright, *Abstracts of York County, Pennsylvania, Wills, 1749–1819* (Westminster, Md.: Heritage Books, 2009), p. 38.

83. Will of Bartholomew Zell, proved August 14, 1779, York County, in Wright, *Abstracts of York County, Pennsylvania, Wills*, p. 62. Will of Abraham Sell, written March 8, 1786, proved July 26, 1786, Germany Township, York County, in *Abstracts of York County, Pennsylvania, Wills*, p. 99. See also Kenneth D. Sell, *The Sell Families of Adams and York Counties, Pennsylvania, and Carroll County, Maryland, 1685–1995* (Camden, Me.: Penobscot Press, 1998). Weiser, *Saint Mary's Church*, p. 100.

84. Strassburger and Hinke, *Pennsylvania German Pioneers*, 1:48–49. Prowell, *History of York County*, 144. Will of Erasmus Holsable (Holtzappel), written December 6, 1792, proved December 10, 1793, Manchester Township, York County, in Wright, *Abstracts of York County, Pennsylvania, Wills*, p. 142. *The History of Tuscarawas County, Ohio* (Chicago: Warner, Beers, and Co., 1884), p. 496.

85. The 1766 inlaid clock was sold at Christie's East, New York, *The Emma Reichard Collection of American Furniture and Folk Art*, January 19, 1988, lot 365. A tall clock with white painted

dial signed by Henry Wismer of Bucks County has a double-headed eagle inlaid in the tympanum; it is in the collection of the Mercer Museum in Doylestown, Pa. A fraktur with double-headed eagle was drawn circa 1785 by Mennonite schoolmaster Andreas Kolb of Montgomery County, Pa.; it is in the collection of Winterthur Museum, acc. no. 2013.31.71; for an image, see Minardi, *A Colorful Folk*, p. 50.

86. Wright, *Abstracts of Lancaster County, Pennsylvania, Wills, 1786–1820*, p. 146.

87. Fabian, "Sulfur Inlay," p. 5. Findagrave.com; Mrs. Harry Pennington, *History of the Switzer Family* (n.p., 1938). Wright, *Early Church Records of Lebanon County*, p. 34, 36.

88. The kitchen cupboard was sold, without any provenance, at Pennypacker Auction Centre, Reading, Pa., *Pennsylvania Dutch Folk Art: The Outstanding Collection of Lamb's Mill for the Estate of John (Jack) W. Lamb*, September 11–12, 1972, lot 698. Sowers, *Colonial Taxes, Lebanon Township*, pp. 1, 6, 8, 11, 14, 19, 22, 25, 28, 31. Egle, *History of Lebanon County*, p. 172. Will of Adam Brandt, Bethel Township, Dauphin (now Lebanon) County, written April 6, 1799, proved January 5, 1804, Dauphin County Courthouse, Register of Wills, will book b, p. 197.

89. Garvan, *Pennsylvania German Collection*, p. 28. The "B R" hanging cupboard was sold by Conestoga Auction Company, Manheim, Pa., *Collection of Barbara Breininger and the Late Lester Breininger*, October 3, 2015.

Book Reviews

Christopher Long. *Kem Weber: Designer and Architect*. New Haven and London: Yale University Press, 2014. ix + 293 pp.; 96 color and 205 bw illus., list of projects, bibliography, index. $65.00.

Kem Weber (1889–1963) is widely recognized as one of the leading figures in American modern design in the first half of the twentieth century. An architect, designer, and teacher, Weber was perhaps the most outspoken and passionate advocate for modernism on the West Coast between the two world wars. His early adoption of streamlining and designing for mass production marked him as an innovator in the field and earned him a national reputation during his lifetime.

Today, Kem Weber's name is regularly cited by curators and collectors to represent early modern design in California, and his precariously cantilevered wooden Air Line Chair of 1935, arguably his most iconic design, is displayed in at least a dozen museums across the country as the quintessential expression of the American streamlined aesthetic. But that is only part of the Kem Weber story.

In *Kem Weber: Designer and Architect*, Christopher Long reveals a much more complex and intriguing narrative of Weber's life and career. We learn that, despite the respect and praise Weber received from critics and his peers, Weber's zealous, at times obsessive, quest to develop an American modernist style was fraught with obstacles and failures. Although some of these impediments were self-imposed and others were beyond Weber's control, Long clearly demonstrates how all the hurdles placed in the designer's path played a key role in shaping his career, and, most important, his designs.

The impact of this enlightening monograph on Weber is reminiscent of Long's previous study entitled *Paul T. Frankl and American Modern Design* (New Haven and London: Yale University Press, 2007), a detailed look at Weber's contemporary and friend. Much of what was written about the Frankl volume rings true for this book on Weber. Surprisingly little in-depth scholarly attention had previously been devoted to either man, despite their extensive name recognition. For Weber, the only earlier publication dedicated to his work is *Kem Weber: The Moderne in Southern California, 1920 through 1941* (Santa Barbara, Calif.: Printed by Standard Print, 1969), a hard-to-find small exhibition catalogue written by David Gebhard and Harriette Von Breton for the Art Galleries of the University of California, Santa Barbara. Both of Long's comprehensive studies fill major gaps in the field. In each, he strives to address a wide audience by using an engaging narrative style to tell a personal biography at the same time as a larger story about American modern design. As with his monograph on Frankl, Long recounts Weber's life chronologically, offering contextualizing information to fill out the story along the way.

One notable difference between the two studies, however, is the deep familiarity with which Long is able to depict Weber's life. This intimacy stems from a treasure trove of personal correspondence and family photographs Long discovered that was still in the hands of Weber's youngest daughter, Erika Plack, living in Santa Barbara. This personal archive, in combination with Long's extensive research into archival collections and period publications, allowed him to provide a much richer and more nuanced understanding of the designer's life and career than he had been able to do with Frankl. One of the wonderful qualities of this book is Long's ability to share Weber's own thoughts on his work, fellow designers, supervisors, and clients. Long's description of the sometimes cantankerous relationships within California modernism circles and their inability to work together to advance their cause is intriguing and begs further study.

Most important, Weber's personal correspondence documents his (many) disappointments and failures. Although it is sometimes depressing to read about Weber's constant frustration and rejection, they make his persistence and successes all the more impressive. Weber's struggles poignantly illustrate the slow and difficult introduction of modern design into American culture and which events and people helped to turn the tide.

From the beginning, Long establishes Weber's mercurial personality and restless nature. Born Karl Emmanuel Martin Weber to middle-class parents in Berlin, Kem (a nickname taken from the first letter of his first three names) was a rebellious and unhappy child despite being raised in a comfortable home and supportive family. After a three-year apprenticeship with a traditional cabinetmaker, Weber pursued a degree in design at Berlin's School of the Royal Arts and Crafts Museum under Bruno Paul, its radical new director. Long's thorough knowledge of European design history is evident as he deftly describes Weber's training under Paul and contemporaneous trends in avant-garde design in Germany, such as the rise of industrial design.

Weber's work for Paul's personal studio sent him to the United States in June 1914 to supervise the installation of the German exhibitions for the 1915 Panama-Pacific International Exposition in San Francisco. This trip would change the course of his life. With the outbreak of war in Europe, Weber was stranded in this country and had to fend for himself in a foreign culture increasingly hostile to Germans. As Long recounts, Weber befriended other Germans and found work wherever he could. He opened an art studio, designed theater sets and party decorations, worked as a farmer and a lumberjack—anything to survive. The bright light in his life during these years was his marriage to fellow German immigrant Erika Forke.

After the war, Weber and his new wife decided to stay in the United States and moved to Santa Barbara to pursue his dream of opening a modern design studio. Weber's enthusiasm was soon met with disappointment, as he found few clients interested in modern design—a trend that continued for many years. To earn a living and support his rapidly growing family, Weber designed furnishings in the popular historic-revival styles but never found satisfaction in his work. He joined California's leading furniture store, Barker Brothers, in 1921. Yet his attempts to introduce modern design were rebuffed time and again. To temper the constant strain of Weber's discontent and to contextualize Weber's experience, Long introduces Weber's contemporaries working in modern styles in the Los Angeles area. Weber mingled with Rudolf Schindler, Frank Lloyd Wright, Richard Neutra, and others, allowing Long to offer an insightful look into the early years of West Coast modernism. The tantalizing glimpses Weber's correspondence provides into the complicated, and sometimes rancorous, relationships of the California moderns leave one wishing that topic was fleshed out more.

Weber's first big break came in the summer of 1925, when positive reactions to European modern designs at the Paris world's fair prompted Barker Brothers to finally give Weber a chance. Weber opened his highly influential Modes and Manners division in Barker Brothers in August 1926, featuring modern designs primarily of his own creation, supplemented with works by Frankl and others. His designs at the time followed French and German trends with busy patterns and angular shapes. Weber's dreams were coming true—his designs and efforts to introduce modernism were getting national attention.

However, even when things were going well, Weber's relentless ambition kept him striving for more, sometimes sabotaging his own progress. In 1927, just as the Modes and Manners shop was taking off, Weber left Barker Brothers to open his own studio again. As Long notes: "restlessness rather than constancy would become a defining hallmark of his production" (p. 64). At first, Weber flourished—the recognition he had achieved at Barker's led to new commercial commissions in Grand Rapids and New York, many interiors, and even some entire architectural projects. He was not only included but given prime space (over Frankl and other New York designers) and consistently wowed the critics at prominent modern design exhibitions on the East Coast. Weber hired assistants and expanded his shop. It was during this time, Long explains, that Weber starts transitioning his style toward streamlining, creating ever more spare designs that focused on geometries.

Then the stock market crashed. If you only read the critical reviews about Weber's work during the early 1930s, you would think Weber survived the Depression reasonably well. However, Long's access to his personal correspondence proves otherwise. The Depression hit Weber, and the entire modern design community, hard. His practice shifted from commissions to speculative endeavors, and he spent an enormous amount of time on the road, trying to convince manufacturers to produce his ideas. It was during this time that he produced one of his most innovative designs—the Bentlock line manufactured by Higgins Furniture. These inexpensive, practical home furnishings were designed for easy mass production and combined a constructivist and streamlined aesthetic. However, though critically acclaimed, sales were poor. He supplemented his income by developing a course on industrial design at the Art Center School in Los Angeles and serving as a set designer for Paramount Studios, before he reluctantly returned to Barker Brothers to redecorate their interiors and launch a new line of more conservative modernized classical furniture called Tempo.

Work picked up in the middle of the decade, as more manufacturers hired industrial designers to design for machine production. Two of Weber's most famous mass-produced designs were developed in this period: a line of curving tubular steel furniture for Lloyd Manufacturing Company, and his innovative wooden Air Line Chair. Made with bow construction to support a cantilevered, streamlined silhouette, the Air Line Chair could be broken down, shipped flat, and easily assembled by the buyer, like IKEA furniture of today. After unsuccessfully pitching the design to many firms, Weber attempted to manufacture the chairs on his own. Despite their innovation, only several hundred were ever produced.

During this productive period in the middle of the decade, Weber received his most ambitious commission: the deluxe modern interiors for insurance executive Walter E. Bixby Sr., of Kansas City. With a healthy budget and an open-minded client who gave him free rein, Weber created a sophisticated, yet casual interior using curvilinear spaces and designs, lively colors, and new materials, such as aluminum and cork paneling. Long proclaims that "Weber's work [at the Bixby House] stands as a triumph—one of the last great ones before the coming war—of the ambitions of American designers of that era to harness all of what seemed to be modern and to do so in a manner that was distinctive" (p. 179). To many, the Bixby House was the peak of Weber's career.

The economic recession of 1937 resulted in fewer commissions. His work on developing the new Disney campus in Burbank got him through, but Walt Disney's micromanagement and strict attention to efficiency resulted in a moderated version of modernism. At the outbreak of World War II, Weber attempted to harness the war effort to promote modern design by developing a prefabricated housing system to address government defense housing needs. Despite initial interest in his idea and months of discussions, no firms were ultimately willing to take the risk.

After World War II, Weber was tired. Though his creative energy had not failed him, he no longer pushed as hard as he had done for the previous thirty-five years. After 1948 most of his work was single-family houses in Southern California—less ambitious, but more secure. Long illustrates how, during these postwar years, Weber experimented with numerous styles, eventually settling into more angular and fragmented shapes with textured, layered surfaces. His most important work in this final decade was the studio and house that he built for himself. Perched on a rocky, wooded hillside, these two buildings reveal what Long calls "a new modernism—aggregate and complex" (p. 237). Somewhat reminiscent of Russel Wright's Manitoga, the Mission Canyon studio and Tunnel Road house have an organic and warm feel. Weber was now rebelling against standardization and striving to create a more personal version of modernism.

Throughout the book, Long reminds us that there were many interpretations of modernism and that Weber's own style was constantly changing. Much of this change was prompted, or even forced, by real-world issues: economic crisis, wartime needs or restrictions, and personal life experiences. Long's access to Weber's own voice through his personal correspondence allows for a much deeper understanding of these practical matters. This depth of information sometimes made the chronology hard to follow, and, at times, the author may have provided too much detail (at one point I felt that I was reading an annoying post on Facebook when I learned Weber ate rubbery chicken for dinner). However, these minor quibbles do not detract from the importance of this publication. Long admirably weaves together a personalized view into the early years of modern design in the United States. Attractively organized and lavishly illustrated, the book greatly enriches our understanding of both Kem Weber and American modern design.

Nonie Gadsden
Museum of Fine Arts, Boston

Jean M. Burks and Philip Zea, eds. *Rich and Tasty: Vermont Furniture to 1850*. Shelburne, Vt.: Shelburne Museum, 2015. 180 pp.; numerous color illus., bibliography. $29.95 pb.

Vermont, like much of northern New England, labors under something of an identity crisis. Earnest Vermonters (like Mainers and New Hampshirites) tell themselves that theirs is a land of stern and stolid Yankees eking a spare existence from a rocky landscape within a marginal economy. What they tell outsiders is that their homeland is a cosmopolitan, four-season playground of the rich and famous. Nowhere is this existential dichotomy more deeply ingrained or more naturally acculturated into a successful, symbiotic ecosystem than in Vermont.

Born of a colonial turf war between New Hampshire and New York, with periodic incursions from Massachusetts and Quebec, Vermont relishes its otherness, treasures its history as an independent republic after the Revolution, and is quite content with its pick-and-choose, neither-nor cultural identity. Just a quick flip through the lushly illustrated pages of *Rich and Tasty: Vermont Furniture to 1850* demonstrates empirically that Vermont's forthrightly chameleon self-identification and self-expression have ever been thus.

The title of the exhibition and catalogue is taken from a newspaper advertisement by cabinetmaker Hastings Kendrick in the Burlington *Vermont Gazette* for June 2, 1829, announcing his intent "to manufacture a variety of rich and tasty FURNITURE from the best materials and in the best manner" (p. 11). A search of the newspaper archive of genealogybank.com reveals more than 260 instances of the phrase "rich and tasty" in advertisements before 1850. The earliest cited use of the phrase comes from a *New York Evening Post* translation from a Paris paper of September 10, 1820, of a report of a prize awarded to French carpet manufacturer Mr. Chenavard, who was "particularly celebrated for his rich and tasty paper and stuff hangings." This account was quickly reprinted in Philadelphia, Washington, D.C., Albany, and, undoubtedly, throughout America. The phrase was picked up by Boston upholsterer William Hancock, who advertised "French Curtain Bands, an uncommon, rich and tasty article, designed for window curtains, for French beds, &c." Hancock's ads appeared in papers from Boston to Keene, New Hampshire, to Bellows Falls, Vermont, so it is no wonder that the term crept into local parlance (p. 25) in Vermont.[1]

Shelburne Museum Director Thomas Denenberg states in the foreword that the Green Mountain State is "the perfect microcosm for studying the creolization of furniture, the creation of a communal aesthetic that is unique, yet made up of influences from near and far" (p. 9). The essays and seventy-four catalogue entries that follow help to define that communal aesthetic and describe elements of the microcosm that created it.

In an essay coyly entitled "A Primer for Light Grade Amber and Pure Vermont Furniture," a reference to the state's famous maple syrup, Philip Zea lays out a rubric for the connoisseurship of furniture, citing design, precedent, materials, craftsmanship, workmanship, ornamentation, innovation, technology, rarity, originality, condition, and provenance as the twelve standards by which to evaluate any object, and he applies each criterion in turn to Vermont furniture illustrated in the catalogue. Like the objects and artisans it describes, Zea's essay is peculiar and refreshing in the way it addresses a philosophical and academic thesis in an accessible, conversational manner. Like everything about this publication, it is both disarming and delightful.

This is followed by Jean M. Burks's essay documenting the lives and work of two Vermont cabinetmakers: Zachariah Harwood of Rupert and John Marshall of nearby Royalton. Typical of cabinetmakers outside major urban markets, Harwood and Marshall each had alternative occupations to supplement their income from cabinetwork. Harwood's furniture is known only through documentary evidence, but Marshall's contribution to the region's artistic heritage survives in a number of well-made pieces that have been passed down in his family. Foreshadowing what is to follow in catalogue entries featuring the work of numerous other craftsmen, Marshall's documented products exhibit recognizable stylistic influences, first-rate craftsmanship, and peculiar assertions of individual aesthetic taste, which ground them to a particular time and place. They prepare the reader to expect more examples of furniture with highly figured veneers, madly turned and carved features, and masterfully made, but with wholly unexpected embellishments of fit and finish.

The essays and catalogue entries draw on major research published to accompany exhibitions of Vermont furniture in the 1990s and bring that scholarship up to date with important new discoveries and many examples that have not been previously exhibited or published. A noticeable difference in *Rich and Tasty* is the emphasis on pieces that exhibit the very highest quality and craftsmanship.[2]

In *The Architecture of Country Houses* (1850), Alexander Jackson Downing remarked on seeing, "with pain and mortification, the suburban villa of a wealthy citizen, a narrow, unmistakable 'six-story brick,' which seemed, in its forlornness, and utter want of harmony with all about it, as if it had strayed out of town, in a fit of insanity, and had lost the power of getting back again." Little of the furniture illustrated in *Rich and Tasty* would be mistaken for coastal city furniture gone astray, but, as Zea effectively argues in his essay, it should not be considered inferior or dismissed as "country." The best Vermont furniture was made by impeccable craftsmen for well-heeled customers who were well aware of the latest styles and current taste.[3]

These ambitious and competitive consumers were not trying to keep up with the tastemakers in Boston or New York; instead, they were trying to stay one step ahead of the wealthy merchant up the road in Windsor or Middlebury. It is this petri dish of a local economy that produced the marvelous innovations that are the delight of this display of what talented and imaginative makers can devise to entice a purchase from a targeted clientele.

One demonstrable innovation is the half-sideboard, to which a chapter in the catalogue is devoted. Furniture forms that combine the functions of desk and sideboard are common in coastal Maine and New Hampshire, but there they take the form of a typical sideboard that includes a writing secretary drawer or a typical secretary-bookcase that has bottle drawers and a linen cupboard. The epitome of this sort of Swiss Army knife furniture is a Sheraton secretary from the Portland, Maine, area, which combines elements of a secretary, bookcase, sideboard, and shelf-clock case in a single, compact unit. In Vermont, the disparate functions of business desk and dining-room server are accommodated in a purpose-built form, the half-sideboard or "locker," which is slightly wider than a bureau or secretary but substantially smaller than a full sideboard. What is most surprising is that the six examples illustrated (p. 13, fig. 2; cat. nos. 18, 40–43) are from sites all over the state and are very different from one another in arrangement and ornamentation. This seems to indicate that appreciation of the utility of the form spread throughout the region, but different cabinetmakers adapted the type to suit their local taste.[4]

Another local trend is for furniture in a neoclassical form but that incorporates decorative elements that are not at all classical. In the exuberant wave-like scrolled crests and backsplashes found on everything from bureaus to secretaries to worktables, one may yet trace a Greek meander that has just meandered off on its own. Catalogue number 36 is a lyre-based table made circa 1825 by Lyman Briggs of Montpelier that incorporates distinctly Gothic-looking acorn drops and applied bosses, the latter exhibited on a number of pieces in the catalogue. Many of the bureaus, secretaries, and sideboards illustrated from central Vermont feature engaged columns that in their wildly turned and carved vases and reels more closely resemble Jacobean bedposts than classical columns. A dressing table from the Champlain Valley (p. 21, fig. 6) even boasts split-spindle turnings with acorn drops applied to the stiles above the legs. Rather than being viewed as flaws, these can just as easily be seen as evidence of the self-assured smorgasbord aesthetic that a localized market can germinate.

That this catalogue even includes a chapter titled "Vermont Uncorked" should forewarn the reader where this thoroughly scholarly inquiry is going, and the aforementioned chapter will not disappoint. From a whimsical desk table by Alonzo Stowell of Londonderry that features drawer fronts carved and painted to look like book spines, to a worktable by James Richardson of Poultney that looks as if it belongs on the set of the Starship *Enterprise*, "Vermont Uncorked" demonstrates quite vividly that furniture can be at the highest levels of all twelve of Zea's criteria of connoisseurship and still be utterly different from anything else you've ever seen.

Another refreshing surprise is the inclusion of a chapter entitled "Three Vermont Furniture Puzzles," outlining some loosely related objects from western Vermont for which the documentation or common denominator is lacking. Catalogues of regional furniture typically present attributions as absolute and neatly omit any anomalies that do not confirm the thesis. Perhaps because this is a revisiting of earlier research and a reevaluation of what has been learned in the interim, the authors might be more comfortable in disclosing discoveries still waiting to be made, in hope that a future publication might reveal the answers. Perhaps, as well, it is a sly nod to the classic Yankee yarn about "the one that got away."

The book's print quality is first rate, and the extraordinary photography by J. David Bohl reveals the individuality and superb craftsmanship of each object. The one disappointment of the work is that the only map of Vermont—a hand-colored plate from Thomas G. Bradford's *Illustrated Atlas, Geographical, Statistical, and Historical, of the United States and the Adjacent Countries* (1838)—is reproduced at such a reduced scale (p. 10) that it is all but illegible. If one did not know one's Burlington from one's Brattleboro, the gentle reader would be at wits' end trying to trace the locations of the objects illustrated in the catalogue. A simple outline map noting the towns mentioned in the text would have been helpful.

Rich and Tasty: Vermont Furniture to 1850 makes a substantial contribution both to the scholarship on Vermont furniture and to the way regional furniture is assessed. It shows us that provincial furniture need not be considered inferior and that fine furniture can still be fun.

Tom Hardiman
Portsmouth Athenaeum

1. *Poulson's American Daily Advertiser* (Philadelphia), November 20, 1820, p. 3. *City of Washington Gazette*, November 21, 1820, 2; *Albany Gazette*, December 1, 1820, p. 2. *Boston Daily American*, September 8, 1825, p. 1. *Keene Sentinel*, March 2, 1827, p. 3: "Has finished and is constantly manufacturing a variety of rich and tasty CABINET FURNITURE, made of the best materials and in the best manner—consisting in part of Sideboards; Secretaries; BUREAUS, with top drawers and Looking Glasses; common and French, &c. Sideboard, Pier, Sofa, Center, Card, Loo, Dining, Pembroke, Extension, Breakfast and Work TABLES, with and without bags; Sofas, Couches, Lounges, Chairs, &c. covered in crimson, green and blue plush; figured, striped and plain hair seating; Moreens, &c, Looking Glasses; Fire Setts; patent Time Pieces; Refrigerators; Portable Water Closets; Night Cabinets; Cradles; Cribs; Wash stands; Hat do.; Portable Desks; Counting Room do.; Bootracks; Bookshelves; Music Seats; Foot Benches; Canterburys; Hearth and Crumb Brushes; Spring and squab Seats; Rocking Chairs, Dressing and Toilett Tables; Mahogany and stained do.; high and low post Field and French BEDSTEADS; Mahogany and stained do.; Easy Lolling, Mahogany, Rosewood and Fancy CHAIRS, &C. . . ."

2. Charles A. Robinson, *Vermont Cabinetmakers & Chairmakers before 1855: A Checklist* (Shelburne, Vt.: Shelburne Museum, 1994), Kenneth Joel Zogry, *The Best the Country Affords: Ver-*

mont Furniture, 1765–1850 (Bennington, Vt.: Bennington Museum, 1995), and Janet Houghton and Corwin Sharp, *Made in Woodstock: Furniture in the Collection of the Woodstock Historical Society* (Woodstock, Vt.: Woodstock Historical Society, 1997).

3. Alexander Jackson Downing, *The Architecture of Country Houses* (New York: D. Appleton & Co., 1850), p. 33.

4. Private collection; Stamford Auctions, April 2, 2006, lot 366a.

Kemble Widmer and Joyce King, with essays by Glenn Adamson, Daniel Finamore, Dean Thomas Lahikainen, and Elisabeth Garrett Widmer. *In Plain Sight: Discovering the Furniture of Nathaniel Gould*. Salem, Mass.: Peabody Essex Museum in association with D Giles, London, 2014. 284 pp.; numerous color and bw illus., appendixes, bibliography, index. $70.00.

In Plain Sight: Discovering the Furniture of Nathaniel Gould by Kemble Widmer and Joyce King, with essays by four other scholars, is a sumptuous volume exploring the furniture and shop ledgers of Salem cabinetmaker Nathaniel Gould (1734–1781). It joins Robert D. Mussey Jr.'s monograph, *The Furniture Masterworks of John and Thomas Seymour* (2003), and Dean T. Lahikainen's study, *Samuel McIntire: Carving an American Style* (2007), as the third in a trio of exhibitions and books organized and published by the Peabody Essex Museum focusing on the life and works of eastern Massachusetts cabinetmakers and carvers equally recognized now and in their day as masters of their craft. Like the other two books, *In Plain Sight* is beautifully produced. The title page opens to a large-format, two-page color spread of Gould's account book that leaps off the page. Long "hidden in plain sight" in the papers of Nathan Dane (1752–1835), a Danvers, Massachusetts, lawyer—donated to the Massachusetts Historical Society in 1834—in this image the account book appears tactile and substantial, its yellowed pages replete with ledger entries key to the authors' project of reconstructing Gould's career and redolent with promise for future research. The book is divided into three parts: interpretive essays, a catalogue of furniture, and appendixes containing selective transcripts of the ledgers. Evocative, full-page images of Gould's furniture front each essay and are distributed throughout the catalogue, adding to the book's visual appeal.

Gould's ledgers, consisting of two daybooks covering the years 1758–63 and 1767–81, and an account book spanning the years 1763–81, record the output of a prolific shop. They document the sale of 1,399 chairs (93 percent of which were side chairs, the authors note), more than 300 different types of table, 56 low chests of drawers, 77 cases of drawers (high chests and chests-on-chests), 110 desks for the domestic market, and 616 pieces of export furniture. The authors linked furniture from his shop that has survived with histories of ownership to the ledgers, enabling them to pinpoint purchases and gain greater insight into Gould's business practices. Through genealogical sleuthing, they uncovered family-based patterns of patronage that, in several cases, extended through several generations. And they traced Gould's participation in the export furniture trade that secured his financial security.

Born in Danvers, Massachusetts, in 1734, Nathaniel Gould was the fifth son of cabinetmaker, housewright, and joiner Nathaniel Gould and his wife,

Elizabeth (French) Gould. Orphaned at age twelve, he came under the legal guardianship of his uncle, wheelwright James Gould, who apprenticed him with an unidentified cabinetmaker, possibly Thomas Wood of Charlestown (Gould married Wood's daughter, Rebecca Wood, in 1760). In 1756 he sold his inherited share of his parents' estate and began working independently as a cabinetmaker, first in Charlestown, then, by 1758, in Salem. In 1761 he bought from peruke maker John Ward, a half share of a "mansion house," where he lived with his family, opposite Ward, who occupied the other half of the house. In 1773 he sold his share of the house and bought two tracts of land: a house lot "in the Back Street" and approximately $3^{1}/_{4}$ acres of tillage "in the north field," as recorded in an inventory of his estate, taken after his death. Apparently, he opted to live in a rented house elsewhere in town. Extrapolating from a radical change in record-keeping practices in his ledgers after 1776, Gould entered into semiretirement, giving over the day-to-day operations of the shop to another worker. In 1781, at age forty-seven, he died in Rutland, Massachusetts, leaving an estate valued at £663.5.8—an extraordinary sum for a cabinetmaker. In addition to land and a house full of mahogany furniture, his inventory enumerated a shop (valued at £50), woodworking tools (£20.14.11), partly finished furniture (£44) "Chipendale Designs" (Thomas Chippendale's *The Gentleman and Cabinet-Maker's Director*, 3rd ed. [1762], £1.8), and thousands of feet of lumber including mahogany, cedar, and pine.

Few of Gould's peers were able to achieve a similar level of financial security. Immigrant Scottish chairmaker James Graham (1726–1808) of Boston, for example, spent most of his life in debt and died a pauper. Cabinetmaker John Needham (act 1758–1798) worked briefly for Gould and lived hand-to-mouth, finding work in Salem and Boston well past retirement age. Salem cabinetmakers John Chipman and Elijah Sanderson fared little better. What were Gould's strategies for success where others struggled? Widmer and King observe, first, that Gould was fortunate to receive an inheritance that enabled him to buy tools and establish a shop. They identify his decision to practice cabinetmaking in Salem as an equally important early factor in his success. Having trained in Charlestown, he may have been discouraged from seeking work in Boston by a perceived lack of opportunity in the crowded and competitive furniture trade of that city. Perhaps he recognized that Salem's leading cabinetmaker, Abraham Watson (1712–1790), was easing out of the business, creating an opening for an ambitious young craftsman to bring new-style furniture to a seafaring community actively building on its mercantile wealth. His ledgers reveal that during his first year in Salem he found a market eager for a wide variety of furniture forms as well as riding chaises.

Gould gained customers by exclusively offering rococo furniture designs that had recently gained favor in Boston. No furniture in an earlier baroque (or Queen Anne) style has yet been attributed to his shop. He introduced the bombé form to Salem, then blockfront designs; he offered decorative features of his own design such as elaborately scrolled bracket feet and knee brackets and applied pendant shells; he translated designs illustrated in plates from English print sources; and he copied the work of such émigré cabinet- and chairmakers as Scottish chairmaker James Graham who arrived in Boston in 1764. The authors note that Gould's "owl's-eye" and "C-scroll-and-diamond" chair splats were lifted directly from Graham's most popular designs. They also observe that Gould's chairs featuring "double C-scroll" splats, copied from a design that Robert Manwaring published in *The Cabinet and Chair-Maker's Real Friend and Companion* (London, 1765), are the only known American examples to use this distinct pattern. Gould offered his design in 1762, fully three years before the publication of Manwaring's book and four years before the book was offered by Boston bookseller John Mein. A copy of the design in the Phillips Library at Peabody Essex Museum, believed to have been owned by Gould, bears an ink inscription "From London 1762," suggesting Gould obtained the plate as a single-page imprint, well ahead of its publication in book form. Gould also adapted designs from the third edition of Thomas Chippendale's *Gentleman and Cabinet-Maker's Director* (1762). His focus on new designs paid off: starting in 1761, members of the merchant elite in Salem, Marblehead, and surrounding towns, such as the Derbys, Cabots, Pickmans, Dodges, Higginsons, and Lees, patronized his shop. Over the next twenty-one years, he supplied three generations of Cabots alone with furniture valued at £660.

The authors partly attribute his success to his early involvement in the furniture export trade. Over the course of his career, he sold or consigned 382 desks (62 percent by number and 74 percent by value), 114 tables, 105 chairs, and a smattering of other forms to Salem shipowners involved in the Caribbean trade. Busy with domestic furniture commissions, he typically contracted export furniture, mainly desks made from native hardwoods such as maple, cherry, and, most commonly, red cedar, from journeymen and outside cabinetmakers such his father-in-law, Thomas Wood, and brother-in-law, Thomas Wood Jr., of Charlestown. Gould substantially marked up these goods, for example, purchasing a maple desk for £1 and selling it for £3.6.8—a 300 percent increase above his purchase price. (In turn, the shipowner might sell the desk in the West Indies for £14.) Widmer and King conclude: it was Gould's export business that "accounted for his greatest profits . . . and allowed him semiretirement as a gentleman" (p. 16).

Between 1758 and 1781 Gould employed at least twenty-two journeymen cabinetmakers, either as shop hands or as subcontractors engaged in piecework. He hired many workers for short periods, to help execute large commissions and to make export furniture; he assigned only the most skilled workers to important orders, thereby retaining a high degree of quality control over his best work and exerting little control over the quality of the furniture made on speculation and destined for foreign buyers. Noting that half of Gould's journeymen began work in their late teens or early twenties, the authors surmise that Gould may have trained many of these young men as apprentices before hiring them, and that their terms of apprenticeship may have been more fluid than heretofore understood. Only three workers served for longer periods in his shop. Philemon Parker, his "most trusted and longest-serving employee" (p. 79), began receiving payments as an eighteen-year-old journeyman in 1763 and continued through Gould's death; thirty-six-year-old John Ropes Jr., who primarily made cedar and maple desks for export between 1761 and 1773; and twenty-year-old journeyman John Ross, who specialized in making chairs and carving claw-and-ball feet between 1765 and 1776.

One of Gould's most striking strategies for success was his willingness to supply furniture to clients on both sides of the acrimonious political divide that pitted loyalist against patriot, neighbor against neighbor, in the decade leading up to the American Revolution. Right through the outbreak of war, he continued to serve both sides, making furniture for the likes of General Gage, commander of the British Army on the one hand, and for members of the Cabot family, who had grown rich on privateering on the other. How did he navigate between the two? The authors contend that his modus operandi was to stay above the fray and remain "diligent in avoiding association with either side" (p. 19). But how difficult that must have been when most clients and colleagues were actively siding with each camp, publicly declaring their allegiances in many ways, including as signatories to open letters either in support of or in protest of Salem as an alternative port after the closing of Boston Harbor. Gould signed neither letter. Nor did he join any political group such as the Sons of Liberty, nor did he support the war effort in other ways (a number of Salem craftsmen, some eager to pocket a £10 bounty, joined the militia). How did he avoid alienating partisans on both sides or, worse, becoming a target of violence, vandalism, or arson?

Perhaps one way he protected his business was to hire and subcontract work with craftsmen outside Salem—not only, as the authors contend, to minimize the possibility of competition from local cabinetmakers who might have used his designs and templates in their own nearby shops, but also to keep "diligent in avoiding association" with potentially politicized artisans who might have drawn him out of his closely guarded neutrality. Perhaps another way he gained favor—or at least tolerance—among the locals was to sell to most of Salem's cabinetmakers, colleagues in allied trades, and employees a variety of commodities including "sugar and textile products, even shoes . . . at a very low markup and significantly below prevailing market prices in Salem" (p. 82). Elsewhere, the authors characterize Gould's low purchase prices and steep markups of contract export furniture and his hard bargaining with employees over wages and charges for room and board as evidence of a "tough and disciplined manner of conducting his business" (p. 81). This soft behavior, then, would seem to fly in the face of such an assessment. It seems to make sense, however, that Gould would forgo monetary profit if what he was "buying" with his below-market prices for these goods was fealty from those who might otherwise have acted on their resentments against him. Perhaps for similar reasons, he eschewed involvement in Salem's civic life—he appears not to have held any public offices or served in voluntary organizations.

Four essays by outside authors provide useful context for understanding Gould's furniture, business practices, and patronage. In "'Desks took on bord' in Nathaniel Gould's Caribbean Furniture Trade," Daniel Finamore provides an overview of Salem's involvement in the Caribbean trade and strategies that captains and shipowners deployed to circumvent restrictive British maritime acts. He notes that Salem's outbound vessels typically took on board only small consignments of furniture—two or three desks and a few other small articles at a time—for sale in the West Indies. Finamore concludes that stylistic preferences, the imprimatur of specific cabinetmakers, and the exact origins of furniture—attributes that may have been important to consumers on the mainland—lost all relevance to Caribbean customers. Dean T. Lahikainen, in "Grand Houses and Rural Retreats," describes the town houses and country estates of Salem's elite that provided the architectural setting for much of Gould's best furniture.

Taking up the theme of home life, consumption, and conspicuous display in the mansion houses of Salem's elite merchant class, Elisabeth Garrett Widmer focuses attention on the role of women in Gould's furniture commissions. Her essay, "Brides, Housewives, and Hostesses: Acquiring, Using, Caring for, and Enjoying Mr. Gould's Furniture," explores how the rituals surrounding marriage, childbirth, and death influenced furniture patronage directly and indirectly driven by women. She observes that 80 percent of Gould's domestic furniture orders were for marriage portions and that, starting in the 1760s, elites established a pattern of enormous commissions consisting of multiple case pieces, tables, and sets of chairs, made in a range of materials and designs for use in rooms of ranked importance within the home. She notes that during weddings, and for weeks afterward, "everything as well as everyone was on view" (p. 58) in the homes of newlyweds. Likewise, the home was "on view" during the postpartum sitting-up visits that mothers expected in the third and fourth weeks after childbirth and in the vigils surrounding deaths. Aware that their homes would be seen and judged by "a sizable, frequent, and observant public" (p. 59), elites relied on Gould to provide furniture that he, and they, together, deemed stylish and appropriate.

Glenn Adamson opens his essay, "Behind the Curve: Putting Nathaniel Gould in Perspective," with an image of contemporary Dutch designer Jeroen Verhoeven's *Cinderella Table*, a dramatic, curvaceous work sculpted with a computer-assisted router of plywood, referencing the past to delight with the shock of the new. Might Boston and Salem elites have first experienced bombé designs in a similar way? Adamson explores the origins of the bombé form, tracing the idea from fifteenth-century Italian cassoni to rarefied "ogee-curve" German and French furniture of the early eighteenth century, executed in precious metals, veneers, even repurposed Chinese lacquer panels. By the mid-eighteenth century, the design had gone mainstream, stripped-down versions of which informed the design of pulpits (such as that built for the First Church of Ipswich in 1749), the bases of window seats, and case furniture. Boston and Boston-trained cabinetmakers, including Gould, copied the design not from print sources, but from imported objects, further simplifying the form in the process. In Adamson's view, Gould "was a kind of genius," producing masterworks of "simplicity and tact" within a provincial, circumscribed context of acceptability (p. 31). Why did elites turn to Gould rather than order these forms from Boston or London? What remains to be explained is how client and craftsman worked together to calibrate design, materials, and workmanship with perceived needs and a desire for prestige.

The second half of the book consists of a catalogue organized by form starting with case furniture and proceeding to seating furniture, tables, and bedsteads, and featuring eighteen examples of Gould's work, most with provenances tracing back to original owners and identified in the ledgers. Appendixes containing select transcriptions of the ledgers round out the volume. Using a methodology similar to that developed by Thomas and Alice Kugelman and Robert Lionetti to classify case furniture of the Connecticut River valley, the authors created a list of features to identify Gould's work. Noting that, at present, twenty-seven examples of Gould's furniture have been identified in museum collections, they prepared the catalogue as a guide to support future attributions, focusing on diagnostic details such as stock size; glue block arrangement, size, and nailing patterns; and the shape and character of claw-and-ball carving. Readers will learn about features unique to Gould, such as blocking with squared corners on case façades, fan carvings with gouged curlicues at their lower ends, and punches on the bottoms of chair splats and their shoes that indicate the chair number in a set. Along the way, the authors share small discoveries, such as their insight that rather than use a template to trace the profile of knee returns and drop bases for pendant shells on the skirts of case furniture, Gould laid out designs for these features with a compass. Though similar in style, each skirt is unique in execution.

Studying the objects in tandem with the ledgers has enabled the authors to document Gould's shop practices, to explicate potentially confusing terminology in the ledgers, and to understand material, design, and price options available to customers. Widmer and King have achieved a remarkable accomplishment not only in clarifying otherwise opaque ledger entries but also in allowing for a deeper reading of these shop records than might otherwise have been possible without access to the objects. They explain the meaning of furniture names, such as "bureau table," that less-informed readers might not even flag as potentially confusing. In common usage, bureau table refers to what is now called a "kneehole dressing table." In Gould's ledgers, it meant a low case of four drawers. Further, the authors were able to extrapolate that bureau tables priced at £6 referred to bombé designs in mahogany with claw-and-ball carved feet; examples priced at £5.6.8 sported ogee bracket feet. They also learned that, in elite households, these bureau tables took the place of dressing tables in wedding commissions also containing high chests. Other names, such as "case of drawers," remain ambiguous. Gould applied this term to chests-on-chests, bonnet-top high chests, and flat-top high chests. No high chests have been attributed to his shop to help clarify this name's meaning—although certain extrapolations can be made: an October 1767 notation, "1 case of draw of mahogany sweld ends," referred to a bombé chest-on-chest.

The volume concludes with appendixes containing the names of Gould's clients and their furniture orders, arranged chronologically by form. Additional appendixes provide information on journeymen and apprentices in

Gould's shop, export furniture, and furniture associated with weddings and childbirth. As transactions not relating to the production of furniture are omitted, researchers interested in issues beyond the scope of this study, including Gould's substantial involvement in the mahogany and native hardwood lumber trade, will want to examine the original.

In the end, what emerges from Widmer and King's research is a portrait of a master craftsman blessed with creativity and talent, driven by ambition, and guided by a keen business sense. The same words the authors use to describe Gould's masterworks—monumental, meticulous, inventive, substantial, and well-crafted—equally apply to this book. Widmer and King's research has yielded a foundational work extending what we know about one Salem cabinetmaker's extraordinary furniture, his involvement in the export furniture trade, and his business practices. It deserves a place on every furniture reference shelf.

Joshua W. Lane
Winterthur Museum, Garden & Library

Dennis Carr, with contributions by Gauvin Alexander Bailey, Timothy Brook, Mitchell Codding, Karina H. Corrigan, and Donna Pierce. *Made in the Americas: The New World Discovers Asia*. Boston: MFA Publications, 2015. 160 pp.; 100 color illus., bibliography, index. $50.00.

It is stated in this small but rich volume that the opening of Spanish trade through what is now Mexico in 1565 placed New Spain at the crossroads of global trade routes. This is undoubtedly true of nearly every entrepôt in the worldwide rush to open ocean trade routes between Europe and Asia that began in earnest in the sixteenth century. What is unique about the influences in the Americas, as opposed to those in other parts of the world, is the more specific subject of this book. Donna Pierce, one of the contributors to the volume, relates that a "Mexico City household that was inventoried in 1645 included furniture constructed of luxury materials such as mahogany, ebony, and ivory from Germany, Cuba, China and the West Indies, along with a Turkish carpet and velvet pillows from China" (p. 56). This is an important acknowledgment that New Spain has its own place in the history of decorative arts and that it bows to no other entrepôt as being lesser.

The content of *Made in the Americas* is not a comprehensive response to the implications of the title, but it is a most admirable survey. How could it be comprehensive with the geographically head-spinning commission of discussing the interaction between Chinese, Japanese, Indian, Spanish, Portuguese, and North American–based British, Dutch, and French markets, not to mention a span of more than two hundred years—all in 122 pages of text interspersed with images?

But this is an immensely important task to undertake in this age, as the model of the European focus in art history fades and the recognition of indigenous and colonial cultures, as unique artistic centers on their own merits, rises. Although it is not explicitly stated, the real focus here is New Spain. Of the works illustrated (with 21 details), 63 are made (or modified) in the

Americas. Of those, 43 are from New Spain (including Mexico, Columbia, Peru, and Ecuador), 5 from Brazil, and 13 from what became the United States. Three are from French Canada or France, 6 from the Philippines, 6 from China, 4 from India, and 4 from Japan. The rest (one each) are from Spain, Italy, Switzerland, and Belgium. It is obvious that the heart of this book lies in the Spanish- (and less so, Portuguese-) speaking New World.

Made in the Americas has the look of a nonthreatening book for the general public, in line with a series of other publications the MFA has done recently for a certain level of readership. Other titles along this line include *Looking East: Western Artists and the Allure of Japan*, by Helen Burnham, with contributions by Sarah E. Thompson and Jane Braun (2014), and various "highlights" books on segments of the collections, including American paintings, American decorative arts, Native American art, European decorative arts, musical instruments, classical art, and so on.

But Dennis Carr has gathered an impressive roster of authors representing expertise in the fields of American decorative and Asian export arts, and the melding of the two. Each contributor makes an effort to include as much on his or her subject as possible, which can lead to a bullet-point style that nevertheless results in a succinct and clear exposition of a tremendous amount of information. Add to this the healthy footnotes and you have a valuable resource that allows thorough follow-up on salient points. If you are interested in furniture, you will find, for one example, references to publications by María Campos Carlés de Pena and Jorge F. Rivas that are not listed in the bibliography (see p. 134 note 22).

European and North American chinoiserie has been well researched and published over the decades since the first wave of scholarly interest in the 1960s. It is time now for serious attention to the same theme in Middle, Central, and South America. The cover illustration depicts a detail of a lacquered desk inspired by Asian and Turkish designs, setting the stage for what may interest readers of *American Furniture* most. For readers of this journal, the index will guide you to such topics as "furniture," "lacquerware," and "wood," as well as to individual furniture forms (cabinet, desk, headboard, etc). Using Spanish terms, you will be equally well directed to the points of interest.

The salon for women (*estrado*) and master bedrooms seem to have been the primary locations where Asian furnishings and local productions reflecting those influences could be found in Latin American homes. The paintings of interiors from New Spain included in the book illustrate the extensive use of Asian materials and the manifestations of their impact in these rooms.

Biombas (locally made folding screens) are particularly well known in Mexico, Venezuela, and Ecuador, and seem to be among the most prevalent and popular symbols of the influence of Asia on interiors in Latin America. The first documented arrival of a Japanese screen is in 1614, and by 1784 the inventory of the count of Xala in Mexico City listed four large screens from China, three short ones (*rodaestrado*), and eight painted screens, two of which had chinoiserie (*achinado*) figures.

One style of decoration that was applied to furniture as well as to other arts was invented in New Spain (Mexico): a merger of inlay, japanning, and painting in a style called *enconchado* (shell inlay). The shell inlay work was inspired by examples from Japan and India (Goa and Gujarat) that was mixed with the Spanish-Moorish traditions in the hands of Latin American craftsmen in what is now Mexico, Peru, Ecuador, Columbia, Venezuela, Guatemala, and Paraguay.

Lacquer is of particular note since there was an indigenous tradition of such work dating back two thousand years using *mopa mopa* in a lacquerware style referred to as *barniz de Pasto* (Pasto varnish), which had been produced in Columbia, Ecuador, and Peru, and then Mexico, particularly in Michoacán. Mitchell Codding provides detailed and precise descriptions of various lacquer techniques in use in New Spain.

The most ubiquitous piece of furniture may be the locally made chest, although examples found in the New World were imported from Germany, Holland, Spain, Italy, or Asia (Korea, Japan, and India). Is there any doubt that New Spain was anything but a "backwater"?

I suppose no review would be complete without raising an issue or two. There is an inevitable repetition of some story lines, facts, and descriptions of certain techniques. Despite these redundancies, the repetition of this basic information can be seen as a helpful feature if you are not reading cover to cover. The map is missing Canton, Nagasaki, Cape Town, and directional arrows, which would have helped the reader to understand the flow of traffic and goods. Wallpaper is a particular interest of mine, and there is one sentence on the topic; using the footnote leads to more information, but the term is not found in the index. The same is true with "fan." The footnotes are extensive and delve much further into resources than the selected bibliography implies, so don't pass up reading them.

Carr reminds us that rather than seeing these "outposts" of art as "cultural backwaters" (the old way of thinking perhaps, but who would say such a thing these days?), they were each vibrant centers of creativity receiving their influences from Asian, indigenous, and European cultures to create a new style of art. This concept makes me think of the *casta* (caste) paintings, one of which is included, which depict spouses of different cultures and the child they bear that is a melding of the parents' heritage.

The only indication that this accompanies an exhibition is a passing reference in the director's foreword, but indeed this book is associated with a show that carries the same title as the book. The exhibition is a gem. The small photographs in the book do not do justice to the extraordinary objects which can be seen on display. There are, however, some inexplicable differences between the two. I tried to make a list of what was in one and not in the other, but therein lies madness. The installation follows a different format as well.

For furniture enthusiasts, there are at least eight objects in the exhibition that are not illustrated or discussed at length in the book. For example, a Gardner family japanned chair is mentioned in the book (but not illustrated, and not referenced in the index), but two examples are on display.

Also in the exhibition are a Japanese nanban domed coffer; a New England high chest, armchair, and tea table; an English Chinese Chippendale chair (from the Moffatt-Ladd House in Portsmouth, New Hampshire); and a japanned mirror. Other surprisingly beautiful pieces in the exhibition and not in the book include a cluster of Talavera ware, some superb textiles, and more American silver. The exhibition runs until February 15, 2016, at the MFA, and then travels to the Winterthur Museum, where it will be seen in a slightly different iteration from March 26, 2016, to January 3, 2017.

You could hardly ask for a more informative and beautiful record of the interior of an upper-class home than the 1751 ex-voto painting of the house of a Mexico City merchant, Don Juan Garcia Truxillo. This one image says volumes about the importance of Asian art and its influences in New Spain. Timothy Brook said it best in his essay: "we too must look onward, beyond conventional narratives of European influence and toward America's key role in the more expansive, multicultural world" (p. 16). Looking beyond conventional narratives is the purpose of this book and exhibition, and they succeed admirably, rising to the daunting challenge to create a cohesive look at a very complex subject.

This is the first book for the general public, and the first exhibition, to specifically examine the influence of Asia on the arts of all the Americas, and it arrives roughly in time to celebrate the 450th anniversary of the Spanish galleon trade between the Philippines and New Spain (the first ship sailed in 1565). There were, recently, similar exhibitions planned by three or four other museums, but they have not materialized. Luckily, Dennis Carr and the Museum of Fine Arts, Boston, have succeeded.

William Sargent
Bonhams (USA)

Leroy Graves. *Early Seating Upholstery: Reading the Evidence*. Williamsburg, Va.: Colonial Williamsburg Foundation, 2015. ix + 227 pp.; 371 color illus., index. $65.00.

The publication of Leroy Graves's *Early Seating Upholstery: Reading the Evidence* stands as a particularly noteworthy moment for the fields of furniture history, material culture studies, and furniture conservation. For more than four decades this largely self-taught craftsman and scholar has basically both founded and then led the field of historic upholstery conservation through his work at the Colonial Williamsburg Foundation. Central to Graves's accomplishments has been the pioneering development of sophisticated methods of noninvasive furniture upholstering that preserve the material integrity of fragile historic chair and sofa frames. At the same time, this approach pays heed to the aesthetic conventions of period upholstery, which he uniquely understands because of his unmatched experience in rediscovering and implementing long-lost methods of webbing, padding, upholstering, and the like. As a living throwback to the craftspeople of centuries past whose expertise came from actual hands-on practice rather than secondhand scholarship, Graves is the holder of the keys to understanding the craft ways of early European and American upholsterers whose techniques disappeared with the advent of new materials and methods in the industrial age. For these reasons and many more, the publication of his book is crucial.

We live in a time when a simple click of a computer key will yield from the major retail online bookstores any number of popular, do-it-yourself upholstery publications that will allow you to reupholster a chair or sofa. But these "craft" books inevitably either veer away from or fully ignore the use of traditional materials and methods. One simply learns modern upholstery approaches to apply to old objects, which is not only ahistorical but also potentially very damaging to the actual furniture frames that are being attacked by the contemporary use of staples, nonreversible glues, nails, and toxic foams and padding. As for more substantive scholarship on the art of historic upholstery, the last three decades have seen the publication of a number of important historical and cultural overviews, including *Upholstery in America and Europe from the Seventeenth Century to World War I* (1987), edited by Edward S. Cooke Jr., and *Culture and Comfort: People, Parlors, and Upholstery, 1850–1930* (1988) by Katherine C. Grier. There also have been a number of important conferences that have focused on conservation issues, including "The Forgotten History: Upholstery Conservation," the first international conference in Europe devoted to the subject, held May 12–13, 2005, in Vanstena, Sweden. These gatherings, as well as some formal presentations at American Institute of Conservation meetings and other decorative arts annual conferences, have yielded useful insights into new possible approaches, although the overall information tends to be specialized, project-oriented, and therefore episodic in nature.

Graves's groundbreaking publication, done with the dedicated and skilled research assistance of Margaret Beck Pritchard, Colonial Williamsburg Curator of Prints and Maps, lays the foundation for an entirely new type of historic upholstery study that merges the history of styles and techniques with a more synthetic consideration of the potential of using newer, noninvasive conservation techniques that are rooted in a deep understanding of period upholstery conventions and tastes. At some 225 pages in length, this book is not encyclopedic in content; indeed, it really could not be a comprehensive overview without being thousands of pages long. But far from being a shortcoming, its well-planned thematic clarity and descriptive brevity are what make the book succeed. What also makes *Early Seating Upholstery* successful is the rather zoom-lens type of experience it provides the reader, as the focus moves back and forth from a larger macroscopic description of early styles, methods, and ideas to much closer microscopic examinations of actual techniques and surviving bits of evidence. For anyone interested in understanding this early trade, learning to "read" this physical evidence is a crucial skill. Often it is the only way that we today can gain insight into the actual methods and designs used by the original upholsterer.

Through the broad thematic and categorical sweep of the main chapters, this publication provides a useful foundation on which future scholars of historic furniture, upholstery, and upholstery conservation can expand. For example, the opening chapters—"A Brief History of Upholstered Seating Furniture" and "The Eighteenth-Century Upholsterer"—provide the reader with a basic understanding of the origins of high-style furniture upholstery as it evolved in Europe and America in the seventeenth and eighteenth centuries (true, there was historic upholstery much earlier, but the orientation of the Colonial Williamsburg collection centers on these two centuries that saw the most dramatic improvements and, arguably, the highest expression of the art before or since). The intrepid scholar who is seeking a fuller comprehension of particular furniture forms, stylistic trends, or particular makers can follow these leads and simply dive deeply into other publications, including historical treatises and period design books that increasingly are available online.

Early Seating Upholstery: Reading the Evidence then pivots into the nitty-gritty of historic upholstery—"Structure and Components of Upholstered Seating Furniture"—by offering up thoughtfully described and well-illustrated examples of the elements of furniture frames and upholstery materials. This includes a primer on wood and wood preparation, joinery methods, and the minutiae of blocks, peaks, and bracing that were central to the upholsterer's craft. Similarly, the introductions to slip-seat techniques, webbing, leatherwork, tacking and taping, and stuffing literally unpack the elemental parts that help us today understand the general methods and individual mindsets of artisans working two or three centuries ago. In some instances, the book's inevitable reliance on static photography, even beautifully detailed close-ups, falls short of what might be gleaned through video presentation of some of these approaches. I speak firsthand in this respect having had the great privilege of mentoring under Graves initially as a conservator and then as a curator. The art of historic upholstery is often a complicated kinetic dance in which the artisan's hands are working both with and against the material limitations of the physical wooden chair or sofa frame and the attributes of the actual foundation materials or top fabrics being manipulated or applied. An expanded online video series on the Colonial Williamsburg website showing the specific upholstery techniques detailed in this chapter would certainly be most welcome both by working conservators and craftspeople trying to understand and replicate the original upholstery traditions and by scholars whose grasp of the craft would be greatly enhanced by seeing in real time the upholsterer at work. This is not only possible in our digital age but also, in fact, economically feasible and wise.

Chapter 4 moves into the concept of "Reading the Evidence" and suggests the importance of studying surviving upholstered seating furniture frames and textiles, early alterations and faking techniques, and the importance of taking into account the information available in early paintings, prints, and other forms of evidence. This last area is by no means definitive but, rather, merely suggestive of the potential for a far more expansive consideration of early Anglo-American pictorial and textual evidence. In this regard, again, the Colonial Williamsburg Foundation conservators, curators, researchers, and archivists should take a proactive role in the planning, implementation, and long-term support of a substantive and thoughtfully ordered digital database of images and information that would then become a primary and ever-growing repository for historic upholstery researchers and practitioners of all sorts.

The book then finishes with a close look at a number of specific upholstery projects that Graves has done over the years. These case studies offer up a novel and highly upholstery-centric type of furniture cataloguing that yields a wondrous amount of useful information for the upholsterer, historian, conservator, and curator alike. Again, keep in mind there was no "how-to" book for Graves to use when he got started decades ago. Instead, it was his own diligent and intuitive consideration of the visual and physical evidence before him on old chair and sofa frames, as well as delving into period design sources and descriptions, that led to his ability to bring back to life such important traditional craft methods. All of the specific topics explored in the earlier chapters of the book are brought into play in the various projects that are explored in chapters 5 and 6, the latter being a specific examination of Graves's noninvasive approach to doing historic upholstery.

After reading *Early Seating Upholstery: Reading the Evidence*, one feels a great sense of gratitude to Leroy Graves for his contributions to our understanding of the Anglo-American material past. He quietly and modestly has provided contemporary and future scholars with a way to think both about and to conserve historic upholstered objects. The need for a next generation of historic upholstery conservators to fully embrace his method is pressing. Perhaps in the months and years to come, we might see the introduction of some specialized symposia centered on Graves's scholarship and conservation practice, as well as a dedicated expansion of educational articles and especially online videos that present even more instances of his many different noninvasive projects and techniques. As it stands, however, *Early Seating Upholstery: Reading the Evidence* is a brilliant start and a great contribution to many different fields of study.

Jonathan Prown
Chipstone Foundation

Recent Writing on American Furniture: A Bibliography

Compiled by Gerald W. R. Ward

This year's list primarily includes works published in 2014 and roughly through November 2015. As always, a few earlier publications that had escaped notice are also listed. The short title *American Furniture 2014* is used in citations for articles and reviews published in last year's edition of this journal, which is also cited in full under Luke Beckerdite's name.

Once again, many people have assisted in compiling this list. I am particularly grateful to Luke Beckerdite, W. Fronia Simpson, Jonathan Fairbanks, Mark Arnold, Dennis Carr, Caroline Cole, Nonie Gadsden, Tom Hardiman, Darcy Kuronen, Steve Lash, Johanna McBrien, Dennis Pickeral, Jay Robert Stiefel, Hilary Tress, Kem Widmer, and Barbara McLean Ward, as well as to the scholars who have prepared reviews for this issue. I am also indebted to the librarians of the Museum of Fine Arts, Boston, Sotheby's Institute of Art, the Portsmouth Athenaeum, and the Portsmouth Public Library for their ongoing assistance.

I would be glad to receive citations for titles that have been inadvertently omitted from this or previous lists. Information about new publications and review copies of significant works would also be much appreciated.

Albert, Gary. "Probability and Provenance: Jacob Sass and Charleston's Post-Revolution German School of Cabinetmakers." *Journal of Early Southern Decorative Arts* 36 (2015). Online at www.mesdajournal.org (accessed September 9, 2015).

Alegiani, J. B. "The Unlikely Path from Physicist to Furnituremaker." *American Period Furniture: A Publication of the Society of American Period Furniture Makers* 14 (December 2014): 10–15. Color illus. (Re W. Patrick Edwards, the Society's Golden Cartouche recipient for 2014.)

American Period Furniture: A Publication of the Society of American Period Furniture Makers 14 (December 2014): 1–120. Numerous color illus., line drawings. (See also individual articles cited elsewhere in this list.)

Andrews, John. *Arts and Crafts Furniture*. 2005. 2nd ed. rev. Woodbridge, Eng.: Antique Collectors' Club, 2015. 328 pp.; illus.

Arnold, Mark. "Follow the River's Bend." Online at www.360woodworking.com. 9 pp.; color illus. (accessed October 10, 2015).

——— "Herms, Terms, and Therms: Synonymous Terms?" Online at www.360woodworking.com. 9 pp.; color illus. (accessed October 10, 2015).

——— "Reeding between the Lines: The History of Reeded Furniture." Online at www.360woodworking.com. 7 pp.; color illus. (accessed October 10, 2015).

Bailey, Chris H. "Affordable Time: America's Contribution; Significant Events in the Development of Mass Production of Clocks from 1750 to 1850." *Watch & Clock Bulletin* 56, no. 6 (November–December 2014): 606–20. 57 color and bw illus.

Bailey, Janet, ed. *100 Objects, 100 Stories, 100 Years at Fruitlands Museum*. Harvard, Mass.: Fruitlands Museum, 2014. viii + 151 pp.; numerous color and bw illus.

Baker, Emerson W. *A Storm of Witchcraft: The Salem Trials and the American Experience*. New York: Oxford University Press, 2015. xv + 398 pp.; bw illus., 3 appendixes, index. (Includes brief reference to Pope family cabinet attributed to the Symonds shop at the Peabody Essex Museum.)

[Baten collection]. *The Jill and Mickey Baten Collection of Important American Furniture*. Portsmouth, N.H.: Northeast Auctions, August 15, 2015. 32 pp.; color illus.

Batley, Tania. "A Different Way of Sitting: American Patent Folding Chairs of the Nineteenth Century." *Material Culture Review/Revue de la culture matérielle* 74–75 (2012): 57–69. Illus.

Beach, Laura. "Chipstone Foundation Acquires a Notable Lancaster Tall Clock at Successful Pook Sale." *Antiques and the Arts Weekly* (October 30, 2015): 44–45. bw illus.

——— "Le Style Shaker: Will a Fresh Look Stimulate the Market?" *Antiques and the Arts Weekly* (April 24, 2015): 52–53. 7 bw illus.

——— "Notes of an Early Philadelphia Joiner Spark Institutional Bidding at Swann." *Antiques and the Arts Weekly* (October 23, 2015): 38. 5 bw illus. (Re drawings and notations of John Widdifield [1673–1720]; see also article below cited under Widdifield.)

——— "The Richest and Handsomest at Hirschl & Adler Galleries." *Antiques and the Arts Weekly* (January 25, 2015): 36–37. bw illus.

Beckerdite, Luke. "Pattern Carving in Eighteenth-Century Philadelphia." In *American Furniture 2014*, 86–141. 110 color and bw illus.

——— ed. *American Furniture 2014*. Milwaukee, Wis.: Chipstone Foundation, 2014. vii + 298 pp.; numerous color and bw illus., bibliography, index. Distributed by University Press of New England, Hanover and London.

Bell, Michael W. "'First Rate and Fashionable': Handmade Nineteenth Century Furniture at the Tennessee State Museum." *Tennessee Historical Quarterly* 62, no. 1 (spring 2003): 5–96. Numerous color and bw illus.

——— "What Freedom Wrought." *Antiques* 182, no. 2 (March–April 2015): 104–11. 12 color illus. (Re furniture from the 1880s and 1890s by Lewis Buckner of Tennessee.)

Belolan, Nicole. Review of *We Sit Together: Utopian Benches from the Shakers to the Separatists of Zoar*, by Jonathan Cape. In *American Furniture 2014*, 257–59.

Benton, Tim, Manuel Fontán Junco, and Maria Zozaya, eds. *Modern Taste: Art Deco in Paris, 1910–1935*. Madrid: Fundación Juan March and Editorial de Arte y Ciencia, 2014. 501 pp.; 358 color and bw illus., checklist, bibliography, index.

Birchfield, James D. "Porter Clay, 'A Very Excellent Cabinetmaker': Part One; Biographical Account." *Journal of Early Southern Decorative Arts* 35 (2014). 22 color and bw illus., appendix. Online at www.mesdajournal.org (accessed January 6, 2015).

[Blum collection]. *The Mr. and Mrs. Jerome W. Blum Personal Collection.*

Portsmouth, N.H.: Northeast Auctions, August 15, 2015. 136 pp.; color illus.

Boom, Irma. *Making Design: Cooper Hewitt, Smithsonian Design Museum Collections*. New York: Cooper Hewitt, Smithsonian Design Museum, 2014. 780 pp.; 1,100 color illus., bibliography, index.

Boston Furniture Archive, 1630–1930. Online at http://bostonfurniture.winterthur.org (accessed October 13, 2015). (Established by Winterthur Museum, Garden & Library.)

Bowett, Adam, ed. *100 British Chairs*. Woodbridge, Eng.: Antique Collectors' Club, 2015. 144 pp.; numerous color illus., index.

Bradbury, Dominic. *Mid-Century Modern Complete*. New York: Abrams, 2014. 544 pp.; 1,000+ color illus.

Breaking Ground: A Century of Craft Art in Western New York. Rochester, N.Y.: Memorial Art Gallery of the University of Rochester in association with Hudson Hills Press, 2010. 157 pp.; numerous color and bw illus.

Breen, Amanda. "Artifact of the Month." *Banke Notes* (Strawbery Banke Museum newsletter) (September 2015): 4. 1 color illus. (Re liquor chest, probably Dutch, with a history in the Wendell family of Portsmouth.)

Brett, Vanessa. *Bertrand's Toyshop in Bath: Luxury Retailing, 1685–1765*. Wetherby, Eng.: Oblong Creative, 2014. 363 pp.; 212 color and 32 bw illus., 13 maps, 2 graphs, tables, bibliography, index.

Breward, Christopher, Fiona Fisher, and Ghislaine Wood, eds. *British Design: Tradition and Modernity after 1948*. London: Bloomsbury Academic, 2015. 352 pp.; 30 color and 41 bw illus., bibliography, index.

[Brooklyn Museum]. "Current and Coming . . . Period Rooms in Brooklyn." *Antiques* 181, no. 6 (November–December 2014): 24. 3 color illus. (Re reinstallation by Barry Harwood of two 1850s rooms from the Robert J. Milligan home of Saratoga Springs, N.Y.)

Brown, Nell Porter. "Preserving Heirs and Airs." *Harvard Magazine* 117, no. 2 (January–February 2015): 16H–16L. 9 color and bw illus. (Re Boston's Gibson House, 1859–1860.)

Burks, Jean M. "Furniture Made in Woodstock, Vermont, before 1850." *Antiques* 182, no. 4 (July–August 2015): 118–23. 12 color illus.

——— "Rich and Tasty: Vermont Furniture to 1850." *Antiques and Fine Art* 14, no. 3 (autumn 2015): 168–73. Color illus.

Burks, Jean M., and Philip Zea. *Rich and Tasty: Vermont Furniture to 1850*. Shelburne, Vt.: Shelburne Museum, 2015. 180 pp.; numerous color illus., bibliography.

Carr, Dennis. "Asian Encounters." *Antiques* 182, no. 5 (September–October 2015): 94–101. Color illus.

——— Review of *A Surviving Legacy in Spanish America: Seventeenth- and Eighteenth-Century Furniture from the Vice Royalty of Peru*, by María Campos Carlés de Peña. In *American Furniture 2014*, 267–69.

Carr, Dennis, et al. *Made in the Americas: The New World Discovers Asia*. Boston: MFA Publications, 2015. 160 pp.; 100 color illus., bibliography, index.

Carruthers, Annette. *The Arts and Crafts Movement in Scotland: A History*. New Haven: Yale University Press, 2013. xix + 404 pp.; 169 color and 173 bw illus.

Carso, Kerry Dean. *American Gothic Art and Architecture in the Age of Romantic Literature*. Cardiff: University of Wales Press, 2015. xviii + 247 pp.; color illus.

Charney, Noah. *The Art of Forgery: The Minds, Motives, and Methods of Master Forgers*. New York: Phaidon Press, 2015. 294 pp.; color and bw illus., glossary, bibliography, index. (Primarily concerned with paintings, but of comparative interest.)

Cheek, Richard. *Selling the Dwelling: The Books That Built America's Houses, 1775–2000*. New York: Grolier Club, 2013. 287 pp.; numerous color illus., bibliography.

Cole, Caroline. Review of *Paul Evans: Crossing Boundaries and Crafting Modernism*, edited by Constance Kimmerle. In *American Furniture 2014*, 270–74.

Colman, Benjamin W. "The Painted Chests of the Connecticut Shore." *American Period Furniture: A Publication of the Society of American Period Furniture Makers* 14 (December 2014): 72–77. Color illus.

[Concord Museum]. "Exhibition Review." *Magazine of the Decorative Arts Trust* (fall 2014): 19. 1 color illus. (Re "Behind Closed Doors: Asleep in New England" at Concord Museum.)

——— "New Acquisition: The Hosmer Daybed." *Concord Museum Newsletter* (fall 2015): 3. 1 color illus. (Re maple daybed made in Concord, ca. 1745–1765.)

Condon, Katy Kiick. "The Marketplace . . . Massachusetts Tall-Case Clock." *Antiques* 181, no. 6 (November–December 2014): 54. 1 color illus. (Re western Massachusetts clock, ca. 1810–1815, with dramatic mahogany inlays, acquired by a private collection.)

[Connecticut Historical Society]. "Connecticut Historical Society Acquires Signed Stonington Chest on Chest." *Antiques and the Arts Weekly* (September 11, 2015): 34. 1 bw illus. (Re a ca. 1790 example signed by Ephraim Grant of North Stonington.)

—— "Connecticut Historical Society Adds Signed Belden Chest to Collection." *Antiques and the Arts Weekly* (July 3, 2015): 34. 1 bw illus. (Re cherry and pine chest of drawers, ca. 1790–1815, signed by George Belden of Hartford and Windsor.)

Coutinho, Maria Inês Lopes, ed. *Museo de Arte Sacra de Sao Paulo*. São Paulo: Museu de Arte Sacre de São Paulo, 2014. 336 pp.; numerous color illus.

Cross, John M. "The Joiners of Port Royal and Early Furniture Making in Jamaica." *Furniture History* 50 (2014): 127–45. 4 color illus.

Culp, Brandy. "Museum Accessions." *Antiques* 182, no. 1 (January–February 2015): 98. 1 color illus. (Re Charleston, S.C., linen press, ca. 1800–1810, acquired by Historic Charleston Foundation.)

Cunningham, Joseph. "Revolving Music Stand and Holder by Charles Rohlfs." In *Design Masters* (New York: Phillips, December 16, 2014), lot 103. 3 color illus.

D'Agostino, Carl. "An FDR Gallery." *Watch & Clock Bulletin* 57, no. 2 (March–April 2015): 145–47. 11 color illus.

D'Ambrosio, Paul, et al. *American Folk Art, Lovingly Collected*. Worcester, Mass.: Worcester Art Museum, 2015. 79 pp.; color illus., index.

Davis, Hollie. "The Cincinnati Wing." *Antiques and the Arts Weekly* (October 23, 2015): 1C, 16C–17C. Color illus.

——— "A Tradition of Progress: Ohio Decorative Arts, 1860–1945." *Antiques and the Arts Weekly* (April 13, 2015): 1, 30–32. Color and bw illus.

Davis, Hollie, and Andrew Richmond. "A Steady Growth of Independence: Joshua Shipman and the Economy of Frontier Craftsmanship." In *American Furniture 2014*, 202–23. 16 color and bw illus.

Davison, Elizabeth A. "Research Note: Scottish Bedroom Tables from Scotland to the American South." *Journal of Early Southern Decorative Arts* 35 (2014). 34 color and bw illus. Online at www.mesdajournal.org (accessed January 6, 2015).

Delphia, Rachel. "The Allure of Leeds House." *Antiques* 182, no. 2 (March–April 2015): 70–87. 31 color illus.

——— *Nakashima Revealed: The Carnegie Mellon Collection*. Pittsburgh, Pa.: Regina Gonger Miller Gallery, Carnegie Mellon University, 2007. 44 pp.; color and bw illus.

Demeter, David, and Andrew Demeter. *Chelsea Clock Company: The First Hundred Years*. 2nd rev. ed. Topsfield, Mass.: Demeter Publications, 2014. 360 pp.; numerous color and bw illus., indexes.

Dervan, Andrew H. "The Bicentennial Commemorative Clock." *Watch & Clock Bulletin* 56, no. 6 (November–December 2014): 624–28. 16 bw illus.

——— "Small Mantel, Boudoir, Large Mantel, Mirror, and Wall Clocks from Waltham Clock Co." *Watch & Clock Bulletin* 57, no. 2 (March–April 2015): 172–76. 14+ bw illus.

Design: The Definitive Visual History. New York: DK Publishing, 2015. 480 pp.; numerous color illus., index. (Published in cooperation with the Smithsonian Institution.)

Dew, Eleanor Sarah. "Lenygon & Morant: The American Connection." *Furniture History Society Newsletter*, no. 200 (November 2015): 2–7. 4 color illus.

Dilnot, Clive, Susan Stewart, and Tony Fry. *Design and the Question of History*. London: Bloomsbury Academic, 2014. 224 pp.

"The Dominy Craftsmen Collection." http://digital.library.wisc.edu/1711.dl/Dominy. (Archival materials and related resources now available online through the efforts of Charles Hummel, University of Wisconsin–Madison Digital Collections Center, Chipstone Foundation, and Winterthur Museum, Garden & Library.)

Donnelly, Max. "'Rapture and Ridicule': Furniture in the 1862 Medieval Court." *The Decorative Arts Society: 1850 to the Present* 38 (2014): 107–31. 20 color illus. (In special issue devoted to the International Exhibition of 1862 in London.)

Dorward, Thomas. "A Clock Returns Home." *Watch & Clock Bulletin* 57, no. 4 (July–August 2015): 340–44. 7 color illus.

Dotson, Steffanie. "Green Furniture: An Assessment of Furniture Society Member Work." *Journal of Green Building* 10, no. 3 (summer 2015): 47–66. Illus.

Eames, Demetrios, et al. *Eames: Beautiful Details*. Los Angeles: AMMO Books, 2012. 408 pp.; numerous color and bw illus.

Edwards, W. Patrick. "European Influences on American and Colonial Design." *American Period Furniture: A Publication of the Society of American Period Furniture Makers* 14 (December 2014): 4–9. Color illus., bibliography.

Eerdmans, Emily Evans, with Dave Barry, Glenn Adamson, and Jane Adlin. *Wendell Castle: A Catalogue Raisonné, 1958–2012*. New York: Artist Book Foundation, 2014. 515 pp.; numerous color and bw illus., bibliography, index.

Ehrenpreis, Diane. "Family Life at Monticello: The 2nd 2nd and 3rd Floors Revealed." *Antiques and Fine Art* 14, no. 4 (winter 2015): 142–49. 11 color illus.

Emlen, Robert P. "A Note about the Manning Chair at Brown University." *Furniture History Society Newsletter*, no. 197 (February 2015): 1–5. 5 color illus.

Emmett, Ric. *American Art Deco Furniture*. [Miami, Fla.]: Art Deco Pros Books, 2014. 567 pp.; numerous color and bw illus., bibliography.

Englund, Alyce Perry. "Speaking through Wood." *Antiques* 182, no. 4 (July–August 2015): 92–95. 6 color illus.

Evans, Nancy Goyne. "Documentary Evidence of Colored Finishes and Decoration on Bedsteads and Cornices: Late Colonial and Federal Periods." In *American Furniture 2014*, 224–56. 22 color illus.

Ewing, Heather. *Life of a Mansion: The Story of Cooper Hewitt, Smithsonian Design Museum*. New York: Cooper Hewitt, Smithsonian Design Museum, 2014. 155 pp.; 110 color and 50 bw illus., line drawings, index.

Fairbrother, Trevor, John T. Kirk, et al. *Collecting and Sharing*. Hanover, N.H.: Hood Museum of Art, 2015. 164 pp.; 183 color and bw illus., checklist. Distributed by University Press of New England, Lebanon, N.H.

Feld, Elizabeth, and Stuart Feld. *Very Rich and Handsome: American Neo-classical Decorative Arts*. New York: Hirschl & Adler Galleries, 2014. 144 pp.; numerous color illus., bibliography.

Fiske, John. "East Comes West: Boston's MFA Shows the Oriental Influence upon the Decorative Arts of the Americas." *New England Antiques Journal* 35, no. 4 (October 2015): 36–40. Color illus.

——— "The Innovator of Ipswich: Abraham Knowlton, 'workman of rare skill.'" *New England Antiques Journal* 34, no. 7 (January 2015): 36–40. Color and bw illus.

Flanders, Judith. *The Making of Home: The 500-Year Story of How Our Houses Became Our Homes*. New York: Thomas Dunne Books, St. Martin's Press, 2015. xii + 346 pp.; 32 color and bw illus., bibliography, index.

Forman, Bruce Ross. "Laurence Birnie and the Apprentice Griffith Owen." *Watch & Clock Bulletin* 57, no. 2 (March–April 2015): 170–71. 2 bw illus.

Franklin, Jamie. "Examining America's Artistic Grass Roots." *Antiques and Fine Art* 14, no. 3 (autumn 2015): 160–67. 12 color illus.

Frishman, Bob. "Horology in Art: Part 18." *Watch & Clock Bulletin* 57, no. 1 (January–February 2015): 46. 1 color ilus. (Re Genre painting *Family Life on the Frontier*, 1845, by George Caleb Bingham, depicting a Connecticut shelf clock.)

———. "Horology in Art: Part 21." *Watch & Clock Bulletin* 57, no. 4 (July–August 2015): 328. 1 color illus. (Re painting by Eric Green.)

Fuller Craft Museum. *Crafting a Collection: Fuller Craft Museum Recent Acquisitions*. Brockton, Mass.: Fuller Craft Museum, 2014. 36 pp.; color illus., checklist. (With essays by Jonathan L. Fairbanks and Beth C. McLaughlin.)

"The Furniture Issue." *American Craft*, digital bonus issue, 2015. 83 pp.; numerous color illus. Available at http://craftcouncil.org/content/2015-digital-bonus-issue-furniture-issue (accessed November 1, 2015).

Garnier, Richard, and Jonathan Carter. *The Golden Age of English Horology: Masterpieces from the Tom Scott Collection*. Winchester, Eng.: Square Press, 2015. 480 pp.; numerous color and bw illus., index.

Gaskill, Malcolm. *Between Two Worlds: How the English Became Americans*. New York: Basic Books, 2014. xxviii + 484 pp.; bw illus., maps, bibliography, index. (Includes illustration of a Hadley chest.)

Gerritsen, Anne, and Giorgio Riello, eds. *Writing Material Culture History*. London: Bloomsbury Academic, 2015. xiv + 338 pp.; illus.

[Gould, Nathaniel]. "A Salem Cabinetmaker Comes into Sharper Focus." *New York Times,* November 7, 2014, C32. 2 color illus.

Granston, Willie. "Influences from Abroad: Biedermeier Chairs in a New York Town House." In *52nd Annual Delaware Antiques Show* [catalogue] (Wilmington, Del.: Delaware Antiques Show, 2015), 103–6. 4 color illus.

Grant, Daniel. "Museum Acquisitions: Top Picks of 2014." *Antiques and Fine Art* 14, no. 1 (winter–spring 2015): 128–37. 17 color illus. (Includes joined table, ca. 1690, given to the Fogg by Anne H. and Frederick Vogel III, and a Byrdcliffe chair, 1904, given to the St. Louis Art Museum by Mr. and Mrs. Edward J. Nusrala.)

Graves, Leroy. *Early Seating Upholstery: Reading the Evidence*. Williamsburg, Va.: Colonial Williamsburg Foundation, 2015. ix + 227 pp.; 371 color illus., index.

Guérin, Polly. *The General Society of Mechanics and Tradesmen of the City of New York: A History*. Charleston, S.C.: History Press, 2015. 219 pp.; bw illus., two appendixes, bibliography.

Guichon, Françoise, ed. *100 Masterpieces of Design*. Centre Pompidou. Paris: Éditions du Centre Pompidou, 2011. 120 pp.; 100 color illus., index.

Haaff, Rainer. *Magnificent 19th-Century Furniture: Historicism in Germany and Central Europe*. Atglen, Pa.: Schiffer, 2014. 656 pp.; 3,000 color illus., bibliography. (Pictorial survey useful for Continental related works.)

Haas, Nikolai, Simon Haas, Laura Dern, and Vincent Gallo. *The Haas Brothers*. Bologna, Italy: Damiani, 2014. 176 pp.; illus.

Habib, Vanessa, Jim Gray, and Sheila Forbes, eds. *Making for America: Transatlantic Craftsmanship; Scotland and the Americas in the Eighteenth and Nineteenth Centuries*. Edinburgh: Society of Antiquaries of Scotland, 2013. xxvii + 236 pp.; numerous color illus., maps (See essays on furniture by Michael K. Brown, Alexandra A. Kirtley, Stephen Jackson, and David Jones.)

Hall, Toby. "Boston Furniture at the Colonial Society." *Colonial Society of Massachusetts* [newsletter] 20, no. 1 (September 2015): 1–3. 2 bw illus.

Hawkes, Jeff. "Scholar Leaves 112 Tall Clocks as Part of a $9.7 Million Legacy." *Antiques and the Arts Weekly* (March 27, 2015): 43. (Re Pennsylvania clocks bequeathed to seventeen institutions by the estate of John J. Snyder Jr.)

Heal, Oliver S. *Sir Ambrose Heal and the Heal Cabinet Factory, 1897–1939*. Wetherby, Eng.: Oblong Creative, 2014. 312 pp.; numerous color and bw illus.

Heckman, Bruce, and Lynn Heckman. "Spruce Gum Boxes: Folk Art for Sweethearts." *Maine Antique Digest* 43, no. 11 (November 2015): 19C–22C. Color and bw illus.

Henion, Paul, with contributions from Mary Jane Dapkus and Russell Oechsle. "Lithographs: A Follow-Up Article with New Information from Ledger Books and Other Speculation." *Watch & Clock Bulletin* 57, no. 2 (March–April 2015): 140–44. 4 color and bw illus.

Herring, Scott. The *Hoarders: Material Deviance in Modern American Culture*. Chicago: University of Chicago Press, 2014. xii + 185 pp.; illus., bibliography, index.

Herzberg, Lesley. *The Shakers: History, Culture, and Craft*. New York: Shire, 2015. 64 pp.; color and bw illus., bibliography, index.

[Hirschl & Adler Galleries]. "Current and Coming: 'Very Rich and Handsome' at Hirschl & Adler Galleries." *Antiques* 182, no. 1 (January–February 2015): 22. 3 color illus.

[Historic Deerfield, Inc.]. "Historic Deerfield Acquires 1803 Tall-Case Clock." *Antiques and the Arts Weekly* (July 10, 2015): 33. 1 bw illus. (Re example by William Lloyd of Springfield, Mass.)

———. "Historic Deerfield Acquires 1803 Tall-Case Clock." *Maine Antique*

Digest 43, no. 8 (August 2015): 8A. 1 bw illus.

———. "Recent Acquisitions." *Historic Deerfield 2014 Annual Report* (Deerfield, Mass.: Historic Deerfield, 2014), 13–17. (Includes tall-case clock by Aaron Willard, ca. 1800, with case attributed to Stephen Badlam, and with history of ownership by Asa Stebbins.)

———. "Recent Acquisitions." *Antiques and the Arts Weekly* (October 2, 2015): S20. 7 bw illus.

Hodge, Susie. *When Design Really Works*. Hauppauge, N.Y.: Barron's, 2014. 223 pp.; color and bw illus., index.

Hofer, Margaret K., Roberta J. M. Olson, et al. *Making It Modern: The Folk Art Collection of Elie and Viola Nadelman*. New York: New-York Historical Society in association with D Giles Limited, London, 2015. 376 pp.; numerous color and bw illus., catalogue, appendixes, bibliography, index.

Hornberger, Patrick, and Joe Kindig III. *Masterpieces of the American Longrifle: The Joe Kindig, Jr., Collection*. Trappe, Md.: Eastwind Publishing, 2015. ix + 149 pp.; numerous color and bw illus., bibliography, index.

Hosley, William. "Folk Art in New England." *Antiques and the Arts Weekly* (August 14, 2015): 1C, 5C–7C. Color illus.

Hunt, Michael John. *Historic Rooms of Winterthur: Paintings by Michael John Hunt*. Winterthur, Del.: Henry Francis du Pont Winterthur Museum, 2015. 128 pp.; color illus., index.

Hurst, Ronald L. "Southern Furniture Studies: Where We've Been, Where We're Going." *Journal of Early Southern Decorative Arts* 36 (2015). Available online at www.mesdajournal.org (accessed September 9, 2015).

[Irving & Casson–A. H. Davenport]. "Irving & Casson–A. H. Davenport Carving Promotes Political Amity." *Historic New England News* (March–April 2015): 4. 1 color illus.

Johnson, Bruce E. *Tales of the Grove Park Inn*. Fletcher, N.C.: Knock on Wood Publications, 2013. 373 pp.; illus.

Johnson, Don. "*Tradition of Progress* Exhibit." *Maine Antique Digest* 43, no. 5 (May 2015): 25B–27B. bw illus.

Johnson, Kathleen Eagen. "Rich and Tasty: Vermont Furniture to 1850." *Antiques and the Arts Weekly* (July 17, 2015): 1C, 30–31. Color and bw illus.

———. "Every Variety of Painting for Lodges: Decorated Furniture, Paintings, and Ritual Objects from the Collection." *Antiques and the Arts Weekly* (June 12, 2015): 1C, 10C–11C. Color illus.

———. "In Plain Sight: Discovering the Furniture of Nathaniel Gould." *Antiques and the Arts Weekly* (November 21, 2014): 1C, 10C–12C. Color illus. (See also Kathleen Eagen Johnson and Kemble Widmer, "For Scholars of Nathaniel Gould, Questions Remain," 12C.)

———. "Made in the Americas: The New World Discovers Asia." *Antiques and the Arts Weekly* (August 21, 2015): 11, 30–31. Color and bw illus.

———. "The Shakers from Mount Lebanon to the World." *Antiques and the Arts Weekly* (August 29, 2014): 1C, 8C–9C. Color illus.

Johnson, Steven. *How We Got to Now: Six Innovations That Made the Modern World*. New York: Riverhead Books, 2014. 293 pp.; bw illus., bibliography, index. (With sections on the significance of looking glasses and clocks.)

Johnston, Patricia, and Caroline Franks, eds. *Global Trade and Visual Arts in Federal New England*. Durham: University of New Hampshire Press; Hanover and London: University Press of New England, 2014. x + 325 pp.; 27 color and numerous bw illus., index.

Katz, Allan, Americana. *Allan Katz Americana*. Woodbridge, Conn.: by the gallery, 2015. Unpaged; color illus.

Keim, Laura C. *Logania: Stenton Collections Reassembled*. Philadelphia: National Society of the Colonial Dames of America in the Commonwealth of Pennsylvania, 2015. 52 pp.; 41+ color illus., chart, line drawing, bibliography.

———, comp. and ed. *Stenton: A Visitor's Guide to the Site, History, and Collections*. Philadelphia: National Society of the Colonial Dames of America in the Commonwealth of Pennsylvania, 2014. 64 pp.; color illus., chart, line drawings.

Kelly, Andrew, ed. *Kentucky by Design: The Decorative Arts and American Culture*. Lexington: University Press of Kentucky, 2015. xiv + 311 pp.; 207 color illus., catalogue.

Kenny, Peter. "Ark of the Covenant: The Remarkable Inlaid Scrutoir from the Brinckerhoff Family of Newtown, Long Island." In *American Furniture 2014*, 2–29. 34 color illus.

Kirtley, Alexandra Alevizatos. "Looking Both Ways." *Antiques* 182, no. 1 (January–February 2015): 146–53. 12 color illus.

Kirtley, Alexandra Alevizatos, and James Gergat. "Subject to Debate: Response." *Antiques* 182, no. 3 (May–June 2015): 54–56. (See also article by Jay Robert Stiefel listed below.)

———. "Two New Names in Delaware Valley Furniture." *Antiques* 182, no. 1 (January–February 2015): 88, 90. 5 color illus. (Re signed pieces by Henry Finney and Henry Carter.)

Klein, Joshua A. "From Head, Heart, and Hand." *American Period Furniture: A Publication of the Society of American Period Furniture Makers* 14 (December 2014): 34–41. Color illus. (Re Jonathan Fisher [1768-1847] of Blue Hill, Maine.)

Kopf, Silas. Review of *To Make as Perfectly as Possible: Roubo on Marquetry*, by André-Jacob Roubo, Don Williams, Michelle Pietryka-Pagán, and Phillipe Lafargue. In *American Furniture 2014*, 260–62.

Korvenmae, Pekka. *Finnish Design: A Concise History*. Rev. ed. Helsinki: Aalto ARTS; London: V&A Publishing, 2014. 343 pp.; color and bw illus., bibliography, indexes.

Krakowski, Adam. Review of *Harbor and Home: Furniture of Southeastern Massachusetts, 1710–1850*, by Brock Jobe, Gary R. Sullivan, and Jack O'Brien. In *Historical Journal of Massachusetts* 41, no. 1 (winter 2013): 147–48.

Kristoffersson, Sara. *Design by IKEA: A Cultural History*. London: Bloomsbury Academic, 2014. viii + 148 pp.; 17 color and 22 bw illus., bibliography, index.

[Lane, Joshua W.]. *Cultivating Style in a Multiethnic World: New York Furniture, 1640–1860*. Winterthur, Del.: Henry Francis du Pont Winterthur Museum, 2015. 40 pp.; color illus.

Lange, Amanda. *Historic Deerfield: Art and Life in an Extraordinary New England Village*. Deerfield, Mass.: Historic Deerfield, 2014. 64 pp.; color illus.

Lasc, Anca I., Georgina Downey, and Mark Taylor, eds. *Designing the French Interior: The Modern Home and Mass Media*. London: Bloomsbury Academic, 2015. 272 pp.; 50 bw illus., index.

Lash, Steven M. "Double-twist Turned Chair." *American Period Furniture: A Publication of the Society of American Period Furniture Makers* 14 (December 2014): 48-55. Color and bw illus.

Leath, Robert A. "50 Years of MESDA: A Colorful Past, a Bright Future." *Antiques and Fine Art* 14, no. 3 (autumn 2015): 144-51. 13+ color illus.

[Leeds Art Foundation]. "Acquisitions." *Decorative Arts Society Newsletter* 23, no. 2 (fall 2015): 10. 2 bw illus. (Re settle and side chair, ca. 1903, by Gustav Stickley.)

[Louisiana State Museum]. "Gothic Revival Armoire Donated by M. S. Rau to the Louisiana State Museum." *Maine Antique Digest* 43, no. 10 (October 2015): 37C. 5 bw illus.

"Loyola Museum of Art Presents Three Shaker Exhibitions." *Antiques and the Arts Weekly* (March 20, 2015): 20. 3 bw illus.

[Lyndhurst]. *Three Parlors: The Furniture of A. J. Davis, J. and J. W. Meeks, and the Herter Brothers at Lyndhurst*. Tarrytown, N.Y.: Lyndhurst, 2015. 36 pp.; color illus.

MacCarthy, Fiona. *Anarchy and Beauty: William Morris and His Legacy, 1860–1960*. New Haven: Yale University Press, 2014. 184 pp.; 174 color and bw illus., biographies, bibliography, index. (Published for the National Portrait Gallery, London.)

Margolin, Victor. *World History of Design*. 2 vols. London: Bloomsbury Academic, 2015. 1,600 pp.; 181 color and 716 bw illus., bibliography, index.

Markey, Shaun. *Folk Art in the Attic: Adventures from a Lifetime of Hunting for Antiques and Folk Art*. Ottawa: Sonderho Press, 2014. 184 pp.; illus.

Mayer, Roberta A. *All the Raj: Frederic Church and Lockwood de Forest: Painting, Decorating, and Collecting at Olana*. Hudson, N.Y.: Evelyn and Maurice Sharp Gallery at Olana, 2014. Unpaged; color illus. (Small pamphlet accompanying an exhibition.)

McCracken, W. Michael. "From Unique to Concomitant: The Evolution of the Furniture Produced by the Stickley Firms; Part 1." *Notes from the Farms: The Journal of the Craftsman Farms Foundation* 23, no. 4 (winter 2014–2015): 6–7. 2 color illus.

——— "From Unique to Concomitant: The Evolution of the Furniture Produced by the Stickley Firms; Part 2." *Notes from the Farms: The Journal of the Craftsman Farms Foundation* 24, no. 1 (spring 2015): 6–7. 4 color illus.

McPherson, Anne S. "Fans, Fish, and Tassels: Idiosyncratic Inlaid Furniture of Northeastern Tennessee; Part I." *Antiques and Fine Art* 14, no. 1 (winter–spring 2015): 200–207. 9 color and 1 bw illus.

——— "Fans, Fish, and Tassels: Idiosyncratic Inlaid Furniture of Northeastern Tennessee; Part II." *Antiques and Fine Art* 14, no. 4 (winter 2015): 166–71. 9+ color and bw illus.

Miller, Alan. "Flux in Design and Method in Early Eighteenth-Century Philadelphia Furniture." In *American Furniture 2014*, 30–85. 68 color and bw illus.

Minardi, Lisa. "Adam Hains and the Philadelphia–Reading Connection." In *American Furniture 2014*, 142–201. 97 color and bw illus.

——— *A Colorful Folk: Pennsylvania Germans and the Art of Everyday Life*. Winterthur, Del.: Henry Francis du Pont Winterthur Museum, 2015. 69 pp.; 84+ color illus., checklist.

——— "'A Colorful Folk': Pennsylvania Germans and the Art of Everyday Life." *Antiques and Fine Art* 14, no. 2 (summer 2015): 154–61. 12+ color illus.

——— "Drawn with Spirit: Pennsylvania German Fraktur from the Joan and Victor Johnson Collection." *Antiques and Fine Art* 14, no. 1 (winter–spring 2015): 138–47. Color illus. (Includes furniture from the same region.)

Molesworth, Helen, with Ruth Erickson. *Leap Before You Look: Black Mountain College, 1933–1957*. New Haven: Yale University Press in association with Institute of Contemporary Art, Boston, 2015. 400 pp.; 318 color and 170 bw illus., checklist, bibliography, index.

Monkhouse, Christopher. "War, Politics, and the Diaspora of Irish Art and Design." *Antiques* 182, no. 2 (March–April 2015): 88–93. 8 color illus.

Monkhouse, Christopher, et al. *Ireland: Crossroads of Art and Design, 1690–1840*. Chicago: Art Institute of Chicago, 2015. 288 pp.; numerous color and bw illus.

Museum of Fine Arts, Houston. *Bayou Bend Collection and Gardens*. Houston: Bayou Bend Collection, Museum of Fine Arts, Houston, 2013. 100 pp.; numerous color illus., maps.

[New Britain Museum of Art]. "'Shakers: Focus on Enfield' Open at New Britain Museum." *Antiques and the Arts Weekly* (October 30, 2015): 9. 2 bw illus.

[New Hampshire Furniture Masters Association]. "Furniture Masters Present 'Schools of Thought.'" *Antiques and the Arts Weekly* (July 3, 2015): 11. 1 bw illus.

——— "NH Furniture Masters Exhibit at Thorne-Sagendorph Art Gallery." *Antiques and the Arts Weekly* (June 12, 2015): 38. 1 bw illus.

Newman, Richard, and Bruce Forman. "Nathaniel Mulliken and His Clockmaking Tools." *Watch & Clock Bulletin* 57, no. 4 (July–August 2015): 329–38. 21 color illus.

Nichols, Katherine. "Wood into Art." *Harvard Magazine* 117, no. 2 (January–February 2015): 61–64. 5 color illus. (Re studio furniture maker Anthony Giachetti.)

"Noteworthy Sales." *Antiques and Fine Art* 14, no. 1 (winter/spring 2015): 18. 1 color illus. (Re high chest of drawers, ca. 1720, attributed to Rhode Island.)

[Nutt, Roy and Ruth, collection]. *The Collection of Roy and Ruth Nutt: Important Americana and Decorative Arts.* New York: Sotheby's, January 23, 2015. 216 pp.; numerous color and bw illus.

[Nutting, Wallace]. "Wallace Nutting Works from Lecasse Collection at Cahoon." *Antiques and the Arts Weekly* (August 28, 2015): 9. 3 bw illus.

Nylander, Jane C. "From the Cradle to the Grave: Privacy and Comfort in New England Bedrooms, 1675–1875." *Antiques and Fine Art* 14, no. 1 (winter/spring 2015): 208–11. 7 color illus.

Obniski, Monica. "Selling Folk Art and Modern Design: Alexander Girard and Herman Miller's Textiles and Object Shop (1961–1967)." *Design History* 28, no. 3 (2015): 254–73. 7 color illus.

Olesen, Christian Holmsted. *Hans J. Wegner: Just One Good Chair.* Copenhagen: Design Museum Danmark; Ostfildern, Germany: Hatje Cantz, 2014. 254 pp.; numerous color and bw illus., bibliography, index.

Ostroff, Daniel, ed. *An Eames Anthology: Articles, Film Scripts, Interviews, Letters, Notes, Speeches by Charles and Ray Eames.* New Haven: Yale University Press, 2015. xviii + 402 pp.; numerous color and bw illus., index.

Parker, Alexandra. "Seeking American-Made Knife Boxes." *Magazine of the Decorative Arts Trust* (fall 2014): 5. 1 color illus.

Parks, Sarah. "Field Cataloging with Winterthur's Boston Furniture Archive." *Magazine of the Decorative Arts Trust* (fall 2014): 10. 3 color illus.

Peart, Darrell, and Edward Bosley. "Greene & Greene Furniture: Design without Compromise." *American Period Furniture: A Publication of the Society of American Period Furniture Makers* 14 (December 2014): 56–61. Color illus., bibliography.

Podmaniczky, Michael S. "Gragg's Wondrous Failure." *Historic New England* 16, no. 2 (fall 2015): 34. 3 color illus. (Re cache of papers associated with chairmaker Samuel Gragg.)

Puza, Christine. "Reviving the Lustrous History of a Chinese Lacquer Table." *Art Conservator: A Publication of the Williamstown Art Conservation Center* 10, no. 1 (spring 2015): 14–15. 3 color illus. (Re an example in the collection of Historic Deerfield.)

Rice, Albert E. *Four Centuries of Musical Instruments: The Marlowe A. Sigal Collection.* Atglen, Pa.: Schiffer, 2015. 320 pp.; numerous color illus., bibliography, index.

Russack, Rick. "A Colonial Gem in Portsmouth: The Moffatt-Ladd House and Garden." *New England Antiques Journal* 35, no. 4 (October 2015): 62–65. Color illus.

Scherer, Barrymore Laurence. "New Collectors: Children's Chairs." *Antiques* 181, no. 6 (November–December 2014): 40–48. 22 color and 1 bw illus.

Schinto, Jeanne. "Good Fellows: The Walpole Society, Part 1." *Maine Antique Digest* 43, no. 11 (November 2015): 29A–32A. bw illus.

——— "Good Fellows: The Walpole Society, Part 2." *Maine Antique Digest* 43, no. 12 (December 2015): 31C–35C. bw illus.

——— "Made in the Americas: The New World Discovers Asia." *Maine Antique Digest* 43, no. 11 (November 2015): 23B–25B. bw illus.

——— "A New Location for Chelsea Clock Company and a Second Edition of Its History." *Maine Antique Digest* 43, no. 4 (April 2015): 3D. 4 bw illus.

Seydl, Jon L., and Elizabeth Athens. "Room for Folk." *Antiques* 182, no. 4 (July–August 2015): 87–91. 12 color illus.

[Shaker Museum]. "The Small World of Shaker." *Antiques and the Arts Weekly* (July 31, 2015): 62. 1 bw illus.

Shaw, Gwendolyn DuBois, et al., with an essay by Richard J. Powell. *Represent: 200 Years of African American Art in the Philadelphia Museum of Art.* Philadelphia: Philadelphia Museum of Art, 2014. xiii + 210 pp.; numerous color photographs, bibliography, index.

Sherer, Barrymore Laurence. "Bewitching Wood in Salem." *Wall Street Journal*, January 12, 2015. (Re the book and exhibition "In Plain Sight: Discovering the Furniture of Nathaniel Gould.")

[Short, Joseph]. "Documented Joseph Short [1771–1819] Furniture Sought for Research." *Maine Antique Digest* 43, no. 9 (September 2015): 8A. 1 bw illus. (Re the work of a Newburyport, Massachusetts, cabinetmaker; contact Melissa Berry at melissadavenportberry@gmail.com.)

Siegel, Gerald. "Fashion Calendar Clocks Revisited and Updated: Part 1." *Watch & Clock Bulletin* 56, no. 6 (November–December 2014): 572–82. Color and bw illus., bibliography.

——— "Fashion Calendar Clocks Revisited and Updated: Part 2." *Watch & Clock Bulletin* 57, no. 1 (January–February 2015): 27–41. Color and bw illus., bibliography.

——— "Fashion Calendar Clocks Revisited and Updated: Part 3." *Watch & Clock Bulletin* 57, no. 2 (March–April 2015): 130–39. Color illus., biblio.

Sims, Lowery Stokes, et al. *Common Wealth: Art by African Americans in the Museum of Fine Arts, Boston.* Boston: MFA Publications, 2014. 256 pp.; numerous color and bw illus., artist biographies, bibliography, index. (Includes entries by Kelly Hays on a Thomas Day secretary and tall clock by Frank E. Cummings III.)

Sirene, Walt H. "An American Backcountry Tall Clock Made by Four Modern Masters, Part 2." *Watch & Clock Bulletin* 56, no. 6 (November–December 2014): 592–602. 23 color and bw illus., 2 addenda.

Smith, Paul J., photographer. *Masters of Craft: 224 Artists in Fiber, Clay, Glass, Metal, and Wood.* Atglen, Pa.: Schiffer, 2015. 248 pp.; color illus., bibliography, index.

Solis-Cohen, Lita. "Fresh-to-Market Philadelphia Tea Table Sells for

$1,895,000." *Maine Antique Digest* 43, no. 4 (April 2015): 29A–30A. bw illus. (Re example with signature of Henry Clifton and carving attributed to the "spike" carver, auctioned in January 2015 by Keno Auctions.)

— — — "Hooper Family High Chest Sells for $257,000." *Maine Antique Digest* 43, no. 2 (February 2015): 10A. 1 bw illus.

— — — "The Musselmans of Murrell: Pioneer Dealers in Pennsylvania German and Early American Antiques." *Maine Antique Digest* 43, no. 1 (January 2015): 14C–15C. 5 bw illus.

— — — "New York Furniture Forum." *Maine Antique Digest* 43, no. 8 (August 2015): 9C–10C. 4 bw illus.

— — — "Pewter-Inlaid Clock Sells for $192,000." *Maine Antique Digest* 43, no. 11 (November 2015): 10A. 3 bw illus. (Re tall clock dated 1762 by Rudolph Stoner of Lancaster County, Pennsylvania, acquired by Chipstone Foundation.)

— — — "Who Designed the Stickley Furniture Sold at Bonhams?" *Maine Antique Digest* 43, no. 12 (December 2015): 14A. 4 bw illus.

— — — "Winterthur Announces Acquisitions." *Maine Antique Digest* 43, no. 5 (May 2015): 12A. 3 bw illus. (Re dressing bureau by Isaac Vose and Son of Boston, acquired in honor of Wendy A. Cooper, and a John Shearer chest of 1809.)

— — — Review of *American Furniture 2014*, edited by Luke Beckerdite. In *Maine Antique Digest* 43, no. 6 (June 2015): 7B–9B. 1 bw illus.

— — — Review of *Very Rich and Handsome: American Neo-Classical Decorative Arts*, by Elizabeth Feld and Stuart Feld. In *Maine Antique Digest* 43, no. 3 (March 2015): 31D. 1 color illus.

Sperling, David A. "The Hunterdon County Clock Case and the Enigmatic John Guild." *Watch & Clock Bulletin* 56, no. 6 (November–December 2014): 629–37. 11+ bw illus.

— — — "A 'War of 1812' Shannon/Chesapeake Clock." *Watch & Clock Bulletin* 57, no. 3 (May–June 2015): 226–31. 5+ color illus.

[Spitler, Johannes]. "Noteworthy Sale: Extremely Important Johannes Spitler Painted Blanket Chest." *Antiques and Fine Art* 14, no. 3 (autumn 2015): 16. 1 color illus.

Spittler, Tom. "Was It Eli Terry or Was It Napoleon?" *Watch & Clock Bulletin* 56, no. 6 (November–December 2014): 621–23. 1 bw illus., bibliography.

[Stickley Museum at Craftsman Farms]. "A Tale of Two Tables." *Notes from the Farms: The Journal of the Craftsman Farms Foundation* 24, no. 1 (spring 2015): 1–2. 2 color and 1 bw illus. (Re only known No. 410-L with flat hammered tacks and No. 634 by Gustav Stickley.)

Stiefel, Jay Robert. "'Beyond expectation, beautiful, graceful and superb': Inlaid Miniature Chests of the Philadelphia Circus, ca. 1793." *Antiques and Fine Art* 14, no. 2 (summer 2015): 138–45. 10+ color and bw illus.

— — — *Rococo and Classicism in Proprietary Philadelphia: The Origins of the "Penn Family Chairs."* Philadelphia: Library Company of Philadelphia for the Welcome Society of Pennsylvania, 2008. 21 pp.; color and bw illus.

— — — "Subject to Debate: A Reappraisal of 'Two New Names in Delaware Valley Furniture.'" *Antiques* 182, no. 3 (May–June 2015): 50–52. 7 color illus. (See also response by Alexandra Alevizatos Kirtley and James Gergat listed above.)

Stocks, David, Jerry Grant, and Sir Terence Conran. *Shaker: Function, Purity, Perfection*. New York: Assouline in association with Laffanour and Ségalot, 2015. 144 pp.; color illus.

Swigger, Jessie. *"History is Bunk": Assembling the Past at Henry Ford's Greenfield Village*. Amherst: University of Massachusetts Press, 2014. 232 pp.; illus., bibliography, index.

Tartt, Donna. *The Goldfinch*. New York: Little, Brown, 2013. 771 pp. (A long-winded novel featuring in part a discussion of dealing and faking American furniture.)

Tatham, Sandra L., ed. *Treasures of the Athenaeum: 200 Years of Collecting*. Philadelphia: Athenaeum of Philadelphia, 2014. 44 pp.; color illus. (Includes pier table by Anthony Quervelle, 1825–1830.)

Tauber, Mike. *Retro Radio: Six Decades of Design, 1920s–1970s*. Atglen, Pa.: Schiffer, 2014. 176 pp.; color and bw illus., index.

Thomé, Philippe. *Sottsass*. London: Phaidon, 2014. 470 pp.; numerous color and bw illus., bibliography, index.

Trent, Robert F. Review of *Early Seating Furniture: Reading the Evidence* by Leroy Graves. In *Antiques and Fine Art* 14, no. 4 (winter 2015): 174–75. 2 color illus.

[Victoria Mansion]. "Herter Original Returns Home." *Antiques and the Arts Weekly* (August 21, 2015): 26. 1 bw illus.

Vida, Christina. "Strong-Howard House: Touching the Past." *American Period Furniture: A Publication of the Society of American Period Furniture Makers* 14 (December 2014): 22–29. Color illus. (Includes section on "Windsor's 21st-Century Furnituremakers" by Bob Van Dyke.)

Votana, Joseph R. *The Shaker Legacies: Hancock and Mount Lebanon*. Atglen, Pa.: Schiffer, 2015. 160 pp.; 180 color and bw illus., bibliography, index of plates.

[Wadsworth Atheneum Museum of Art]. "Bingham Secretary: A Folk Art Masterpiece Acquired by Wadsworth Atheneum Museum." *Antiques and the Arts Weekly* (March 27, 2015): 40. 1 bw illus.

— — — "Noteworthy Sales: Folk Art Masterpiece." *Antiques and Fine Art* 14, no. 2 (summer 2015): 14. 1 color illus. (Re Bingham family secretary.)

— — — "Wadsworth Atheneum Museum of Art Acquires Bingham Family Civil War Memorial Secretary." *Maine Antique Digest* 43, no. 5 (May 2015): 8A. 1 bw illus.

Ward, Gerald W. R., comp. "Recent Writing on American Furniture: A Bibliography." In *American Furniture 2014*, 275–84.

Watkins, Charles Alan. "The Tea Table's

Tale: Authenticity and Colonial Williamsburg's Early Furniture Reproduction Program." *West 86th: A Journal of Decorative Arts, Design History, and Material Culture* 21, no. 2 (fall/winter 2014): 155–91. 17 color and bw illus.

[Widdifield, John]. "Manuscript Furniture Designs by an Early 18th-century Philadelphia Joiner." *Printed and Manuscript Americana*, sale 2391 (New York: Swann Auction Galleries, September 17, 2015), lot 173. 1 color illus. (Re rare drawings of furniture and other notations by Widdifield [1673–1720], who was trained in England and came to Philadelphia ca. 1705. See also article by Laura Beach cited in this list.)

Willougby, Martha. Review of *Thistles & Crowns: The Painted Chests of the Connecticut Shore*, by Benjamin Colman. In *American Furniture 2014*, 262–67.

Wilson, Kristina. "Like a 'Girl in a Bikini Suit'" and Other Stories: The Herman Miller Furniture Company, Gender and Race at Mid-Century." *Design History* 28, no. 2 (2015): 161–81. 12 color and bw illus.

Wood, Lucy. "Tied Up in Knots: Three Centuries of the Ribbon-Back Chair." *Furniture History* 51 (2015): 241-70. 18 color and bw illus., appendix.

Yoon, Haejeong. "Horn of Plenty: The History and Conservation of a Cornucopia Mirror." *Art Conservator: A Publication of the Williamstown Art Conservation Center* 10, no. 1 (spring 2015): 8–11, 18. 5 color illus. (Re a mirror once thought to be from Salem, now attributed to Germany.)

Yudina, Anna. *Furnitecture: Furniture That Transforms Space*. New York: Thames and Hudson, 2015. 272 pp.; numerous color and bw illus., index.

Yuzna, Jake, ed. *NYC Makers: The 2014 MAD Biennial*. New York: Museum of Arts and Design, 2014. iii + 259 pp.; numerous color and bw illus., bibliography.

Zilber, Emily. *Crafted: Objects in Flux*. Boston: MFA Publications, 2015. 176 pp.; numerous color illus., checklist, bibliography.

Zimmerman, Philip D. Review of *In Plain Sight: The Furniture of Nathaniel Gould*, by Kemble Widmer and Joyce King. In *West 86th: A Journal of Decorative Arts, Design History, and Material Culture* 22, no. 1 (spring/summer 2015): 94–96. 1 bw illus.

Index

Account books: James Logan, 18–19; John Head, 1, 2, 13; Nathaniel Gould, 209; Thomas Chalkley, 9(fig.)
Ache, Samuel, 154
Adamson, Glenn, 209, 213–14
Air Line Chair, 201, 204
Algier, Joseph, 126
Alleman, Anna Maria, 168
Alleman, Christopher and Elisabeth (Shaffner), 168–69
Alleman, Conrad, 168, 169
Alleman, John Christian, 169
Alleman, Margaret, 168, 168(&fig. 169), 198n73
Alleman, Martin, 168–69(&fig. 170)
Allen, Nathaniel, 5
Altar sticks, 114, 115(fig.)
American Institute of Conservation, 219
American Philosophical Society, 91
American Revolution, Gould and, 212
Anderson, Mark, 70, 87
Animal motifs, sulfur-inlaid furniture and, 77
Antiques magazine, 70, 197n68
The Architecture of Country Houses (Downing), 206–7
Arsenic, 71, 91
Art Center School (Los Angeles), 204
Art Galleries of the University of California, Santa Barbara, 201
Asia, influence in Americas, 215–18
Atlantic white cedar: gate-leg table, 13(fig.); scrutoires, 6(fig.), 7(fig. 5)

Bachman, Maria, 104(figs.), 105, 133(&figs.), 134
Bachman, Michael, 133
Bachman, Peter, 104(figs.), 105, 133
Bachman, Veronica, 101
Bachmann, John, 106
Bachmann, Peter, 106
Bailey, Gauvin Alexander, 215
Ball feet, 159

Bamberger, Anna, 109–10, 137
Bamberger, Christian and Maria, 137
Baptists, Philadelphia, 3–4, 5, 14n5
Barker Brothers, 203, 204
Barniz de Pasto, 217
Bartholomew, Nicholas, 126
Bartholomew, Theodore, 126
Bartruff, Andreas, 142(&figs.)
Bassler, Dorothea, 156
Batruff, Andreas, Jr., 142–43
Bauer, Georg (Georgius Agricola), 90
Baum, Adam and Veronica (Gingerich), 166
Baum, Charles, 197n66
Baum, Magdalena, 166, 167(fig. 167)
Bauman, Wendell, 92
Bedwell, Thomas, 71, 85n5
"Behind the Curve: Putting Nathaniel Gould in Perspective" (Adamson), 213–14
Beierle, Andreas and Catharina, 94(&fig.)
Bentlock line, Higgins Furniture, 203
Berg, Andrew, 110
Berg, Veronica, 110, 192n17
Besore, Daniel, 119(fig. 65), 120, 193n27
Besore, David, 120
Besore, Jacob, 120(&fig.)
Betz, Samuel, 157
Biles, Thomas, 5
Biombas, 216
Birch, tall clock case, 82(fig.)
Bird motif, 68(fig.), 128, 129(fig.), 135(&figs.), 178–79(&figs.)
Biringuccio, Vannoccio, 91
Birth and baptismal certificates, 120(fig.), 157–58(&fig. 141), 161, 172(fig.)
Bixby, Walter E., Sr., 204
Bixby House, Weber and, 204
Black walnut: gate-leg table, 13(fig.); sulfur inlay and, 69; tall clock, 94(figs.)
Blimler, Gottlieb, 126
Blockfront designs, 210

Blower & Cogan, 11, 15n16
Blue Book Philadelphia Furniture (Hornor), 1, 7(fig. 5)
Bohl, J. David, 208
Bologna (Italy), chest, 89(figs.)
Bombé form, 210, 213, 214
Bone inlay, 124(figs.)
Boshaar, John, 120
Bower, Anna Maria, 110
Bowers, Rachel, 195n39
Box with drawer, walnut, 189(fig. 216)
Bracket feet, 159(&fig. 145), 210, 214
Bradford, Thomas G., 208
Brandt, Adam, Jr., 185
Brandt, Adam and Anna, 184(fig. 202), 185
Brandt, Barbara, 185
Brandt, Elisabeth, 160–61(&fig. 148)
Brandt, Esther, 161
Brandt, Ludwig, 160–61(&fig. 147)
Brandt, Martin, 160–61
Branson, William, 4, 14n6, 18
Braun, Jane, 216
"Brides, Housewives, and Hostesses" (Widmer), 213
Briggs, Lyman, 207
Britnall, David, Jr., 21
Brook, Timothy, 215, 218
Brotzman, Peter, 126
Brua, Anna Maria, 162
Brua, Elisabeth, 161–62(&fig. 151), 163, 197n69
Brua, Gustavus, 162
Brua, Jacob, 162, 197n69
Brua, Johann Peter, 162
Brua, Johann Theobald/Dewalt, 161–62
Brua, Peter, Jr., 163
Brua,Theobald, Jr., 162
Brunner, Hattie, 87, 88, 95(fig. 15)
Bureau table, 214
Burkhard, George, 126, 127
Burkhard/Burkhart/Burkert, George, 126
Burkhart, Anna Barbara, 181
Burks, Jean M., 205–9
Burnham, Helen, 216
Butter mold, 76(fig. 13)

The Cabinet and Chair-Maker's Real Friend and Companion (Manwaring), 211
Cabot family, 211, 212
Cadwalader, John, 5
Calcite, 81
Calvert, Charles, 171

Candlesticks, 114, 115(fig.)
Caribbean trade, 211, 212–13
Carl, Anna Maria, 172
Carr, Dennis, 215–18
Cazenove, Theophile, 144–45
Chalk, 81
Chalkley, Thomas, 15n15; furniture commission, 9(fig.), 10–11, 13
Chancellor, William, 8
Charleton, R. J., 18
Cherry, tall clocks, 112, 113(figs.), 117(figs.), 119(figs.)
Chest façade, walnut, 80(figs. 28&29), 160(fig. 147)
Chest of drawers, walnut, 173(figs.)
Chest over drawers, 109; walnut, 184(fig. 202), 185(&figs.)
Chests, 130(figs.), 131, 158(figs. 142&143), 160(fig. 148), 161(fig.), 164(figs.), 165–68(&figs.), 178(figs.), 180(figs.), 184(fig. 201)
Chinoiserie, 216
Chipman, John, 210
Chippendale, Thomas, 210, 211
Chipstone Foundation, Widdifield notebook and, 17
Chisel, sulfur inlay technique and, 76–77, 78(fig. 20)
Christ Lutheran Church (Stouchsburg), 155–56(&fig. 138), 157, 162, 165
Christ Lutheran Church (York), 176
Cinderella Table, 213
Claypoole, George, 1
Claypoole, James, 1
Claypoole, Joseph, 1
Claypoole, Josiah, 1
Clemm, Johann Gottlob, 155–56
Clocks. *See* Tall clocks
Codding, Mitchell, 215, 217
Coffman, Beulah Bowers, 176
Collynns, Samuel, 11
Colonial Williamsburg, 219, 220
Colonial Williamsburg Foundation, 218
Color change, in sulfur inlay over time, 83–84(&figs. 36&37)
Colorimetry, of sulfur inlay, 82
Compass star, 158–59(&fig. 143), 165(fig. 161), 166, 167(fig. 166)
Conestoga Auction Company, 199n89
Conestoga Massacre, 116
Conestoga settlement, 92–93
Conewago area: gravestones, 174–75(&figs.); sulfur-inlaid furniture, 170–74(&figs. 175–76, 178–79)

Confectioner's trade, sulfur inlay on furniture and, 75–76(&figs. 12–15)
Connecticut River valley case furniture, 214
Connoisseurship of furniture, 206
Conrad, Frederick, 198n73
Cooke, Edward S., Jr., 219
Corner cupboards: pine, 146(fig. 117); walnut, 72(figs.), 73, 81(&figs.), 179(fig. 189)
Cornice, 152; tall clock, 147–48(&fig. 121)
Corrigan, Karina H., 215
Cradles, walnut, 141–42(&figs. 105&106), 153–54(&figs. 132–34)
Culture and Comfort: People, Parlors, and Upholstery, 1850–1930 (Grier), 219
Customs' House (Oswego, New York), 73
Cypress, corner cupboard, 81(figs.)

Dane, Nathan, 209
Das Bergbüchlein, 90
Dauphin County, sulfur-inlaid furniture, 157–69(&figs.)
Daybooks, Nathaniel Gould, 209
Debye Scherrer x-ray diffraction of sulfur inlay, 82–83(&fig. 35)
DeHuff, Catharine, 194n34
DeHuff, Henry, 194n34
De la pirotechnia (Biringuccio), 90(fig. 6), 91, 99
Denenberg, Thomas, 206
De re metallica (*On the Nature of Metals*), 90
Desk, slant-front, 171(figs.)
Desk-and-bookcase, 12(&fig.)
"'Desks took on bord' in Nathaniel Gould's Caribbean Furniture Trade" (Finamore), 212–13
Dettenborn/Tetteborne, Ludwig Heinich, 127
Dietrich, Daniel Webster, 131, 195n39
Dietrich, Elizabeth Stager, 131
Dietrich, George Sanderson, 131, 195n39
Digges, John, 170–71
Digges Choice tract, 170–71, 174
Disney, Walt, 204
Disney campus, Burbank, 204
Doggett, John, 76
Doll, Catharina (Hartmann), 127
Doll, Conrad, 127
Doll, Johannes, 127
Doll, Johannes, Jr., 127
Doll, Joseph, 127

Doll, Mary, 126, 127
Door lintel, 157(fig.), 197*n*66
Door pediment, 146(fig. 116), 147
Double C-scroll splats, 211
Double eagle group, of sulfur-inlaid furniture, 178–80(&figs. 188–91)
Dovetails, 164
Downing, Alexander Jackson, 206–7
Doyle, Thomas, 194*n*34
Dressing table, Vermont, 207
Dunckel, Anna Barbara, 112
Dunckel, Johannes, 111–12(&fig. 51)
Dunckel, Melchior, 112
du Pont, Henry Francis, 87, 88

Eaby, Jacob, 117
Eaby, Jason K., 117
Eaby, Moses, 117
Eaby family, 117; tall clock, 116(fig. 59)
Eaglesfield, Ann, 3, 5, 14*n*6
Eaglesfield, Barnard, 1–15; probate inventory, 4(fig.), 5–9(&fig. 6), 11; shop, 6–9; will of, 2(fig.), 3(&fig.)
Eaglesfield, Benjamin, 14*n*5
Eaglesfield, George, 3–4, 14*n*5
Eaglesfield, John, 14*n*5
Eaglesfield, William, 14*n*5
Early Seating Upholstery: Reading the Evidence (Graves), 218–21
Ebersol, Jost/Joseph, 151
Ebersole, Jacob, 133, 151(&fig. 128)
Eby, Jacob, 117
Ellicott, Andrew, 126
Elton, William, 14*n*5
Emanuel Lutheran Church (Elizabeth Township), 124
Emanuel Reformed Church (Hanover), 172
"Embroidery Artist," 154
Emswiler, Jacob, 176
Enconchado, 217
England, Widdifield in, 17–18(&fig.)
Ephrata Cloister, 161, 172(fig.)
Eschelman, Christian, 88
Escritores, Eaglesfield and, 5, 8
Eshelman, Barbara, 105
Eshelman, Benjamin, 105
Eshleman, Henry, 147(fig.), 151, 153
Euler/Eiler, Maria Dorothea, 171
European origins, of sulfur-inlaid furniture technique, 89–91
Evans, Edward, 5, 6(fig.)
Evans, James, 76
Eyeman, Catharine, 101

Faber, George, 193*n*20
Fabian, Monroe, 70(&fig. 3), 81, 87, 181
Fackler, Gottlieb, 178
Feet: ball, 159; ogee bracket, 112(&fig. 54), 117(&fig. 61), 159(&fig. 145), 214
Ferree, Hannah, 162
Ferree, Jacob, 118
Ferree, John, 116
Ferree, Mary, 118
Ferree, Peter, 118, 162
Finamore, Daniel, 209, 212–13
Fireplace surround, 146(fig. 118)
First Church of Ipswich, 213
First Reformed Church (Lancaster), 96, 111, 126, 127, 130, 133
Fischborn, Johann Philip, 164–65
Fischborn, Ludwig, 165
Fischborn, Lutwig, 164–65(&fig. 157)
Fischborn, Magdalena, 158(&fig. 142), 165
Fischborn, Philip, Jr., 165
Fischborn/Fishburn, Ludwig, 164–65
Fisher, John, 168, 169–70(&fig. 173)
Fisher, Jonathan, 8
Five-plate stove, 156–57
Fleur-de-lis, relief-carved, 90(figs. 7&8), 107(&figs.), 108(figs.), 109, 128, 129(fig.)
Fleur-de-lis, sulfur-inlaid, 91, 92; on chests, 109–12(&figs.); on schranks, 99, 100(fig. 23)
Floral motif, on sulfur-inlaid furniture, 77, 135, 176–78(&figs.)
Flubaker, Jacob, 126
Folding screens, 216
Foliate cartouches, 92
Foliate designs, 97(fig.), 98–99
Fordney, Casper, 96
Fordney, Henry, 96
Fordney, John, 96
Fordney, Melchior, 96
Fordney (Fortineux), Michael, 94, 95(fig. 16), 96
"The Forgotten History: Upholstery Conservation" (conference), 219
Forke, Erika, 202
Forman, Benno, 191*n*4
Forne, Hans Adam, 177
Forney, Louisa Charlotte, 177
Forney, Maria Eva, 172
Forrer, Christian, 116(fig. 59), 117, 148, 149(fig. 123)
Forrer, Daniel, 117

Fourier transform infrared spectroscopy (FTIR) of sulfur inlay, 80(fig. 30), 82
Fraktur lettering, 142(&figs.), 154, 199*n*85
Franciscus, Christopher, 92, 126
Franck, Anna, 185
Franck, Christian, 185
Franck, Elizabeth, 185
Frankl, Paul T., 201, 202, 203
Freuler, Anna Margaretha, 94, 95 (fig. 16), 96
Freuler, Jost, 96
Frick, Peter, 127
Friedrich, Georg, 125
Friendship Fire Company, 115
Frieze, schrank, 152–53(&fig. 131)
Funk, John, 92
Furniture export trade, Gould and, 211, 212–13
The Furniture Masterworks of John and Thomas Seymour (Mussey), 209

Gadsden, Nonie, 201–5
Gage, Thomas, 212
Garmon, Edward, 21
Garvan, Beatrice, 70, 73
Gas chromatography–mass spectrometry, of sulfur inlay, 82
Gate-leg tables, 12, 13(fig.)
Gebhard, David, 201
Geesey, Titus C., 187
Gelwicks, Elisabeth Maria Barbara, 172
Gelwicks, Eva Dorothea, 172
Gelwicks, Friedrich, 174
Gelwicks, Friedrich Heinrich, 171–72
Gelwicks, George, 171(&figs.), 172, 174
Gelwicks, George Carl, 171
Gelwicks, Johannes, 172(&fig.)
Gelwicks, Nicholas, 172
The Gentleman and Cabinet-Maker's Director (Chippendale), 210, 211
Gesso type inlay, 81–82(&fig. 33)
Gibler, Anna Elisabeth Margreth, 175(&fig. 181)
Gibler, Anna Margaret, 175
Gibler, Michael, 175(&fig. 180), 177
Gish, George, 161
Gissy, John, 119
Glue blocks, 159(&fig. 146)
Gochnauer, Catharine, 124
Gochnauer, Christian, 124
Gochnauer, Jacob, Jr., 123–24(&fig. 75)
Gochnauer, Jacob, Sr., 124
Gorgas, Jacob, 188(&fig. 212)

234   INDEX

Gouge work, 77(&figs. 18&19), 78(figs. 21&22), 79
Gould, Elizabeth (French), 210
Gould, James, 210
Gould, Nathaniel, 209–15
Graff, Andrew, 194*n*34
Graff, Hans, 92
Graff, Jacob, 120, 122, 124
Graham, James, 210, 211
"Grand Houses and Rural Retreats" (Lahikainen), 213
Graves, Leroy, 218–21
Gravestones, inlaid sulfur highlights on, 73(&fig.), 74(figs.), 174–75(&figs.), 198*n*80, 198*n*81
Greek key design, 128, 129(fig.)
Grier, Katherine C., 219
Grim, Catharine, 165
Grove, John, 15*n*15; letter of instruction for furniture commission, 9(fig.), 10–13
Grove, Joseph, 15*n*15
Grove, Rebecca, 15*n*15
Growden, Lawrence, 8
Gypsum, 81

Haas, Barbara, 194*n*34
Haas, Conrad, 194*n*34
Haefterich, Magdalena, 193*n*22
Half-sideboard, 207
Hambrecht, Johann Adam, 193*n*22
Hambrecht/Hambright, Anna Maria, 114, 193*n*22
Hancock, William, 206
Hanging cupboards, 70, 186(figs.), 187, 197*n*70, 199*n*89
Hardiman, Tom, 205–9
Hard pine, scrutoire, 7(fig. 5)
Harris, John, Jr., 157
Harris, John, Sr., 157
Harwood, Zachariah, 206
Head, John, 4, 5, 12, 14*n*6; account book, 1, 2, 13
Hearts and flowers group, of sulfur-inlaid furniture, 180–81(&figs. 192–94)
Heart-shape cutouts, 153(figs.), 154
Heck, Ludwig, 194*n*34
Heilman, Henry, 149
Heinselman, John, 150–51
Henry, William, 91(&fig.), 116, 127, 194*n*34
Hensel, William, 126
Heritage Center Museum, 82
Herr, Abraham, 127–28

Herr, Christian, 92(&fig.), 98(fig.), 101–2, 106
Herr, Emanuel, Jr., 102
Herr, Emanuel and Mary, 68(fig.), 78(fig. 23), 105–6(figs. 34–37)
Herr, Hans, 92
Herr, Maria, 106
Herr, Veronica, 92, 98(fig.), 101–2
Hershey, Mary, 132
Hess, Clarke, 87
Hesselius, Gustavus, 9
Heyl, Elisabeth Barbara, 193*n*22
Heyne, Johann Christoph, 114, 115(fig.)
Hidden drawers, 160(fig. 150)
Hiestand, Elisabeth, 119
Hiestand, John, 132
Hiestand, Magdalena, 132
Hiester, Daniel, Sr., 90
Higgins Furniture, 203
High chest, 97–99(&fig. 18)
Hine, Thomas, 5
Hinge, 109(fig. 46)
Historiography of sulfur-inlaid furniture, 70
A History of Newcastle-on-Tyne (Charleton), 18
Hoff, George, 118(fig. 63), 119(&fig. 65), 136, 139, 149, 150(fig. 125), 187(&figs.), 194*n*34
Hoff, Michael, 119
Holl, Johannes, 128
Holl, Peter, I, 127–28
Holl, Peter, II, 127, 128
Holl, Peter, III, 70, 73, 127, 128
Holtzappel, Anna Barbara, 178
Holtzappel, Erasmus, 178
Holtzappel, Hans Leonard, 178
Holtzappel, Maria Barbara, 178
Holtzappel/Holsapple, Peter, 178(&fig. 186)
Hook, Benjamin, 197*n*64
Hornor, William McPherson, Jr., 1, 7(fig. 5), 19
Horst, Michael, 149–50(&fig. 125)
Hostetter, Jacob, 133
Hubbard, Robert, 18
Huber, Christian, 70, 73, 128, 130, 195*n*38
Huber, George, 70(&fig. 3), 195*n*38
Huber, Georg/George, 128–30(&fig. 79)
Huber, Johannes, 128–29
Huber, John, 129, 195*n*38
Huber, Jonas, 129–30
Hubley, Michael, 194*n*34
Hühn, Anna Maria, 133

Hühn, Johann Valentin, 133–34
Hühn, John Nicholas, 133
Hühn/Huhn/Hun, John, 133–35
Hummel, Charles, 70, 73
Hummel, Frederick, Jr., 161

Ickes, Peter, 172
Il libro dell'arte (The Book of Art), 71
Illig, Andreas, 156
Illig, Georg Michael, 156
Illig, John, 156–57(&fig. 139)
Illig, Leonard, 156
Illig, Margaret, 156
Illig, Philippina, 156
Illustrated Atlas, Geographical, Statistical, and Historical, of the United States and the Adjacent Countries (Bradford), 208
Imbsweiller/Imschwiller, Peter, 176
Inlay. *See* Mixed-wood inlay; Pewter inlay; Sulfur-inlaid furniture
In Plain Sight: Discovering the Furniture of Nathaniel Gould (Widmer & King), 209–15
Instrumental data analysis of sulfur inlay, 82–83(&figs.)
The Italian Confectioner, 76
Italy: fleur-de-lis motif in, 91; orpiment and, 71, 89
Ivory, 89

Jerg, Dorothea, 147
Joiners, 20
Jones, Jenkin, 3
Juliana Library Company, 91, 116, 126
Jundt, Georg and Magdalena, 125

Karmene/Kitzmiller/Kemmerer/Kimmerling, Christian/Christopher, 166
Kauffman, Andrew, 132
Kauffman, Anna, 102–3(&figs.), 137, 139, 192*n*17
Kauffman, Anna Elisabeth, 138(fig. 99)
Kauffman, Christian, 127–28
Kauffman, Elisabeth, 107, 192*n*17
Kauffman, Eva (Sneveley), 133
Kauffman, Jacob, 180
Kauffman, Jacob, Jr., 105, 132, 133
Kauffman, Jacob, Sr., 105
Kauffman, Johannes, 102–3(&figs.), 138(fig. 99), 192*n*17
Kauffman, John, 102, 105, 107, 109, 119, 137, 192*n*17
Kauffman, John, Jr., 137
Kauffman, Mary, 133

Kauffman, Michael, 109–10(&fig. 47), 137, 192*n*17
Kauffmann, Christian, 105
Kauffmann, Jacob, 105
Kauffmann, Johannes and Anna, 119
Kaufman, Henrich, 131–32(&fig. 82)
Kem Weber: Designer and Architect (Long), 201–5
Kem Weber: The Moderne in Southern California, 1920 through 1941 (Gebhard & Von Breton), 201
Kendrick, Hastings, 205
Kettner, George Michael, 90
Kilheffer, Jacob, 192*n*12
Kilheffer, Johannes, 123
Kimmerling, Anna Maria, 164
Kindig, Martin, 92
King, Joyce, 209–15
Kinser, Henry, 197*n*69
Kinsports (Kihports/Keeports), Daniel, 180
Kitchen cupboard, 199*n*88; walnut, 184(fig. 202), 185(figs.)
Klein, Christiana Sophia, 142
Kline, Maria Barbara, 126
Klinger, George, 165
Klinger, Maria, 165–66(&fig. 159)
Knife, sulfur inlay technique and, 76–77(&figs. 18&19), 78(figs. 20&22)
Knoll, Christian, 143
Knotwork pattern, 78(fig. 23)
Kohler, Jacob, 192*n*12
Kolb, Andreas, 199*n*85
Koppenhefer, Eva, 155(&fig. 136)
Koppenhefer, Henrich and Anna Catharina, 155
Koppenhefer, Henrich and Christina, 155
Koppenhefer, Johann Thomas, 155
Koppenhefer, Simon and Maria Elisabeth, 155
Koppenhefer, Thomas, 162
Kugelman, Alice, 214
Kugelman, Thomas, 214
Kunigunda, Anna Maria, 120
Kurtz, Susanna, 117

Lacquer, 217
Laeder, Hannah, 117
Lahikainen, Dean Thomas, 209, 213
Lamb, Benjamin, 122(fig. 70)
Lancaster County Courthouse, 93(&fig.)
Lancaster County (Pennsylvania). *See* Lebanon-Lancaster County border region; Sulfur-inlaid furniture

Lancaster Library Company, 91, 115, 116
Lancaster (Pennsylvania), 93
Landis, Elisabeth, 161(&fig.), 197*n*68
Landis, Felix, I, 161
Landis, Felix, III, 161
Landis, Felix, Jr., 161
Landisville Mennonite Meetinghouse, 100, 101(fig. 25)
Lane, Joshua W., 209–15
Lang, Barbara, 132–33(&figs. 84–86), 134, 195*n*41
Lang, Christian, 132
Lang, Joseph, 195*n*41
Lang/Long, John, 132
Latrobe, Benjamin Henry, 93(fig.)
Lauer, Eva Magdalena, 144(&figs.), 145(fig. 115), 147
Lawrence, Mary, 18
Lawrence, William, 18
Lebanon-Lancaster County border region, sulfur-inlaid furniture, 143–44; Ley schrank, 144–47(&figs. 111&112); star inlay group, 147–54(&figs. 119–34)
Lenhere, Elizabeth, 194*n*34
Ley, Christopher, 145
Ley, Michael, 144(&figs.), 145(fig. 115), 147, 155–56, 162
Lichten, Frances, 84, 87, 128
Lichten, Frank, 70
Lightwood stringing, 117
Lignum vitae, router plane, 76(fig. 14)
Lind, Anna Maria, 127
Lind, Conrad, 127
Lind, John, 127
Lind, Juliana, 126–27
Lind, Michael, Jr., 126, 127
Lind, Michael, Sr., 126–27, 194*n*34
Linen fold panel, 107
Linseed oil, 81
Lionetti, Robert, 214
Little Cocalico (Pennsylvania), 88
Lloyd, Peter, 10
Lloyd Manufacturing Company, 204
Loeser, John Jacob, 194*n*34
Logan, James, 2–3, 6, 14*n*5, 14*n*6; Widdifield and, 18–19
Logan & Shippen, 9
Long, Ada, 141
Long, Anna Elisabeth, 137, 192*n*17
Long, Barbara, 195*n*41
Long, Christopher, 201–5
Long, Henry, 122
Long, Hermann, 141

Long, Isaac and Susanna (Kauffman), 197*n*70
Looking East: Western Artists and the Allure of Japan (Burnham), 216
Loose, Conrad, 196*n*52
Loose, Isaac, 196*n*52
Lowden, Hugh, 1
Lucan, Jonathan, 21
Lyford, Thomas, 20–21, 23*n*9
Lyre-based table, 207

Made in the Americas: The New World Discovers Asia (Carr), 215–18
Mahogany: high chest, 97(fig.); spice boxes, 21(figs.)
Manheim Township (Pennsylvania), 92; chests, 132–35(&figs. 84–89)
Manitoga, 204
Mann, Frederick, 126
Mantel, 94, 95(fig. 15)
Manwaring, Robert, 211
A Map of the British Empire in America with the French and Spanish settlements adjacent thereto (Popple), 10(fig.)
Marlys, Elizabeth, 17
Marriage portions, 213
Marshall, John, 206
Maryland, tombstones inlaid with sulfur in, 73(&fig.)
Masonic Hall (Lancaster), 126
Mass, Jennifer, 70, 87
Massachusetts Historical Society, 209
Meily, Martin, 120
Mennig/Minnich, John and Mary, 152(fig. 131), 153, 154
Mennonite families: in Pequea and Conestoga settlements, 92–93; sulfur-inlaid furniture and, 87, 100
Mercer Museum (Doylestown, Pennsylvania), 199*n*85
Mertz, D. I., 127
Metallurgy, sulfur's use in, 89, 90–91
Metz, Elisabeth, 107
Meyer, Philip, 174
Meyer/Meier, Philip, 172
Meyli, Samuel, 194*n*28
Meyli/Meily, Samuel, 120, 121(figs.)
Millar, William, 76
Miller, Barbara, 180
Miller, Christian, 180
Miller, Esther "Hester," 157
Miller, Eva, 153
Miller, George and Maria Catharina, 154(&fig.)

Miller, Heinrich, 162(fig. 152), 163–64
Miller, Henry, Jr., 164
Miller, Henry, Sr., 164
Miller, Jacob, 92
Miller, Magdalena, 164
Miller, Michael, 154, 156
Miller, Nicholas, 180
Miller, Susanna, 117
Miller, Veronica, 180, 181(figs.)
Miniature chests, walnut, 86(figs.), 87, 88, 136–37(&figs. 95&96), 142–43(&figs. 107&108), 176–77(&figs. 184&185)
Minnich, Anna Maria, 153
Minnich, Johannes, 153
Minnich, John, 161
Minnig, John, 153
Mixed-wood inlay: box with drawer, 189(fig. 216); chests, 122–24(&figs. 72–76), 158(figs. 142&143), 162(fig. 152), 164(figs.), 165(figs.), 166(figs.); corner cupboard, 179(fig. 189); tall clocks, 113–14(figs.), 116(figs.), 119(&figs.), 139(figs.), 179(fig. 188)
Modernism, Weber and, 201–5
Modes and Manners division, Barker Brothers, 203
Moffatt-Ladd House (Portsmouth, New Hampshire), 218
Molds, confection, 75–76(&figs. 12–14)
Mopa mopa, 217
Morris, Anthony, 8–9, 18, 21
Morrow, Francis, 126
Moser, Anna Elisabeth, 88
Moser, Cadarina, 137(&fig.)
Moser, Catharina, 137
Moser, Johannes, 88, 137
Moser, Johannes, Jr., 88
Moser, Margaretha Moser, 137
Moser, Weyerich, 137
Mosser, Johannes, 86(fig. 1), 87, 88
Most Blessed Sacrament Catholic Church (Bally, Pennsylvania), 114
Muhlenberg, Anna Maria, 90
Muhlenberg, Henry, 90, 141–42
Muhlenberg, Henry, Jr., 127, 194n34
Muhlenberg, Henry Melchior, 116
Mullard, Robert, 18
Mumma, Anna, 138(fig. 100), 139
Mumma, David, 138(fig. 100), 139, 192n17
Mumma, John, 139
Museum of Fine Arts, Boston, 216, 218
Musser, John, 191n2

Musser, Veronica and Henry, 191n2
Mussey, Robert D., Jr., 209
Myerstown (Pennsylvania), 144–45
Mylin, Martin, 92

Needham, John, 210
Neoclassical form, in Vermont furniture, 207
Neutra, Richard, 203
New Bristol Hope (ship), 10
Newcastle upon Tyne, Widdifield and, 17, 18
Newman, Daniel, 194n34
New Spain, Asian influence in, 215–18
New York Evening Post (newspaper), 205
Niello, 71
Nissly, C. L., 102
Nolt, Jonas, 105
Nyberg, Laurentius, 115

Oak: chests, 125(figs.); schranks, 104(figs.), 129(fig.), 138(fig. 99); spice box, 21(fig. 5); tall clock, 135(fig. 93)
Oberholtzer, Barbara, 130
Oberholtzer, Christian, 130, 195n38
Oberholtzer, Magdalena, 130
Oberholtzer, Martin, 92
Oberholtzer, Michael, 92
Oberle, Johann Adam, 124
Oberle, Johann Martin, 124
Oberle, Michael, 125
Oberlin/Oberle, Michael, 124
O'Bourne, Margaret, 22n1
Ogee bracket feet, 112(&fig. 54), 117(&fig. 61), 159(&fig. 145), 214
Ogee curve, 213
Orpiment, 71, 89(&figs.), 91
Overholt, Abraham, 153

Panama-Pacific International Exposition, 202
Pancake, Rosina, 169
Paramount Studios, 204
Parker, George, 22
Parker, Philemon, 211–12
Pasto varnish, 217
Paul, Bruno, 202
Paul T. Frankl and American Modern Design (Long), 201, 202
Paxton Boys, 116
Peabody Essex Museum, 209, 211
Pemberton, Israel, 8
Pena, María Campos Carlés de, 216
Pendant shells, 210

Pendulum door, 114(fig.)
Pennsylvania: map of, 88(fig.); sulfur production in, 71–73
Pennsylvania Folklife (journal), 70(&fig. 3)
Pennsylvania Gazette (newspaper), 89–90
Pennsylvania German furniture. *See* Sulfur-inlaid furniture
Pennypacker Auction Center, 192n16, 199n88
Pequea settlement, 92–93
Pewter candlesticks, 114, 115(fig.)
Pewter inlay: chest, 125(&figs.); corner cupboard, 72(figs.), 73; schranks, 94, 95(fig. 16), 96; tall clocks, 112, 113(figs.), 114, 119–20(&figs. 65&66), 124, 193n20
Philadelphia: desk-and-bookcase, 12(fig.); gate-leg table, 13(fig.); mahogany spice boxes, 21(figs.); walnut scrutoire, 6(fig.), 7(fig. 5)
Philadelphia Monthly Meeting, 18, 21
Philadelphia Museum of Art, 1
Phillips Library (Peabody Essex Museum), 211
Pierce, Donna, 215
Pie shelf, 184(fig. 202)
Pine: chest of drawers, 173(figs.); chests, 125(figs.), 130(figs.), 132(figs.), 158(fig. 142), 178(figs.); corner cupboards, 146(fig. 117), 179(fig. 189); door lintel, 157(fig.); hanging cupboard, 186(figs.); kitchen cupboard, 184(fig. 202); miniature chest, 176(figs.); schranks, 95(fig. 16), 106(fig. 38), 129(fig.), 145(fig. 113); slant-front desk, 171(figs.); slide-lid box, 189(fig. 215); tall clocks, 82(fig.), 135(fig. 93)
Plack, Erika, 202
Plasterers' molds, 76
Plastering—Plain and Decorative, 76
Plinth blocks, 112, 113(fig. 55)
Plumley, Charles, 14n4
Polychrome painted chest, 176(&fig.)
Poorman, Johannes, 158(&fig. 141)
Popple, Henry, 10(fig.)
Powel, Samuel, Jr., 8
Powel, Samuel, Sr., 8
"A Primer for Light Grade Amber and Pure Vermont Furniture" (Zea), 206
Pritchard, Margaret Beck, 219
Probate inventory: Eaglesfield, 4(fig.), 5–9(&fig. 6), 11; Plumley, 14n4
Prown, Jonathan, 218–21

Pseudo-Otto Artist, 172(fig.)
Pump-making trade, sulfur inlay on furniture and, 73
Putti, 94(&figs.)
Putty inlay, 81(&figs.)
Pyrite, 72–73

Quakerism, Widdifield and, 18

Rauschenberg, Bradford L., 73
Rausher, Christina, 178
Red mulberry, tall clock, 119(figs.)
Reichard, Salome, 142
Reinecker, Adam and Elisabeth, 172
Reist, Abraham, 102, 105, 106–7(&figs. 38–42), 141, 152, 192n17
Reist, Barbara, 152
Reist, Christian, 192n16
Reist, Elisabeth, 106–7(&figs. 38–42)
Reist, Elisabeth (daughter), 107, 141
Reist, Elisabeth (Kauffman), 141
Reist, John, 107
Reist, Peter, 107
Renaissance, use of sulfur, 71
Renaker, Anna Maria, 175
Renaker, Casper, 175
Renaker, Paul, 175(&fig. 182)
Renaker/Reinecker, Casper, 172–74(&fig. 178)
Renecker, Catherine, 175
Replica, sulfur-inlaid panel, 77(fig. 17), 78–81(&figs. 21, 22, 24–27), 84(figs.)
Rich and Tasty: Vermont Furniture to 1850 (Burks & Zea), 205–9
Richardson, Hannah, 15n12
Richardson, James, 208
Richardson, Joseph, 15n12
Richardson, Joseph, Sr., 15n12
Richardson, Mary, 15n12
Ricker, John, 165
Rieth, Christopher, 156, 197n64
Rieth, Valentin and Eva, 197n64
Ritz, John, 172
Rivas, Jorge F., 216
Rob, William, 21
Roberts, Edward, 5
Rock Ford Plantation, 191n8
Rococo furniture: Gould and, 210; high chest, 97(fig.)
Ropes, John, Jr., 212
Rose motif, 185(&fig. 204)
Rosettes, 117(figs.), 118, 151(&fig. 129)
Rosin, 81
Ross, George, 116

Ross, John, 212
Router plane, 76(fig. 14)
Row, Peter, 194n34
Rudy, Catharine, 120
Rudy, Charles, 132, 195n41
Rudy, Daniel, 132
Rudy, Rudolph, 120
Rupert, Johann Adam, 178
Rupley, Catharina, 163

Sadler, John C., 110
St. Benjamin's Lutheran Cemetery (Carroll County, Maryland), 73
St. Benjamin's (Pipe Creek or Krider's) Church (Westminster), 174
St. James Anglican Church (Lancaster), 116
St. John's Lutheran Church (Littlestown), 174, 198n80
St. Luke's Lutheran Cemetery (Carroll County, Maryland), 73(&fig.), 74(fig. 9)
St. Luke's (Winters) Church (New Windsor), 174
St. Mary's Church (Conewago), 171
St. Mary's Church (Silver Run), 174, 175(figs.), 177, 198n81
St. Mary's Union (Reformed and Lutheran) Cemeteries (Carroll County, Maryland), 73, 74(figs. 10&11)
Salem, Caribbean furniture trade and, 212–13
Salem German Reformed Church, 120
Samuel McIntire: Carving an American Style (Lahikainen), 209
Sanderson, Elijah, 210
Sargent, William, 215–18
Scanning electron microscopy, of sulfur inlay, 82, 83(fig. 34)
Schaeffer, Alexander, 154
Schaefferstown (Pennsylvania), 154
Schindler, Rudolf, 203
Schneider, Christian and Elisabeth, 152(&fig. 130)
Schneider, Johannes, 135, 152
Schneider, Susanna (Bauman), 152
Schoepf, Johann David, 154, 169
School of Royal Arts and Craft Museum (Berlin), 202
Schott, Andrew, 168
Schranks: door panels, 68(figs.), 78(fig. 23); Huber, 128–31(&fig. 79); walnut, 68(fig.), 69(&fig.), 70(fig. 3), 94, 95(fig. 16), 96(&fig.), 98(fig.), 99–107(&figs. 20–24, 26–42), 129(fig.), 138(figs.), 140(figs.), 144(figs.), 145(figs. 113&114), 152–53(&figs. 130&131)
Schwar, Adaline, 141
Schwar, Anna, 119, 141
Schwar, Barbara, 119
Schwar, Catharine, 141
Schwar, Christian, 141
Schwar, Christian, Jr., 141
Schwar, Elisabeth, 141
Schwar, Elizabeth, 119
Schwar, John, 107, 119, 141
Schwar, Maria, 141
Schwar, Peter, Jr., and Ada, 119, 140–41(&fig. 103)
Schwar, Peter, Sr., 141
Schwar/Shwahr, Christian, Jr., 119
Schwar/Shwahr, Christian, Sr., 119
Schwar/Shwahr/Swarr, Christian, 118–19(&fig. 63)
Schweitzer, Friederich, 181
Schweitzer, Magdalena, 181
Schweizer, Frederick, 181
Schweizer, Fridrich, 181
Schweizer, Johann Friederich, 181
Schweizer, Peter and Elizabeth (Heffelfinger), 181
Scrutoires, 11, 15n8; walnut, 5, 6(fig.), 7(fig. 5), 11–12; Widdifield and, 20–21(&fig. 3), 35
Sehner, Johann Gottlieb, Jr., 126
Sehner/Sener, Gottlieb, Sr., 126
Selim, Anthony, 194n34
Sell, Abraham, 176, 177
Sell, Adam, 176–77
Sence, Robert, 126
Shelburne Museum, 206
Shell, Ludwig, 194n34
Shell, Margaret, 194n34
Shell inlay, 217
Shenk, Anna (Schwar), 141(fig. 105)
Shenk, John, 141
Sheraton secretary, 207
Shippen, Edward, 116
Shortel, John, 126
Shwahr, Christian, Jr., 102
Shwahr, Christian, Sr., 102
Shwahr/Schwar, Anna, 102
Silica, 81
Simon, Joseph, 115

Slant-front desk, walnut, 171(&figs.)
Slavery, 15*n*16
Slide-lid boxes, sulfur-inlaid, 181–84(&figs. 195–200), 189(fig. 215)
Sliding batten, 162(fig. 153)
Slough, Matthias, 97–98(&fig. 18), 116
Slugging, 71
Snively, Joseph, 120
Spalling, of sulfur inlay, 84(figs.)
Spangler, W. H., 131
Speicher, John and Regina, 147
Speicher/Spycker, Margaretha Barbara, 147
Spice boxes, Widdifield, 20(&fig.), 21(&figs.), 35
Splint matches, 71(fig.)
Spohr, Johannes and Anna Maria, 96(&fig.)
Spohr, John George, 96
Spread-wing eagle motif, 136(&figs. 95&96)
Stager, Elizabeth, 131, 195*n*39
Stager, John and Sarah (Levengood), 195*n*39
Stahly, Catharine, 156
Staining, Widdifield and, 21–22, 41–61
Stalker, John, 22
Stappleford, Thomas, 18
Star motif, 72(figs.), 131–32, 138(fig. 100), 139, 147–54(&figs. 119–34), 158–59(&fig. 143), 165–66(&figs. 161&163)
Staufer/Stauffer, Barbara, 143(&figs.)
Stauffer, Jacob and Anna, 143
Stauffer, John, 143
Steel, James, 12
Stein, Catharine, 194*n*34
Stein, Frederick, 194*n*34
Stein, Ludwig, 115, 116, 127, 194*n*34
Stein, Ludwig and Maria Catharina, 193*n*22
Steinman, Anna Regina, 114
Steinman, Christian Frederick, 114
Steinman, John Frederick, 114
Stein/Stone, Christina, 193*n*22
Stein/Stone, Frederick, Jr., 193*n*22
Stein/Stone, Frederick, Sr., 193*n*22
Stein/Stone, Johann Heinrich, 193*n*22
Stein/Stone, Ludwig and Maria Catharina, 114
Stein/Stone, Maria Catharina, 193*n*22
Steman, John, 119
Stiegel, Henry William, 142

Stine, Judith, 147
Stoehr, Margaret, 148
Stone, Anna Maria, 114
Stone, Catharine, 114
Stone, Frederick, 113(fig. 55), 114–16, 126, 127, 194*n*34
Stone, Frederick, Jr., 114, 194*n*34
Stone, Ludwig, 114
Stone, Susanna, 114
Stoner, Rudolph "Rudy," 113(fig. 55), 114, 116, 117(fig. 61), 126
Stoves: five-plate, 156–57; rococo patterned, 99
Stowell, Alonzo, 208
Straightedge, 136(fig. 97), 137, 195*n*46
Strap hinges, 159, 161
Strapwork inlay, 116(figs.), 117, 122–23
Studi, Martin, 177
Study, John, 177
Sturgis, Joseph, 148–50
Sulfur, historic uses and sources of, 71–73
Sulfur-inlaid furniture: Alleman chests, 168–69(&figs. 169–71); chests, 70(fig.), 77(figs. 18&19), 78(fig. 20), 80(figs. 28&29), 109–12(&figs.), 130(figs.), 131, 143(&figs.); color shift with age, 69(fig.); Conewago area, 170–74(&figs. 175–76, 178–79); corner cupboards, 72(figs.), 81(figs.), 179(fig. 189); cradle, 141–42(&figs. 105&106); Dauphin County, 157–69(&figs.); double eagle group, 178–80(&figs. 188–91); early Lancaster County, 92, 99–132; early Lancaster furniture and, 93–99(&figs. 19–21); European origins, 89–91; floral group, 176–78(&figs.); furniture forms, 69, 87; gravestones, 73(&fig.), 74(figs.), 174–75(&figs.), 198*n*80, 198*n*81; hearts and flowers group, 180–81(&figs. 192–94); historic uses and sources of sulfur, 71–73; historiography of, 70; Huber schrank, 128–31(&fig. 79); identifying owners, 87–88; late, from Lancaster County, 135–37; Lebanon-Lancaster County border region, 143–54(&figs.); Manheim Township chests, 132–35(&figs. 84–89); miniature chests, 142–43(&figs. 107&108); molds, 75–76(&figs. 12–15); origins of technique, 89–91; periods of, 92; possible makers, 125–28; replica panel, 77(fig. 17), 78(figs. 21&22), 79(figs.),

84(figs.); schrank door panels, 68(fig.), 78(fig. 23); schrank frieze fragment, 69(fig.); schranks, 98(fig.), 99–107(&figs. 20–24, 26–42), 137, 138(figs.), 139, 140–41(&figs. 103& 104), 144–47(&figs. 111&112); singular objects, 185–89(&figs.); slide-lid boxes, 181–84(&figs. 195–200), 189(&fig. 215); table, 134(figs. 91&92); tall clocks, 82(fig.), 112–22(&figs. 61–64, 68–69), 135(&figs.), 139–40(&figs. 101&102), 170(figs.), 179(fig. 188), 187–88(&figs. 210–13); technique, 69, 76–85; technological transfer and, 73–76; York County, 169–74(&figs. 173–76, 178–79), 176–78(&figs.)
Sulfur-inlaid tombstones, 73–74(figs.)
Sulfur inlay, chemical characteristics, 81–83
"Sulfur Inlay in Pennsylvania German Furniture" (Fabian), 70(&fig. 3)
Sulfur molds, 76
Summy, Elisabeth (Shirk), 133
Summy, John, 133
Summy, Peter, 133
Sussel, Arthur J., 197*n*68
Swann Galleries (New York), 17
Switzer, Cornelius, 126
Sycamore, 197*n*70; chest, 162(figs.), 163(&figs.)

Tables: black walnut gate-leg, 12, 13(fig.); walnut, 134(figs. 91&92), 151(&fig. 129), 188(fig. 214), 189
Talavera ware, 218
Tall clocks: black walnut with sulfur inlay, 94(&figs.), 95(fig. 14); cherry, 113(figs.), 117(fig.), 119(figs.); possible makers, 125–26; walnut, 116(figs.), 118(figs.), 121(figs.), 122(figs.), 124, 135(figs.), 139(&figs.), 147–50(&figs.), 170(figs.), 179(fig. 188), 187–88(&figs. 210–13)
Technological transfer, sulfur inlay, 73–76
Tempo furniture line, 204
Thomas, Philip, 126
Thomas Mills Company, 75(fig. 12)
Thompson, Sarah E., 216
Three-leaf clover motif, 135(&figs.)
"Three Vermont Furniture Puzzles," 208
Till compartments, 130(fig. 82), 131, 159(&fig. 144), 160(fig. 149)
Tombstones. *See* Gravestones

A Treatise of Japaning and Varnishing (Stalker & Parker), 22
Trinity Lutheran Church (Lancaster), 94, 98, 114, 115, 116, 119, 126, 127, 193*n*22
Trinity Lutheran Church (New Holland), 124–25, 131
Truxillo, Don Juan Garcia, 218
Tulip motif, 185(&fig. 205)
Tulip poplar: box with drawer, 189(fig. 216); chest of drawers, 173(figs.); chests, 132(figs.), 133(figs.), 155(fig. 136), 160(fig. 148), 161(fig.), 162(fig. 152), 164(figs.), 165(figs.), 166(figs.), 167(figs.), 168(fig. 170), 180(figs.); corner cupboards, 146(fig. 117), 179(fig. 189); cradle, 141(figs.); desk-and-bookcase, 12(fig.); high chest, 97(fig.); kitchen cupboard, 184(fig. 202); miniature chests, 86(figs.), 136(fig. 95), 142(figs.); schrank door panels, 68(fig.), 78(fig. 23); schranks, 95(fig. 16), 96(fig.), 98(fig.), 102(fig.), 104(figs.), 105(figs.), 129(fig.), 138(fig. 99), 140(figs.), 144(figs.), 145(fig. 113); tall clocks, 94(figs.), 113(figs.), 117(figs.), 118(figs.), 119(figs.), 121(figs.), 122(fig. 70), 135(figs.), 139(figs.), 147(figs.), 150(fig. 126), 187(figs.), 188(fig. 212); valuables chest, 70(fig. 4)
Tulpehocken Manor, 144, 145–47(&figs. 115–18)
Tulpehocken Valley chests, 154–57(&figs. 136, 137, 139)
Tuscarawas County (Ohio), 178
Tuthill, James, 4

Uhler, Anastasius, 147
Uhler, Christoph, 144(fig. 111), 145(fig. 113), 146(figs.), 147
University of Wisconsin–Madison, 17
Upholstery, noninvasive furniture, 218–21
Upholstery in America and Europe from the Seventeenth Century to World War I (Cooke), 219
Usher, John and Mary, 18

Valuables chest, sulfur-inlaid, 70(fig. 4)
Varnishing, Widdifield and, 21–22, 41–61
Verhoeven, Jeroen, 213
Vermont furniture, to 1850, 205–9

Vermont Gazette (newspaper), 205
Von Breton, Harriette, 201

Wachseinlagen, 70, 84, 87
Wagner, William, 169(fig. 172)
Waldschmidt, John, 88, 137
Walnut, 155(figs. 136&137), 156(fig.), 158(figs. 142&143), 160(fig. 148), 161(fig.), 164(figs.), 165–68(&figs.), 178(figs.), 180(figs.), 184(fig. 201); box with drawer, 189(fig. 216); chest façades, 80(figs. 28&29), 160(fig. 147); chest of drawers, 173(figs.); chests, 89(figs.), 109–12(figs. 47–54), 122–24(&figs. 72–76), 125(figs.), 130(figs.), 131(fig.), 132(figs.), 133(figs.), 137(fig.), 143(&figs.), 151(fig. 128); corner cupboards, 72(figs.), 81(figs.), 179(fig. 189); cradles, 141(figs.), 153(figs.); desk-and-bookcase, 12(fig.); frieze, 152(fig. 131); hanging cupboard, 186(figs.), 187; kitchen cupboard, 184(fig. 202), 185(figs.); miniature chests, 86(figs.), 136–37(&figs. 95&96), 142(figs.), 176–77(&figs. 184&185); schrank door panels, 68(fig.), 78(fig. 23); schrank frieze fragment, 69(fig.); schranks, 95(fig. 16), 96(fig.), 98(fig.), 99–107(&figs. 20–24, 26–42), 129(fig.), 138(fig.), 144(figs.), 145(figs. 113&114), 152–53(&figs. 130&131); scrutoires, 5, 6(fig.), 7(fig. 5), 11–12; slant-front desk, 171(figs.); slide-lid boxes, 182(figs.), 189(fig. 215); straightedge, 136(fig. 97); tables, 134(figs. 91&92), 151(&fig. 129), 188(fig. 214), 189; tall clocks, 116(figs.), 118(figs.), 119(figs.), 121(figs.), 122(figs.), 124, 135(figs.), 139(figs.), 147–50(&figs.), 170(figs.), 179(fig. 188), 187(figs.), 188(figs. 212&213); use in colonies, 11–13; valuables chest, 70(fig. 4)
Walter, Joseph, 194*n*34
Ward, John, 210
Warder, Jacob, 18
Warren, Jacob, 18
Watson, Abraham, 210
Wax inlay, 70, 84, 87
Weber, Kem (Karl Emmanuel Martin), 201–5
Weiser, Frederick S., 198*n*80
Weiss, Susanna, 194*n*34
Weiss, Susanna (Stone), 194*n*34

Welter, Abraham, 161
West, Benjamin, 91(&fig.)
West Coast modernism, 201–5
White cedar: matches, 71(fig.); spice boxes, 21(figs.)
White pine: chests, 108(figs.), 109, 110(fig. 49), 123(figs.), 137(fig.), 143(figs.), 155(fig. 136), 160(fig. 148), 165(figs.), 167(fig. 167), 168(fig. 170); schranks, 140(figs.), 144(figs.); scrutoire, 6(fig.); table, 134(fig. 91); tall clock, 150(fig. 125)
Widdifield, Ann, 18
Widdifield, Elizabeth, 18, 23*n*1
Widdifield, Hannah, 18
Widdifield, John: career, 18–19; early life of, 17–18; furniture forms, 20–21; immigration to colonies, 18; inventory, 19–20; notebook, 16(fig.), 17, 20–22; notebook facsimile, 23–67; scrutoire, 20–21(&fig. 3), 35; spice boxes, 20(&fig.), 21(&figs.), 35; staining and varnishing instructions, 21–22, 41–61
Widdifield, John, Jr., 18, 20
Widdifield, Mary, 18
Widdifield, Peter, 17, 18, 23*n*1, 23*n*5
Widdifield, Sarah, 18
Widmer, Elisabeth Garrett, 209, 213
Widmer, Kemble, 209–15
Willing & Shippen, 9
Wilson, George, 5
Winterthur Museum, 87, 199*n*85, 218
Wismer, Henry, 199*n*85
Withers, Michael, 126
Witmer, Abraham, 149
Witmer, Michael, 149
Witmer, Ulrich, 149
Wolf, Daniel, 111
Wolf, David, 110(fig. 49)
Wolf, John Nicholas, 110–11
Wood, Rebecca, 210
Wood, Thomas, 210, 211
Wood, Thomas, Jr., 211
Worldly Goods: The Arts of Early Pennsylvania, 1680–1758 (exhibit), 1
Wright, Frank Lloyd, 203
Wright, Russel, 204
Wrought-iron hooks, schrank sections held together using, 100, 101(fig. 26)

X-ray diffraction analysis, of sulfur inlay, 82–83(&fig. 35)
X-ray fluorescence, of sulfur inlay, 82

Yeates, Jasper, 126
Yellow pine: chest, 176(fig.); spice boxes, 21(figs.)
York County, sulfur-inlaid furniture in, 169–70(&figs. 173&174); Conewago area, 170–74(&figs. 175–76, 178–79); floral group, 176–78(&figs.)
York (Pennsylvania), view of, 169(fig. 172)

Zahneiser, Matthias, 126
Zea, Philip, 205–9
Zeisberger, David, 178
Zell/Sell/Sill, Anna, 176–77(&fig. 184)
Zinzendorf, Nicholas Ludwig von, 116
Zion Lutheran Church (Harrisburg), 163, 169, 198*n*73
Zion Lutheran Church (Hummelstown), 165
Zion Lutheran Church (Manheim), 142
Zwecker/Swecker, Christina Barbara, 124